Carlos Montezuma

Carlos Montezuma

and the
Changing World
of
American Indians

Peter Iverson

University of New Mexico Press: *Albuquerque*

Library of Congress Cataloging in Publication Data

Iverson, Peter.
    Carlos Montezuma and the changing world of American
Indians.

    Bibliography: p.
    Includes index.
    1. Montezuma, Carlos, 1866-1923. 2. Yavapai Indians—
Biography. 3. Indians of North America—Government
relations—1869-1934. I. Title.
E99.Y5M6534 1982   970.004′97 [B]   82–13624
ISBN 0–8263–0641–1

Portions of this book have been published in the *Journal of Arizona History* and in *American Indian Leaders: Studies in Diversity,* edited by R. David Edmunds (University of Nebraska Press, 1980). Permission to reprint this material is gratefully acknowledged.

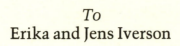

To
Erika and Jens Iverson

Contents

Illustrations

Preface

My interest in the life and career of Carlos Montezuma grew from a more general concern for the history of the Indians of the American Southwest. One of the first published accounts I read which mentioned Montezuma was Edward Spicer's classic overview, *Cycles of Conquest*, which appeared in 1962. Montezuma figured only briefly in that large volume; given the information then available to him, Spicer could present but a fragmented image. Still, Montezuma seemed an intriguing and important character, both for his unusual career and for the impact some of his views had on several Native American peoples. As an M.D. and an outspoken critic of the Bureau of Indian Affairs, he clearly merited more attention than he had received.

While largely forgotten for many years by most Americans, Montezuma during his lifetime ranked as one of the most important Indians in the country. After his death in 1923, he remained a vital figure within the memories of his people, the Yavapais or Mohave-Apaches of the Fort McDowell reservation in southern Arizona; his opinions continued to influence some of the Pimas and Papagos of the same region. But by the time Spicer's book was published, he had receded from the prominence he had enjoyed in the eyes of Arizonans and people interested in Indian affairs.

This blurring of the public memory occurred in part because of the era in which Montezuma lived. While in fact extremely significant, the period of time from the end of the Indian wars, the closing of the frontier, and the passage of the General Allotment Act to the movement to reform Indian policy—from the late 1880s until the early 1920s—had been almost entirely neglected by students of Native American history. When they considered Indian history at all, historians usually focused on the more romantic period that had immediately preceded it: the final days of the Old West and the great struggles by American Indians to save their homelands and their ways of life. When armed confrontation ended, historical investigation essentially halted.

There was another reason for Montezuma's virtual disappearance from the pages of history. After his death, his papers became scattered and unavailable for scholarly research. Since Montezuma not only was important in pan-Indian concerns and in Arizona Indian matters but also wrote prolifically, his papers promised to be an enormously valuable source. And while such sources as the National Archives contained some correspondence and information, a full biography could not yet be drafted. Several writers could not be deterred. Will C. Barnes attempted to round up biographical information on Montezuma in the 1930s. His somewhat tangled narrative of over 200 pages never got into print, but it served as a partial basis for Oren Arnold's *Savage Son*, published by the University of New Mexico Press in 1950. Arnold's novel, as it must be labeled, centered almost entirely on Montezuma's early life and gave little attention to his career. It hardly represented an advance in scholarship, and as the title suggests, left something to be desired as a portrait of Indian life.

In the 1970s prospects improved immeasurably for a proper biography of Carlos Montezuma. In 1972, Hazel Hertzberg published her pioneering study of early twentieth century pan-Indianism, *The Search for an American Indian Identity*. Hertzberg's book gave attention to Montezuma, particularly in terms of his role with the Society of American Indians. While sometimes presenting an unflattering picture of Montezuma, she acknowledged his influence on the national level. During the decade, in addition, two collections of Montezuma's papers were acquired and made available to researchers. These collections, at the State Historical Society of Wisconsin and the Arizona State University Library, made possible a far more comprehensive portrayal. When consulted with other useful collections, such as the Arthur C. Parker papers at the New York State Museum, the Richard H. Pratt papers at Yale University, and the additional Montezuma file at the University of Arizona, the biography became an exciting possibility.

As it happened, I did my graduate work at the University of Wisconsin and taught for a year at Arizona State University following completion of my Ph.D., so I became acquainted with the two new collections. In the fall of 1976, I gave a paper at the American Society for Ethnohistory meeting in Albuquerque. While there, I talked with Professor Alfonso Ortiz of the University of New Mexico's Department of Anthropology. Ortiz, a Tewa, had recently urged more regard be given by scholars to the lives of such Native Americans as Charles Eastman and Carlos Montezuma. Ortiz encouraged me to write the biography and I began to work.

Now that the manuscript has been completed, I am still unsure how definitive a study it is, as parts of Montezuma's life remain essentially unknown or are subjects of conflicting reports. But I am hopeful that my study will tell us something about the man and about the changing world in which he and other Native Americans lived. It was, surely, a critical time. Indians in the American West confronted reservation conditions and a life usually greatly different from the one they had previously lived. They faced central questions about who they were, how they would exist, and what they would believe. They dealt with the powerful arm of the United States government, the Bureau of Indian Affairs, as well as pressures from an expanding Anglo-American population. To what extent could old ways continue? How should their land be used? To what kind of leadership could they turn?

Montezuma's life and career, I believe, inform us about some of the answers that Native Americans were beginning to make to these and other questions. His life as a medical doctor illustrated the potential professional careers Indians could seek and achieve if given the opportunity. His residence in Chicago showed an alternative environment that more and more Native Americans would enter as the twentieth century passed. His involvement in pan-Indian activities reflected, as Hertzberg has demonstrated, the growth of an identity beyond that of tribe or community—identity as an Indian. His deepening concern for the well-being of his people at Fort McDowell disclosed this continuing importance of reservation life. His sharp criticism of the Bureau of Indian Affairs, and the often bitter response it elicited, revealed the way in which the federal government perceived its trust responsibilities and the limits that could be placed on Native American initiative and freedom.

Carlos Montezuma was hardly a typical Indian of his time, nor was he a typical American of his era. Yet the way in which he chose to live his life, the causes he championed, the influence he had, the results he both could achieve and could not accomplish mirror much of Indian life in a transitional age. The rich resources now available, moreover, allow a rare opportunity to delineate a man and his time in a manner not always practicable, to use a word of Montezuma's day.

In the course of my research, I have had the assistance of many people and institutions. After I had started my work, Jack Larner received a grant from the National Historical Publications and Records Commission to put together the far-flung papers of Montezuma. Jack generously allowed me access to papers as his project evolved. He and his assistant, Tom Huppert, proved to be most helpful colleagues. I thank them both for their friendship and their invaluable aid. I also wish to thank a number of people in Arizona. Charles C. Colley, then archivist and field collector at Arizona State University, provided early assistance and encouragement. Carolina Butler of Paradise Valley gave me information about the contemporary Orme Dam controversey involving McDowell land and introduced me to people in the McDowell community. Sigrid Khera, then associated with the Anthropology Department of Arizona State, generously shared with me her material on Yavapai history and culture. Members of the Fort McDowell community tolerated another Anglo inquisitor about Carlos Montezuma and presented me with invaluable stories and perceptions about Montezuma's life and influence. Staff members at the State Historical Society of Wisconsin, Arizona State University, the National Archives, Yale University, Arizona Historical Society, New

York State Museum, Chicago Historial Society, Newberry Library, the University of Wyoming, and other institutions served me well. My colleagues around the country have helped with material, advice, encouragement, and criticism. Among the many I should thank are James Axtell, Vine Deloria, Jr., R. David Edmunds, William T. Hagan, Laurence Hauptman, Hazel Hertzberg, Robert Keller, Lawrence Kelly, Terry Lamb, Geoffrey Mawn, Pamela Oestreicher, Alfonso Ortiz, James Rawls, James Ronda, Margaret Szasz, Robert Trennert, and John Wunder. I appreciate the interest and aid of fellow teachers and students at the University of Wyoming. My department heads at Wyoming, Roger L. Williams and Deborah Hardy, have been most supportive. Virginia Scharff gave the manuscript a careful and critical reading and provided many helpful suggestions. Diane Alexander, Jean Henderson, Sandy Adams, Patti Martin, and Helen Martin typed final drafts of this study. Luther Wilson, director of the University of New Mexico Press, and Elizabeth Hadas, senior editor at the press, have improved the book immeasurably. My research has been assisted greatly by grants received from the National Endowment for the Humanities, the American Philosophical Society, and the University of Wyoming. I am very happy to dedicate this book to my children, Erika and Jens.

Preface to the New Printing

This book emerged in 1982, as the Yavapais of Fort McDowell neared the conclusion of a long fight against Orme Dam, whose construction would have flooded most of their lands. Many had invoked the name and example of Carlos Montezuma as they carried out this extended campaign. In 1983 the Yavapais and their allies won. Orme would not be built. Arrogant Arizonans who had attempted to bribe the Yavapais into accepting the dam now contemptuously dismissed any possibility that Fort McDowell could ever become economically viable.

These proponents of Orme Dam were quite certain that Fort McDowell would never flourish financially. They were also quite wrong. Gaming soon fueled a new prosperity at Fort McDowell. The millions of dollars generated by the Fort McDowell Yavapai Nation's casino made possible many significant new initiatives. One of the most noteworthy is the Wassaja Memorial Health Center.

As with any Indian victory, this triumph has not been easily achieved. In 1992, for example, federal agents raided Fort McDowell and attempted to haul away video gaming machines. Angry Yavapais resisted and thwarted the invasion. Their firm stance forced the state of Arizona to negotiate a compact that allowed almost all of the machines to remain. Each May the people celebrate Sovereignty Day to commemorate that defense of their rights, just as each November they recall the demise of Orme Dam.

Generosity is especially valued in Native communities and the newfound wealth of the Yavapais has permitted them to observe that old value in unprecedented ways. They have given millions of dollars to assist Native students enrolled at Arizona State University, Northern Arizona University, and the University of Arizona. Moreover, they have assumed sponsorship of the Fiesta Bowl Parade and made other substantial contributions to a wide variety of activities and enterprises within Arizona.

Established on September 15, 1903, the Fort McDowell Yavapai Nation will soon be a century old. Its survival is in and of itself an impressive testament to each generation's tenacity and resolve. Yavapai elders know full well that challenges lie ahead. Nevertheless, they share Carlos Montezuma's determination that their land must be defended and they share his belief that their community will continue.

I have been honored to write this biography of Wassaja and I am honored that his community has decided to make this book available to a new generation of readers.

Peter Iverson
Tempe, Arizona
May 12, 2001

Carlos Montezuma

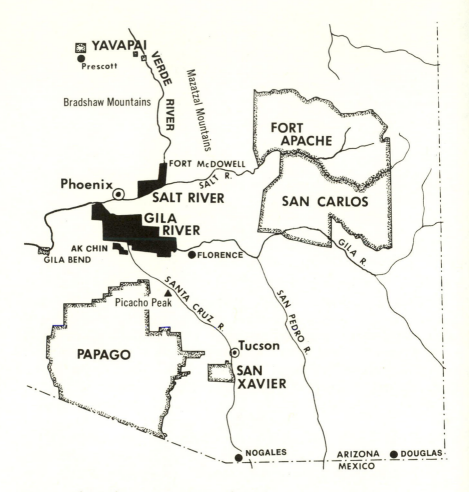

Map 1. The Indian reservations of Southern Arizona. By permission from *A Pima Past*, by Anna Moore Shaw, Tucson: University of Arizona Press, Copyright 1974.

1

The Circle Begins

His life was a circle. Born the son of Coluyevah and Thilgeyah during the 1860s, he lived to see and to shape a world they would never know. He would leave their world as a boy, live in the Midwest and East as a child, graduate from a university and from medical school, and become one of the most famous Indians of his day. As he emerged as a national figure, he became progressively more drawn to the local affairs of the people he had been forced to leave behind. In his final years, he would withdraw increasingly from his medical career and the world of his city, Chicago. Terminally ill with tuberculosis, he returned to the Yavapais of the Fort McDowell community in Arizona. There he died, in January 1923, and there he was buried. His life's circle, which had brought him into contact with the vital issues and personalities affecting American Indians of his day, would be complete.

The world would know him as Carlos Montezuma, but he did not acquire this name at birth. His parents called him Wassaja, which in English could be translated at "signaling" or "beckoning." His people, the Yavapais of central and southern Arizona, also are known as Mohave-Apaches, a confusing and misleading appellation that caused Montezuma no little difficulty late in his life. As a Mohave-Apache, Montezuma inevi-

tably became an Apache in the public eye. His combative nature
would earn him such titles as "the fiery Apache." But he was
not an Apache.

The Yavapais belong to the Yuman family. Ethnologists generally divide them into three geographical subgroups: southeastern, northeastern, and western. The Yavapais called these
groups the Keweyipaya or Wavikopaipa, Wipukyipai, and Tolke-
paya, and divided them further into various bands. These
branches of the Yavapai could be linked linguistically to peoples such as the Walapais, Havasupais, Mohaves, and Yumas.
The Yavapais had some associations with their eastern neighbors, the Tonto and San Carlos Apaches. Those ties, combined
with confusion in early names for them, led to the Mohave-
Apache label, even though the Apaches were of Athapascan
heritage, sharing linguistic similarities only with the Navajos
among peoples of the region.[1]

The Yavapais differed from other Yuman peoples in occupy-
ing a very large geographical area that included a variety of ter-
rain and climatic zones. While never numbering more than a
few thousand in total population, they occupied an area of perhaps twenty thousand square miles. They may have had cultural bonds with other Yuman peoples, but they fought and
raided many of them over the years. The Pimas and Maricopas,
their neighbors in the Fort McDowell area, historically had
been their enemies, and this animosity had not entirely disap-
peared by the time of Montezuma's birth.[2]

During Wassaja's early childhood, in the 1860s, the Anglo-
American world was rapidly enclosing the world of the Indians of Arizona. Resistance would continue into the 1880s, led
by such stalwart people as Geronimo. Still, the Anglo-Americans presence was very strong. The Navajos, for example, had
been confronted by James Carleton, Kit Carson, and others, and
had been forced in 1864 to make the Long Walk to exile at
Bosque Redondo in eastern New Mexico. In addition to existing forts, the Americans constructed such edifices as Fort Bowie
in 1862, Fort Goodwin, and Fort McDowell in 1865. The dis-
covery of gold in the Prescott area in 1863 heightened Anglo-
Indian tensions. The streams of non-Indian prospectors and
settlers disrupted Native American life. As competition made
game and forage scarce, relations among Indian peoples de-

teriorated. They fought each other, in addition to fighting the newcomers.[3]

By 1869 a drought had set in in southern Arizona. The Gila River Pima reservation was enlarged that year by 81,000 acres, but little else could have been encouraging to Indians of the area. East of the Pimas, near Florence, Anglos and Mexicans were farming and starting to take advantage of Gila River water that the Pimas had once had to themselves. In 1871, in one of many clashes between the Pimas and the Yavapais, a group of Pimas surprised some of the Yavapais, killing a number of them and capturing others. Wassaja and his two sisters survived but were among the captives.[4]

According to two Pima reminiscences, such captives normally could expect fair treatment by their captors and would be brought up among the tribe. These, however, were extraordinary times. In these hard times, Anna Moore Shaw noted,

despite his good intentions, sometimes a Pima captor was unable to provide his prisoner with food and other necessities of life. When this happened he had but one logical alternative: sell the captive and use the money to provide for his own family.[5]

Such a future awaited Wassaja, whom the Pimas had dubbed Hejelweiikam ("Left Alone"), and his sisters. The three were separated at this time, and Wassaja would never again see his sisters. They apparently were sold to a man who eventually took them to Mexico, where they died before Montezuma could rediscover them in his adult life. Already divorced from the rest of his family, he likewise would not see any of his other immediate relatives alive. His mother attempted to recover her lost children and was shot by Army scouts; his father was among the Yavapais moved to the San Carlos reservation in the 1870s, and he died at that location. An aunt and cousins would be his closest relatives still living years later at the Fort McDowell community.[6]

Three Pima men took young Wassaja to the village of Adamsville, a small settlement no longer in existence, situated about seven miles from the town of Florence. There, according to most accounts, they encountered a man by the name of Carlo Gentile. An immigrant from Italy, Gentile had been attracted to Arizona by the recent gold strikes. In addition, as a photographer and artist, he doubtless found the Southwest an attractive place to spend some time. Although a bachelor, Gentile became interested in the welfare of the young boy, and proved willing to purchase him for a sum of thirty dollars from the Pimas. In Florence, on November 17, 1871, Gentile had Wassaja baptized as Carlos Montezuma in the Church of the Assumption. The boy's new first name, of course, came from his new benefactor; his last name represented an attempt to give the young Indian some vestige of his Native American heritage. The proximity of Montezuma's Castle in central Arizona may have influenced the particular selection of surname. The baptismal certificate listed the year of Montezuma's birth as 1866. In later life Montezuma would generally use 1867 as his birthdate; available evidence suggests that he was born a little earlier, perhaps in 1865. In any event, Carlos Montezuma was not very old when Gentile adopted him, and he would not return to his homeland for nearly three decades.[7]

In relatively short order, school became an important part of Montezuma's life. He later wrote an article for the Carlisle Indian School paper relating how he had made his way up the educational ladder. As Montezuma told it, he initially was lured into the schoolyard by the promise of winning marbles from other children. When the bell rang, he followed the children into the building and was initiated into the formal educational process. It was no small transition, for he had just been "a small Apache boy in the wilds of Arizona, just as happy as a bird, free from any thought of danger."

Before long, Montezuma had mastered his ABC's, learned to count, and begun to memorize the Lord's Prayer and to sing "Precious Jewels." "I learned as fast as any of the whites," he recalled, "for the reason that the teacher delighted to instruct me." He also did well "by staying at home nights to study, not by playing at corners as did some of the white children." In other words, being around people who believed in you, combined with hard work, could provide enviable results.

He had to be more diligent than the average student, for Gentile moved around. In addition, Montezuma was not in the best of health, so he spent two years at a country school near Galesburg in central Illinois, staying with a friend of Gentile's. Montezuma attended Chicago public schools from 1872 to 1875, then the school in Galesburg from 1875 to 1877, and finally a public school in Brooklyn, New York, during the 1877 to 1878 school year.

Gentile obviously cared a good deal for Montezuma and tried to do his best by him. For several years, his business interests did well in Chicago. He became active in the Chicago Press Club and the Art Institute. But soon after he and Montezuma moved to New York, a fire destroyed Gentile's business. Despondent and uncertain about the future, the photographer finally decided that he had to give up his charge. A Mrs. Baldwin looked after the boy for a while in the New York City area. Ultimately, Baptist missionary representative George Ingalls brought Montezuma to Urbana, Illinois, where a Baptist minister, William H. Steadman, became his guardian.[8]

Both Ingalls and Steadman viewed the latter's role less as a father and more as a transitional overseer who would ensure that Montezuma traveled the proper path. Initially, the arrangement was simply room and board in exchange for a few chores, but it evolved into a meaningful, lasting relationship. Steadman would marry Montezuma and Marie Keller twenty-five years later and would also travel to Arizona to investigate the condition of the Yavapais at Fort McDowell. But Ingalls made his expectations evident at the start:

I want Montezuma to become, first a *real* Christian and then to be a Physician and with a good education and love of Christ in his heart, to go back to his people and labor for their good as a Christian or missionary physician—I want him to have a knowledge of some trade—perhaps a carpenter, or other useful trade, a knowledge of farming so he can direct such branches of industry among his people.

In the spirit of the age, Ingalls said that while Montezuma was "bright in *some* studies, he seems slow when put at work and must be trained and have patience exercised towards him, for his race are disinclined naturally to hard work."[9] Montezuma would go on to become a good Christian, not surprisingly a good Baptist, as well as a physician, though his work for his people may have followed lines different from those Ingalls en-

visioned. Ingalls's attitude about the natural disinclination of
Indians to work hard was one against which Montezuma would
labor all his life.

Following two years of preparatory work, Montezuma enrolled at the University of Illinois. He attained his B.S. degree
in chemistry following a four-year course, which included work
in English, mathematics, chemistry, German, physiology, mi-
croscopy, zoology, mineralogy, physics, physiography, mental
science, logic, constitutional history, political economy, and
geology. His scores ranged from 75 to 91, with his best marks
in chemistry, which he took each quarter. For his degree, Montezuma wrote a seventeen-page thesis entitled "Valuation of
Opiums and Their Products." He apparently was well liked
around campus, participating in several school activities ranging from military drill to speech. The campus paper, *The Illini*,
on May 5, 1883, carried an account of a speech contest in Adel-
phic Hall the night before, during which a large audience heard
Montezuma give "one of the rare treats of the evening, on 'Indian's Bravery;' commencing with the impressive scene of
Themopylae, he likened the Indians to that band of Spartans."
The writer called Montezuma's description of the Indians in
America before the arrival of the white man the "most vivid,
pathetic and beautiful picture ever painted in our Hall."[10]

"Like Napoleon, whose star sunk for war on the battlefield,
so the Indian star sunk to rise no more, on the battlefields of
America," concluded the *Illini* article. At a very early date,
Montezuma clearly had adopted a positive, even romantic view
of the aboriginal past. However, he had concluded with equal
firmness that this period could never return. He would look
back on his childhood in Arizona and speak of it in fond, ideal-
ized terms. Nonetheless, the Indian of today, he began to argue,
could not live in that past and had to move on to the present
and prepare for the future.

Upon his graduation from Illinois, Montezuma faced the
issue of his own future. He returned to Chicago and looked for
work. One of his letters of introduction was to Fuller and Fuller, wholesale druggists in the city. One of the Fullers, who
remembered Montezuma as a young newspaper boy, asked
whether he looked to pharmacy as a career. Montezuma replied
no, he wanted to study medicine, so Fuller provided him in

turn with a letter of introduction to a Dr. Hollister of Chicago
Medical College. Hollister, Montezuma later recalled, was a
bit of a philanthropist and gave him much encouragement.
Montezuma's tuition to the Chicago Medical College would
be arranged, but he needed work. After six months of search-
ing, Montezuma uncovered a job cleaning a drug store and
washing windows about four blocks from the medical school,
then located at 26th Street and Prairie Avenue. He could begin
his medical studies.[11]

It took Montezuma longer than he expected, but he completed medical school in 1889. Receiving his M.D. qualified
him, along with Charles Eastman, as one of the few Native
American physicians. They were difficult years; Montezuma
had to struggle to keep himself in school. He had no money to
spare, and his studies demanded all he could give them. One
of the people he turned to at this time for advice and friendship was the head of Carlisle Indian School, Richard Henry
Pratt. Montezuma first wrote to Pratt on January 16, 1887. His
letter marked the beginning of a lifelong correspondence between the two men.

Pratt was a veteran of many campaigns during the wars conducted against American Indians in the 1860s and 1870s. A director of Indian scouts who later accompanied Indian prisoners
eastward, he became impressed not only with Native American potential but with the injustices being inflicted upon them
as well. At Fort Marion in 1876 Pratt inaugurated his pioneering efforts in Indian education. He firmly believed that Native
Americans could succeed within American society, if given
proper training and if immersed in the right environment. For
Pratt, that meant industrial education in the Northeast. Inspired by the example of Hampton Institute in Virginia, Pratt
brought Indian students first to that school, directed by Gen.
Samuel C. Armstrong. Soon thereafter, he began his own institution, Carlisle Indian Industrial School, in Pennsylvania.
There Pratt hoped to shear Native American pupils of their
Indian identity and to prepare them for a new life in modern
industrial America. "Kill the Indian and save the man" would
be but one of his prevailing sentiments.[12]

Montezuma would receive more letters from Pratt than from
any other individual. Pratt, to be sure, was a tireless corre-

spondent. In addition, he expressed his views in a forceful, dogmatic manner that certainly influenced a young man in a formative stage. Pratt's style and his growing antipathy for the Indian Bureau affected the crusade Montezuma would launch eventually for Native Americans. Initially, at a critical point, Pratt provided encouragement and support when Montezuma needed it.

Pratt wrote to Montezuma January 21, 1887, noting in part:

This world is full of work for those who will undertake it. For your people the Indian race—there is a very large work to be done both ways; not only are the Indians to be educated to better things but the white people are to be educated to allow better things—not for a few, but for all. You and I have something to do with both phases of this work.

Such advice struck a responsive chord. Montezuma's career really would run on two tracks. He would attempt to work with and for Indians, initially through employment within the Bureau of Indian Affairs, and later through the Society of American Indians and with Indians of southern Arizona and elsewhere. Also, however, in part because of his unsatisfactory experience with the Bureau, he would become a kind of missionary to the white world. He would try to demonstrate to the non-Indian population what Native Americans could achieve if given the opportunity. That demonstration, to be visible and effective, had to take place within white, urban America.

The head of Carlisle invited Montezuma to speak to audiences in Philadelphia and New York to show what Indians could do. During the same year, on the occasion of the passage of the General Allotment Act, Montezuma asked Pratt if he would be entitled to land when tribal land was taken in severalty. Pratt suggested he write to the commissioner of Indian affairs. Montezuma, in fact, had already written to the secretary of the interior, identifying himself as "an Apache whom you heard in Philadelphia last winter when Captain Pratt gave his entertainment" and asking under what conditions and where he would be entitled to land. Commissioner J. D. C. Atkins notified Montezuma he would be entitled to an allotment with the Apaches when their reservation was divided, if he was located there at the time, or he could make settlement upon any

vacant land belonging to the United States. In return, Montezuma told Atkins that he wished to secure a place where he
could do the most good for his downtrodden people, especially
the Apaches. "I think," he ventured, "there can be derived some
good out of them."

As 1888 began, Montezuma looked forward primarily to the
prospect of completing medical school. Pratt held forth the op-
tion of starting his medical career in Pennsylvania with a local
physician, and for good measure, the chance from April to June
of accompanying some younger Indian students to England "to
show English people what we are doing in America and con-
tradict Buffalo Bill's Wild West." Plans for the European trip
soon collapsed, however, and at about the same time Montezuma learned that he would not graduate. He wrote twice to
Pratt on March 26, informing him that the faculty had decided
not to grant him a diploma on account of "backstanding" and
also for his "welfare." Sadly and angrily he accused them of
not taking any interest in him and of withholding his diploma
to keep him from being with the Carlisle superintendent. Montezuma expressed his uncertainty about what to do, whether
to stay the requisite period or deny the faculty the satisfaction and finish his studies in the East. He concluded that his
mentors had not been fair; indeed, they were prejudiced. Montezuma offered to work with Pratt but pledged to remain in
Chicago if Pratt thought it best.[15]

Pratt responded immediately and in characteristic fashion.
Montezuma had but one worthy course, he admonished, and
that was to stay. He should insist they award the diploma because of his gains, success, and worth. Climb that mountain,
Pratt said, and then go on to reach the highest honors and place
in the profession. Christ's crucifixion brought eternal life to
man; "Rejoice, my good Carlos, that you are considered worthy
of a little crucifying and may the good Father ever have you
under the shadow of His wing."[16]

Montezuma remained in Chicago and received his M.D. in
1889. In the interim, Pratt sent him the Carlisle school paper,
which Montezuma assured his mentor, gave him "courage to
press forward where the Indians ought to be—man among
men." Being a man would be a favorite theme of Montezuma's
in years to come, whether he was urging a patient to pay a

delinquent bill, stressing to his people the need to keep striv-
ing and working, or addressing a non-Indian audience about
Native American potential. Now, trying to decide how to begin
his medical career, Montezuma again expressed interest in
working "more for the Indians than in the past" and in being
"useful to my people."[17]

Upon graduation, lacking a better alternative, Montezuma
entered private practice. He opened an office near Chicago Medical College, but few patients were willing to try the new doctor. Montezuma later told a congressional committee that he
learned to live "without anything," after a while. After two or
three months, he received a letter from Commissioner of Indian Affairs Thomas Jefferson Morgan inquiring about his interest in a position as physician within the Indian Service.
While not making a definite promise, the commissioner said
that any application would receive serious consideration and
observed he had recently appointed Miss La Flesche as physician among her own people, the Omaha. How had Morgan heard
of Montezuma? His letter, dated August 3, 1889, revealed his
source: "My friend, Captain Pratt, tells me that you have finished your medical studies, and have entered upon the practice
of your profession. He speaks of you in very high terms as a
man of intelligence and perseverance, and it has occurred to
me that you might like a position as physician among your
own people at some Indian Agency."[18]

Montezuma responded to Morgan's inquiry on August 12,
1889. "Nothing else would give me a greater pleasure than to
sacrifice my past experience for the elevation of a nation that
you have at heart." Ever since he had been old enough to appreciate his surroundings, he continued, he had hoped to situ-
ate himself to help his people, and thus he had corresponded
with Pratt. Though he would not have applied for a post, for
fear of being an office seeker, Montezuma pledged to accept
cordially any position that might be offered. He expressed a
desire to "reform them and also to do all I can to set them a
good example."[19]

It was a new day for the American Indian, Montezuma contended. If ever the Indian question, as he called it, could be
settled, it would be in Morgan's administration. Those people
interested in improving the lot of Native Americans no longer
had the wild Indian to contend with "but the influences of civi-

lization. Even though far removed from his original homeland in Arizona and from Native American life in general in the West, Montezuma sensed already that Indians confined to reservations were exposed both to opportunity and to danger. What he perceived as the good aspects of Anglo-American civilization, such as written English, Christianity, and the chance to make one's way into new options and careers, were more accessible to them, but Indians could also be prey to unscrupulous outsiders who could corrupt them and exploit them and their resources.[20]

Such feelings were consistent with the opinions of Commissioner Morgan. Francis Paul Prucha has summarized Morgan's commissionership: "With great energy and absolute conviction he promoted policies of individualization, Christianization, and acculturation of the Indians and their absorption into American white society in a status no different from that of other citizens."[21] A proponent of a greater role by the federal government in Native American education, he doubtless looked to Montezuma as an ideal example of what the Indian could become.

Morgan promptly appointed Montezuma to the post of clerk and physician at the Indian school at Fort Stevenson, Dakota Territory, at an annual salary of $1,000. Although he recalled in later years that he was so eager to assume his new responsibilites that he caught the next train out of town, Montezuma actually waited several weeks to respond to the commissioner's invitation to become an Indian Service employee. He needed time to take care of remaining business in Chicago, but he could start work at Fort Stevenson on September 20. Montezuma offered thanks for such a responsible position and hoped it would be "for the betterment of a nation who linger around the threshold of civilization."[22]

Montezuma left Chicago with genuine enthusiasm for what awaited him. He would be entering new country, and he would have the opportunity to care for Indian people. In addition, he would have the chance to prove to those who had stood in his way during the late stages of his medical studies that he could be a good physician. Montezuma must have been proud of obtaining his M.D. Now he could go on to demonstrate his value as a doctor and worth as a human being to both the Indian and white worlds.

The discipline and determination he had needed to fulfill the requirements for the degree had already shaped the belief he would possess all his life in the power of work. Equally strong was his conviction that each Indian should enjoy the freedom to achieve. Not surprisingly, Montezuma saw in his own life a lesson about Native American potential. If given advantages like his and the same opportunities to learn, how many Indians could reach similar heights?

For the past decade he had supported himself, spending summers at hard labor on various farms and working during school years at a variety of jobs. In June of 1888 he remembered:

As I was thrown on my own resources I was fully aware that I had to climb a mountain of discipline in order to be a man among men. I realized that I belonged to a race who were being driven at the point of the bayonet instead of by persuasion. With these thoughts I felt a rush of indignation which called on me to stand firm to the rights of that race whose blood circulates through my veins.

But his work was just beginning:

Shall I call this done? No! Never! While there is life in me I shall teach my race the values of life from savagery to civilization. I will lead them to the Father that watched over their forefathers when they fell into the hands of their enemies, to the God who permitted the nation to which they belonged to be nearly whipped out of existence. I will teach them that the same Providence guides them today, and requires of them a greater responsibility.[23]

The idealism and optimism that Montezuma carried northward to Dakota Territory, as we shall see, would not survive his first year on the Northern Plains. He would assume four different positions in the next several years, moving from Fort Stevenson to the Western Shoshone Agency in Nevada to the Colville Agency in Washington and finally to Carlisle Indian School in Pennsylvania, where he would at last serve under Richard H. Pratt. Like his time in medical school, these would be awkward, arduous years, but they would teach him lessons crucial to his twentieth-century career of advocate and reformer.

2

An Indian Service Employee

"I do not regret that I went into the Indian Service," wrote Montezuma after his period of service in the Bureau of Indian Affairs. "I went into it with a missionary spirit and I worked for the interest of my people. I enjoyed the work." He became a physician in the Service because he felt that he owed to God and his people a part of his life, having had the privileges of eighteen years of schooling. He resigned because he believed he was going backward in his profession. Thus after seven and a half years, Montezuma quit his government position to face "the competition of life" in Chicago.[1]

Living at Fort Stevenson in North Dakota, at the Western Shoshone Agency in Nevada, and at the Colville Agency in Washington, Montezuma saw for himself the conditions of western reservations at the end of the frontier. His experiences helped shape many of his later writings. Montezuma did not like what he perceived as the consequences of reservation life, and he often opposed the way the Indian Bureau operated. He clashed with Indian Service employees over working conditions, pay, and priorities. His move to Carlisle to work with Richard H. Pratt marked a transition from the first stage of his medical career to the beginnings of his career as a reformer of Indian policy.

15

Initially Montezuma responded with enthusiasm to his new surroundings at Fort Stevenson. Pratt, for one, was greatly pleased and predicted it would be an invaluable experience. Montezuma could as well make himself "invaluable to the Superintendent and together you can make many improvements in the school."[2]

In November 1889, Montezuma reported his early reactions to Fort Stevenson to Mrs. Amelia S. Quinton of the Women's National Indian Association, a philanthropic organization headquartered in Philadelphia. He had "at last reached the first step in my aim in life." Having been a resident of urban American for some years, Montezuma was surprised that there could be a school in such isolated surroundings. Serving primarily Arikara, Gros Ventre, and Mandan children of the Fort Berthold reservation, Fort Stevenson was seventy-five miles from Bismarck, the nearest railroad stop. The children found themselves in a highly structured environment, which included marching to breakfast, "perfect order" at the breakfast table, and morning worship service. Montezuma found the parents a varied lot; some were "respectable," but he thought a great improvement was still desirable.

The new physician went out of his way to praise the superintendent, George E. Gerowe. The school had improved greatly during Gerowe's administration, Montezuma said, and his twenty years of experience would be important in making Fort Stevenson what it should be—the school of the Northwest. It would not be easy, for the students tended to "disregard the opportunities and privilege given to them," but Montezuma pledged to do whatever he could "to impress upon these young minds the duty of life."[4]

In his daily activities and in at least one formal talk, Montezuma attempted to inspire the boys and girls at the school to a nobler and higher manhood and womanhood. Montezuma emphasized the change that had transpired in the thinking of whites. Formerly they had seen the Indians as wild deer, incapable of education. Then some of them conceived the reservation idea to isolate the Indians and protect the whites from them. Now a new era had arrived in Native American education, spearheaded by Pratt's pioneering experiment at Carlisle. And a new time had come for the use of Indian land with the passage of the General Allotment Act. But eighty acres were not enough, "without knowledge, without money, without tools, without a house." Where could young Indians acquire the knowledge and skills they needed? Government schools such as Fort Stevenson could teach them to take care of themselves, to take care of animals, to plow, sow, and reap, to cook, serve, and sweep, to read, and to pray. Montezuma applauded the decision of the Indian Bureau that teaching in the schools be only in English. "We cannot be civilized through the agency of an uncivilized tongue."[5]

The government could assist and the teachers could instruct, Montezuma continued, but the boys and girls of Fort Stevenson must "devote with all your might what is given you to do, whether it be hard or easy. You must help yourself. Then gradually, you shall be equipped for life's struggle and competitions and once equipped you shall be free, and shall not be consigned back or elsewhere for any cause whatever." The school physician had seen a sick student about to leave to go home. Perhaps he would die. Still, Montezuma resolved:

... do you know, children, I would rather die in the struggle for my manhood and the welfare of my people than to remain in ignorance with health. We cannot do any more than run the race as far as we can. God will do the rest. Let the heart within you throb for the betterment of yourselves and of a nation which you claim. You are a part of the American family; children, to be educated for the responsibilities that will surely come to you as a citizen of this country.[6]

By the spring, Montezuma's feelings had altered drastically. He and Gerowe had come to an irrevocable parting of the ways; Gerowe angrily told Montezuma that one of them had to leave the school at the end of the quarter. Though he had worked conscientiously, Montezuma believed he had "been wronged like many of the Indian instructors which have left this institution"; *prejudice, distrustful feeling* and lack of encouragement from the superintendent will always lead an Educated Indian downwards." "As a peacable, Christian Indian physician who has a love for his people and an ambitious desire to benefit them for a nobler aim of life," Montezuma wrote to Commissioner Thomas J. Morgan, asking whether he should transfer or remain at Fort Stevenson.[7]

The day Montezuma wrote to Morgan, Gerowe had written as well, asking that Montezuma be removed from the Indian Service for incompetency. Expressing his interest in Montezuma's welfare and a desire for his success, the commissioner listed the charges made against the doctor and asked for a prompt reply to them. On June 27, 1890, Montezuma reviewed his stint at Fort Stevenson and responded to Gerowe's accusation in a carefully detailed seventeen-page letter.[8]

Gerowe did not mince words. He apparently called Dr. Montezuma inefficient in the practice of medicine; charged him with presenting false reports to the Bureau; labeled him as being disliked by the pupils and being incompetent in his office; and, for good measure, termed him impudent and filthy. Thus, Montezuma's lengthy reply could hardly be startling. If Gerowe's indictments gained any credence whatsoever, it would blight his fledgling medical career in the short run and perhaps permanently harm it. As Montezuma put it, if he were as Gerowe had presented him, he would fully deserve being discharged from the Indian Service.

Upon his arrival at Fort Stevenson, Montezuma said he found the children with chronic eczema. The children had received "this annoying skin affection from the *filthy camp life*" and stayed in school "*without change of clothing and without any help.*" Their beds were not changed; the bathroom was filthy. Montezuma ordered requisite changes be made to improve the environment, but his instructions did not meet with full compliance. Still, the health of the children remained as good as could be expected, and no fatalities had been recorded. If the children disliked him, it might be because he required more from them than did the other employees; "I came here not to be ruled by the untutored Indian children, but I came with love and 19 years of discipline in the white man's way." He could not fairly be called impudent for exercising the right to express his opinions. Of all the charges the one of filth rankled Montezuma the most. He professed astonishment and labeled it a mad man's testimony. Finally, he related examples of prejudice against him during the year, including suspicions of his relations with girl students, which he angrily denied, stating that they had been retracted by those who had made errant observations. Montezuma concluded that rather than be discouraged, he should be encouraged to become more useful to his people.[9]

Fortunately for Montezuma, Commissioner Morgan did not take Gerowe's allegations very seriously, but things had reached such a point at Fort Stevenson that Montezuma could no longer continue his position at the school. A vacancy opened at the Western Shoshone Agency in Nevada, and Morgan appointed Montezuma as physician there at the annual salary of $1,000. Montezuma accepted the post, reporting on July 21, 1890 and thanking the Commissioner for his fatherly advice and encouragements. He had to walk eighteen miles into the agency from White Rock; he would remain in Nevada until January 1893.[10]

At the Western Shoshone Agency, Montezuma apparently was spared the kind of vitriolic confrontations that had characterized his tenure at Fort Stevenson, yet he remained far from satisfied with his working conditions. Initially he requested a horse and saddle in order to visit different villages ten and thirteen miles from the agency. He needed a stove in his room and a properly heated drug room. His vaccine against smallpox was old and not reliable. He asked for a second horse, as "one horse is impracticable and cruel to the poor creature." And he wanted to be able to practice outside the reservation, serving non-Indians who otherwise generally would have to travel sixty-five miles to the nearest physician in Tuscarora.[11]

His most poignant plea was an urgent entreaty for a hospital building. He presented several justifications for the construction of such a facility. Montezuma objected to the medicine man, "the curse of savage life." His complaints here are of interest in part because of the image Montezuma would later acquire in Arizona of being sympathetic to traditional tribal practices. In 1891, however, he inveighed against this "well nigh omnipresent" figure and his "diabolical incantation." Because of the medicine man's influence, Montezuma would be refused admittance to minister to the sick but blamed nevertheless for an individual's death. Second, Montezuma needed to be able to treat the school children away from their families' "miserable and squalid hovels" and the "baleful influence" of the medicine man. He had to be able to treat his patients and not have to worry about exposure or lack of proper care.[12]

Morgan could not bestow the hospital, even if he was moved by Montezuma's pleas. As he later told Henry L. Dawes, Montezuma's letter "evinces intelligence as well as heart." "Of course," Morgan added, "his pitiful appeal in behalf of the humane treatment of the unfortunate sick under his care will be in vain. I have pleaded and urged and begged for money for hospitals, but have been refused, and I am helpless." The commissioner did not expect to achieve anything by sharing Montezuma's letter with the Massachusetts senator, but he forwarded it so "that you may see how an Indian looks at this matter and that you may divide with me the sorrow, which I know you feel as well as I, that we must turn a deaf ear to such calls of humanity."[13]

Two other episodes during Montezuma's sojourn in Nevada shed light on his evolving perspectives and priorities. The first involved his interest in working with Indian students who had completed their schooling, and the second concerned his growing antipathy toward the federal government's administration of Native American affairs. His association with Pratt centrally affected both concerns. Doubtless influenced by the outing system practiced by Pratt at Carlisle, Montezuma attempted to form an association to help Indian returning students or those who wished to work either among white people or at agencies. Pratt believed deeply in the practice of immersing his students in the world of the white man and particularly in the working element of that world. Indian students at Carlisle thus were supposed to gain practical, vocational skills and were to have contact with white families. The families, ideally fully imbued with the work ethic, would serve as models to the Indians of the kind of home atmosphere that one should prefer. Commissioner Morgan endorsed this principle enthusiastically, as it fit in directly with his concept of the main goal of education: "the development of character, the formation of manhood and womanhood" through a course of training "fairly saturated with moral idea, fear of God, and respect for the rights of others; love of truth and fidelity to duty; personal purity, philanthropy, and patriotism."[14]

Writing to Indian agents scattered across the reservations of the United States, Montezuma noted that "our labor must begin with our rising young Indians. For them to lose by idleness means failure; what they want is learning and labor." He asked the agents to forward lists of returned Indian students and of individuals who could speak and read the English language. There is not much evidence that he received a significant response. John Fosher, the agent at the Shoshone (Wind River) Agency in Wyoming, submitted a list "of Indians and half-breeds who speak the English language and nearly all can read and right [sic] there are others not here enumerated who can use enough English for ordinary intercourse." Fifty-four names were on the list, including some who had played and would play important roles in Wind River reservation life: Washakie, Shakespeare, Enos, and Black Coal. The Indian Agent at Sac and Fox-Shawnee Agency cautiously would furnish names, assuming that Montezuma would give the people on the list some literature or had in mind some other philanthropic purpose. But apparently most agents ignored the request, either out of apathy or because they distrusted Montezuma's motives. The association did not become a reality, yet the idea did not expire. Montezuma would again raise the idea of an association at the turn of the century, and, most significantly, would be affiliated with the effort to start the Society of American Indians, an organization that primarily embraced Native Americans who had a good deal of formal education.[15]

Montezuma's tenure in Nevada also marked an expansion of his disenchantment with federal Indian policy. His unhappy experience at Fort Stevenson, of course, had not left him with a high opinion of the way the government carried out its trustee responsibilities. His continuing difficulties with facilities and supplies at the Western Shoshone Agency surely were irksome. In addition, at this time Pratt and Carlisle faced some problems with "sufficient funding." "Stand up and face the foe," Montezuma admonished Pratt, "for you have one Apache in an ambush ready at any moment to rush out and present the Indian question black and white." "It is disgusting," he wrote, "to see how the government ignores the efficient workers in the Indian service."

In the debate over the form Indian education should take, Montezuma unequivocally endorsed the off-reservation boarding school—a position fully squared with that of Pratt. In explaining his stance, he used the very words with which he would later describe the limitations of reservation life:

If the government is so economizing, why not appropriate sufficient money for transportation of Indian children to the east? The children in a few years will be self-supporting, have command of the English language and they will have some idea of the world, and I do not think they will ever return to camp life, but will be a man, not a savage; a citizen, not a pauper. While, if the Indian children remain on reservations and attend day schools, they will lack the above opportunities; at the age of fifteen and sixteen they are married; another family to be added to the ration list, which means expense to the government for years to come as they will be idlers, beggers, gamblers and paupers.[16]

Montezuma went on to suggest that Indian parents might not be able to know what was best for their children. He further argued that reservations shielded their residents from necessary programs:

. . . if the choice of my life remained with my mother and father or myself I would not be writing to you. Ignorance and at the very lowest depth of an uncivilized life of which the reservation bondage bestows would have been my fate. . . . We have enslaved the Indians in ignorance and superstitions long enough and have fed and clothed them without any recompense . . . We have experimented with the Indians by bullets and reservation system, and they are expensive and failures. I know of no way by which the Indians can become like the whites only by the same process, which the whites give to their children and that is, "education." This has never failed to improve any nation. The Indians of today can never prosper or grow great, if they are hid away from the outer world and its sunshine of enlightenment.[17]

Finally, the Baptist physician vented some anti-Catholic feelings. He saw Catholic influence behind congressmen who opposed "the freeing of the Indians from their reservation bondage of degradation and ruin to that of enlightenment and education." And he agonized over the prospect of Native Americans "being made a slave under the crown of Rome." Montezuma's comments must be viewed in the context of late nineteenth-century America, an era that was hardly the heyday of the ecumenical movement. Many Protestant Americans were suspicious of the Catholic church and worried about the country's direction amid the onslaught of southern and eastern European immigrants. Within the field of Indian education, the role of the churches was very controversial. Catholic-Protestant rivalry had characterized the westward movement. Now, in the Americanization period, when, as one Commissioner of Indian Affairs put it, the goal should be to make the Indian feel at home in America, Catholic and Protestant representatives still vied with one another. Given Montezuma's upbringing, it is not surprising that he harbored some anti-Catholic sentiments; Pratt and Morgan shared the bias. Morgan, in fact, was an ordained Baptist minister, and his term as commissioner of Indian affairs had been distinguished by monumental wrangles with the Catholic church, primarily over the issue of contract schools. He steadfastly opposed the notion of the federal government contracting with the churches to provide educational services; his stance, combined with his religious affiliation, guaranteed a lively controversy. Montezuma certainly was but one individual caught up in a widespread, provocative altercation.[18]

After two and a half years in Nevada, Montezuma wearied of the isolation. He "yearned for enlightenment." He had made friends at Western Shoshone, but to "be surrounded by influences which would be for my betterment," he was willing to start anew. On October 28, 1892, he requested a transfer to another agency. Morgan presented him with five alternative positions, either vacant or soon to be so: Warm Springs, Oregon; Umatilla, Oregon; Pawnee, Oklahoma; Nespilem, Colville Agency, Washington; and Blackfeet, Montana. Montezuma telegramed the Commissioner that he would accept Colville. Morgan appointed him physician there at $1,200 per year, to start work January 9, 1893.[19]

Colville proved to be an unhappy choice. Within a few weeks after his arrival, Montezuma complained to Maj. Hal J. Cole, the local agent, about working conditions and petitioned Morgan once again for another post. The doctor lacked respectable shelving for his drugs and a chair in his office, curtains or blinds in the drug room, a table, an office desk, a riding horse, saddle, blankets, and bridle. He informed Morgan that he regretted having made the move and asked "guidance as a lonely Apache who is trying to seek a higher scale in life." Could he move elsewhere?[20]

The new year, however, had brought a change of administration to Washington, D.C. Grover Cleveland had defeated Benjamin Harrison in the fall election, and Morgan had resigned from the Indian Service to become corresponding secretary of the Baptist Home Mission Society and editor of the *Home Mission Monthly*. Acting Commissioner R. V. Belt told Montezuma there were no vacancies at present, but some might occur when the transition in administration had fully taken effect. Montezuma was told he could call the attention of the department to the matter after a few months.[21]

In mid-June, Montezuma expressed his desire to "leave the service in the near future to locate in a civilized community, to show the white people that an Indian—though he be an Apache—can compete in the learned profession." Such an action would be in keeping with his general philosophy that the "best way to solve the Indian question is to put them in a civilized community." He had not sought to be in the Indian Service, but he had tried to help better the lot of his people. He had never had a leave of absence, but requested one now for sixty-one days in order to attend the World's Fair and seek a location to practice. If his plans did not work out, he could then go back to Nespilem.[22]

Clearly he hoped not to return. Even the weather had not been cooperative. He had heard great things about Washington, but in the second half of April snow had still been on the ground. The Nespilem River flowed within a short distance of his house, but he had caught few trout. By contrast, the Nevada climate had been delightful; he had enjoyed good fishing and hunting in the aptly named Duck Valley. More critically, he told Pratt, it was time "to fulfill the higher mission than mere physician, that is to prove to the white people there is the same stuff in the Indians as there is in the White people, it only requires the same environments."[23]

Montezuma had grown weary of what he termed the ignorance and superstition afflicting reservation life. And he sharply disagreed with what he perceived as the basic thrust of contemporary Indian policy. "To my mind," he argued, "we have been nursing the Indians too much with our 'sympathies' . . . To build up good, strong characters we must give away to many of our good intentions." He added:

To bestow on a baby a man's wants is absurd. To continue in our blind kindness toward the Indians means *'let them alone,'* Indians *will be Indians/ 'they cannot be made men and women like us.'*

The Indians do not die because of civilization, they die for want of character, to withstand the evil influence of civilization . . .[24]

Rather than leave the Indian Service entirely, Montezuma embarked on a course that satisfied several of his current desires. In the summer of 1893, he transferred to his final position in the Bureau: physician of Carlisle School under the supervision of Richard H. Pratt. Here he could work with Indian students removed from the reservation and here he could be with the old soldier with whom he had been corresponding. It would not be a permanent arrangement, for Montezuma ultimately wanted to be a kind of missionary to the white community, an example of what Indians could achieve. Still, it represented a logical transition in that direction.

Montezuma arrived at Carlisle July 27, 1893 and remained at the school for nearly two and a half years before resigning, effective January 8, 1896, to enter private practice in Chicago. It would be a period when he could test in practice many of the general theories about Indian life and Indian potential that he had been developing in his years on the western reservations. Undoubtedly he expected to see Native American students free to achieve, now that they had left their home communities. The students would not gamble; they would learn discipline. And these students must be given every assistance and every encouragement. For children to come under the influence of Christian civilization, they must be taken away from their homes. Moreover, Native American students should not just leave home for a few years and then return. There ought to be enough money so that they could attend college. Such additional exposure and training would increase what they could contribute to the world and improve the likelihood that they would be "rescued from the pits into which their parents are sunken."[25]

Montezuma clearly enjoyed his tenure at Carlisle. We know this in part because there is no evidence of the kind of complaining that marked his sojourns on western reservations. His stay cemented the bond between him and Pratt, which would last throughout life. When Montezuma resigned from his position at the school, Pratt noted that the doctor's services "have been most satisfactory." Captain Pratt fully sympathized with his ambition to enter private practice and, of course, saw Montezuma as a shining example of Native American achievement.[26]

Although he fully appreciated the efforts of Pratt and the place of Carlisle in the overall program of Indian education, Montezuma probably left the school with a better sense of the institution's natural limitations. Carlisle's enrollment had reached 800 by the time of his arrival. While this represented an increase and was in itself a substantial number, it paled by comparison to the total number of Native American children in the country. Although schools such as Haskell in Kansas and Genoa in Nebraska would be established in great part because of Carlisle's success, no new schools would be founded in the East. Transportation costs alone militated against enlarging upon the Carlisle precedent. In addition, the students who enrolled at Carlisle often did so with little preparation. The instructors and staff at the school therefore faced a tremendous challenge in the limited time afforded them to educate their pupils. Generally students attended Carlisle for a maximum of five years, though some left sooner and a few remained longer in an effort to graduate. Pratt's critics emphasized that most Carlisle students did not graduate and that even fewer entered college or university. They also observed that most Carlisle students did not, in fact, permanently relocate in the East. Rather they returned to the reservation environment from which they had come and away from which Carlisle was designed to direct them.[27]

Nonetheless, relative to other Indian schools of the era, Carlisle probably came closer to achieving its particular aims than most. Montezuma could point with pride to individual lives that had been transformed there. He had the satisfaction of being at Carlisle during its real heyday, before Pratt fell into disfavor and was forced out in 1904. As a physician, for example, Montezuma served as medical adviser to the famous Carlisle football team. He accompanied the squad on its trips to compete with the leading university teams in the United States. Montezuma recognized that the sport had brought more publicity and attention to Carlisle than any other factor, and he believed that the Indians' remarkable gridiron prowess won over many non-Indians to the school's side. He wrote to Pratt from Chicago in the year he moved there:

I can give no words that will express the amount of good, the awakening power of what Carlisle is doing for the rising generation of the Indians by your football team and band coming to Chicago. The football team fought and won the Laurel of the West; the Band instilled into the hearts of the cultured and refined that delicate and most sacred character in the Indian.[28]

At another time he responded to a query about the qualities of Carlisle players:

When anything happens to the Indian, we have always heard; "well, it is the same old story." or "He is only an Indian;" but now, "It is suprising!" Carlisle Indian Industrial School is a bundle of surprising facts, and one of them is its football team. My recollection goes back to the time when these new boys shyly and awkwardly entered the gymnasium hall. By skillful management and instruction they have developed into splendid athletes . . . Contrary to the old idea that most of the football players are rough and uncouth, in the fiercest scramble or in the parlor Carlisle boys are gentlemen. To be silent and indifferent under showers of applause and honor is the Indian character.[29]

Football, as Montezuma noted from Chicago, was not Carlisle's sole claim to public acclaim. Musical accomplishments of the students also caught the national eye. An Oneida, Dennison Wheelock, directed the young musicians. Wheelock, who later became involved in pan-Indian affairs, was trained at an eastern conservatory. He composed music as well as conducted it, including a piece entitled, "From Savagery to Civilization." But perhaps the most heralded Indian musician at Carlisle was not Wheelock, but a Sioux woman named Zitkala-sa, an accomplished violinist whose abilities earned her much attention. One article describing the school said in part:

. . . the fact of an Indian girl being able to play so marvelously well on so difficult an instrument as the violin is regarded as showing clearly the possibilities of not only lifting the Indian race completely out of the slough of despond in which they have been so long sunk,

but elevating them to the same plane as that which the advanced
white man occupies.[30]

Zitkala-sa later emerged as both a writer and activist. She
continued to use her Dakota name in her public life and as Gertrude (Simmons) Bonnin, she would figure prominently in Indian life of the early twentieth century.

Being at Carlisle afforded Montezuma the opportunity to
meet many of the people centrally involved in Indian policy
and concerns. At the annual conference hosted by Albert K.
Smiley on the shores of Lake Mohonk, Commissioner Morgan
had mentioned Montezuma as an example of education Native
American adulthood who could have a powerful, beneficial influence. Now Montezuma could attend the conference, as he
did in 1893 and 1895. On both occasions he addressed the assembled audience, sharing his convictions about reservation
life. In words he often recycled, he criticized the effects of such
existence, labeling the reservation a demoralizing prison, a barrier to enlightenment, and a promoter of idleness, gamblers,
paupers, and ruin. Montezuma urged the conference participants to open the reservations and allow white settlers to set a
good example for the Indians. In another instance, Indian Rights
Association President Herbert Welsh asked Montezuma for his
assistance in judging essays on the topics "How Shall We Civilize the Indians?" and "Indian Education." Contacts with people like Welsh and Smiley generally would be helpful in the
career of reformer that soon would blossom for Montezuma.
He would ask for their opinion and their aid and often receive
it, though not always; Indian Rights Association representative
S. M. Brosius would oppose Montezuma years later in the
Southwest.[31]

"Captain Pratt has not loaded me to come here and fire at
you," Montezuma told the 1895 Lake Mohonk Conference.
"He knows that I stand independent." Despite such assurance,
one may ask legitimately about the extent to which Pratt influenced or even controlled Montezuma. As has been shown
and as will be evident, the two men were very close. They
shared many perspectives; they cheered each other on. "He and
I," Montezuma once remarked, "always hit the same nail."
They admired each other's dedication, character, and person-

ality. Indeed, they often received the same accolades and the same epithets. Pratt, who outlived Montezuma, wrote to him frequently and freely offered his opinions and advice. Many of the ideas that Montezuma advanced were in fact ideas that Pratt also presented, either before him or concomitantly. There can be little question that Pratt's influence was significant.[32]

Yet while Montezuma remained steadfastly loyal to Pratt, the 1890s were the years in which the Carlisle superintendent influenced him the most. When Montezuma left Carlisle and returned to Chicago, he entered a new phase of his life and career. He would become a physician on his own, rather than under the sponsorship and supervision of the Indian Bureau. In addition, he would come into increasing contact with other Indians like himself—well-educated, articulate individuals who cared deeply about the fate of Native Americans in this transitional time. Some of these people had been uprooted early in life, as had Montezuma, but many had not. While Montezuma would never be a great admirer of Indian tradition and lore, he steadily would gain a better understanding of the importance of tribe. His association with the Yavapais at Fort McDowell would soon commence, and this affiliation would be critical in his broadening outlook on reservation life. Montezuma's views on Indian land and water rights became pronounced, and they differed greatly from those of Richard Pratt. And so he would indeed "stand independent," but that stance would not truly be evident until years after he had left Carlisle.

3

Chicago, Zitkala-sa, and the Creation of the Fort McDowell Reservation

Carlos Montezuma returned to Chicago in 1896, intending to establish a private practice in medicine. As before, his patients were few. Then, a stroke of good fortune altered his career. Walking along State Street one day, Montezuma encountered Dr. Fenton B. Turck, a prominent physician who specialized in internal medicine. Montezuma had met Turck at Carlisle. Turck had given a demonstration of his diagnostic work in stomach and intestinal diseases, and Montezuma had been impressed. Upon learning of the Yavapai's meager fortunes to date, Turck invited him to assist at his clinic in Chicago. The next day, Montezuma went to work for Dr. Turck. Turck apparently instructed him, encouraged him, and opened doors for him in Chicago that might otherwise have opened more slowly, if at all, to a young Indian doctor. Dr. Montezuma was on his way to becoming established in the city.[1]

While specializing in stomach problems and related internal medical concerns, Montezuma also engaged in a more general practice. He initially had an office at 100 State Street. The city was expanding to the south and Montezuma chose the South Side for his residence. He lived at 3135 South Park Avenue, with his home serving as an office as well. The doctor would have hours from 8:00 to 11:00 A.M. at home, then head north

31

to the Loop. He would be on State Street from noon to 1:00 or
2:00. After dinner, he would again take patients from 7:00 to
8:30 P.M. He maintained his home at the same address for many
years, though early in the twentieth century he moved his
downtown office to a nearby location at 72 Madison Street. [2]

The evidence concerning Montezuma's medical career is
fragmentary and rather problematic. There are not records that
indicate incompetency, but there is also little to demonstrate
excellence. He belonged to the requisite societies, including
the American Medical Association and the Illinois and Chicago
medical societies. He was associated with several Chicago medical institutions as an instructor in his special areas of interest.
Montezuma told a congressional committee in 1911 that he
was an expert on the nonsurgical treatment of appendicitis,
claiming that he had "gone deeper into that than any man in
the United States." On the same occasion, he commented that
he "could have made a splendid quack years ago. I could have
made millions, you might say, but I would not disgrace my
colleagues."[3]

No one ever thought Montezuma was a millionaire. To the
contrary, his financial records continually reflect monetary
difficulties. His patients would often write expressing an ina-
bility to pay their overdue fees. Sometimes, of course, they
would not write at all. Montezuma would write a delinquent
patient, telling him that he badly needed the money, and urging him to "be a man" and pay. An old friend of Montezuma's
recalled that he moved in high social circles and was invited
to all the social events of importance in the city. She suggested
that if he had not given highest priority to Indian rights, his
life could have been far easier. While her testimony about Montezuma's standing in high society is suspect, she no doubt was
correct in her assessment of his commitment to Native American well-being.[4]

Being a good doctor was important to Montezuma. As a missionary to white America, he wanted to prove that Native
Americans could become skilled professionals. This desire affected his choice of career and his decision to practice in Chicago. But he could not be just another doctor. He was an Indian
doctor, and his ethnic identity could not be erased, either in
the eyes of Chicagoans or in his own eyes. And as the twenti-

eth century began, he entered a period of intensive activity in Indian affairs that would last until his death in 1923. It would be his primary concern, transcending his vocation as a physician.

For a time, it appeared that he would carry on that concern in partnership with the young Sioux woman Gertrude Simmons, or Zitkala-sa ("Red Bird") who had taught at Carlisle. Born February 22, 1876, at the Yankton Sioux Agency, the third child of Ellen Simmons, Zitkala-sa had received a traditional upbringing on the reservation before leaving with Quaker missionaries for "the land of red apples," Indiana. She stayed for three years at White's Indiana Manual Labor Institute in Wabash, returning at the age of eleven to South Dakota. As she recorded so vividly in *American Indian Stories*, she disliked much about the school. She "felt the cold blades of the scissors against my neck, and heard them gnaw off one of my thick braids." She experienced "the iron routine," she "trudged in the day's harness heavy-footed, like a dumb sick brute." Gertrude Simmons watched a classmate die and grew bitter at her teacher: "I blamed the hard-working, well-meaning, ignorant woman who was inculcating in our hearts her superstitious ideas."[5]

The ideas had some effect, for Zitkala-sa was not happy when she returned home. At fourteen, she came back to Wabash to complete her training, and again, against her mother's advice, enrolled at Earlham College in Richmond, Indiana. She had the great satisfaction of winning the college oratorical contest and one of two prizes at the state oratorical competition, but an illness left her unable to continue her college studies. Her pride kept her from going back to her mother, who "had she known of my own condition . . . would have said the white man's paper's [sic] were not worth the freedom and health I had lost by them." She went on to Carlisle to teach. Before going back to her mother and her home country at the turn of the century, she studied further at the New England Conservatory of Music. She had become an accomplished musician; she aspired to become a writer.[6]

It is not certain when Zitkala-sa and Montezuma became seriously interested in each other. Carlisle records show that they were not employed at the school at the same time. Montezuma had left the institution by the time Zitkala-sa accepted a position there. They both were featured in an article about the school that made them appear as contemporaries. It is possible, indeed likely, that they met in the East, while Montezuma still lived in Pennsylvania. Given his continued attachment to Carlisle superintendent Richard H. Pratt, he surely would have heard about her.[7]

We owe our knowledge of the courtship between Montezuma and Zitkala-sa to a number of her letters in the Montezuma collection recently acquired by the State Historical Society of Wisconsin. During their lifetime and afterward, very few people knew that these two people who would become so important in Indian life were nearly married. The Zitkala-sa letters in the Wisconsin papers begin in early 1901. By that time Montezuma was far more than a mere acquaintance. He clearly was in love with her and wanted to be married. She remained intermittently unconvinced about the prospects of matrimony, though by March 1901, they were engaged. She wrote in early June about a traditional Sioux wedding, then later that month of being married by a justice of the peace in Chicago. He asked her to accompany him on a trip to Arizona, but she declined. By August 1901, Zitkala-sa had broken the engagement. She kept the door open to a closer relationship in the future. Then Montezuma apparently overstepped whatever boundaries she had in mind, and she backed off once again. By the summer of 1902 she was married to Raymond Bonnin, a Sioux.[8]

Her engagement to Montezuma ended unhappily. The proud Yavapai physician did not like being spurned, and, to make matters worse, Zitkala-sa lost the engagement ring he had sent her. In a year's time, love letters had become curt notes; Zitkala-sa no longer signed her name, "Lovingly, Z" but "Sincerely, Mrs. Gertrude Bonnin." Eventually they became friends once again, if not always ideological companions. By 1913, she would reminisce cheerfully about Montezuma's "narrow escape" and speak very favorably of him. Still, one suspects it took years for the wounds to heal, if they ever did heal, and that this affected their dealings with each other, particularly within the Society of American Indians.[9]

To say the least, it was a mercurial relationship, and we will probably never have a complete picture of it. Except for a few brief notes after the engagement had ended, Montezuma's letters to Gertrude Bonnin are not available in collections of his papers. They may not have been kept; it is difficult to imagine Gertrude Bonnin carefully filing them away. Montezuma, predictably, kept a great many of her letters, though the Wisconsin collection is incomplete. What we do have, however fragmentary, is fascinating and revealing about both people.

While Zitkala-sa did not date many of her letters, one still can piece together the outlines of their engagement and why it faltered. Even though she agreed at one point to marry Montezuma and even though she did marry Raymond Bonnin, Gertrude Simmons expressed strong misgivings about the prospect of marrying anyone. She did not lack for admirers. In one letter, indeed, she enumerated a long list of applicants—by occupation, unfortunately, rather than by name. She was determined to lead her own life and follow her own convictions. Perhaps only partly in jest, she once reassured Montezuma that she would remain interested in him only so long as they remained incompatible. She feared the confines of her era's marriages: "I know absolutely nothing about housekeeping," she wrote. "I would be restless and a burden—see?" And another time: "I know so little about keeping a home in running order that the undertaking is perfectly appalling to me."[10]

But as she did marry Raymond Bonnin so promptly, there had to be other reasons as well for her not to marry Montezuma. Zitkala-sa had ties to her aging mother and to Sioux country. She wanted to be with Indians rather than "a missionary to the whites." She urged Montezuma to accept a physician's job at the agency. If he were truly in love with her, he would accept, she argued. But, as we have seen, Montezuma had had more than enough of isolated Indian Bureau posts, let alone of the Indian Bureau itself. He had established himself in Chicago and he obviously did not relish the prospect of again being a Bureau employee. He declined. Ironically, Gertrude Bonnin married an Indian Service employee and she spent much of the rest of her life in Utah and in Washington, D.C., removed from her home area. She wrote to Montezuma that she had "a friend out here who claims all I can give by the laws of natural affinity." That must have been Raymond Bonnin. Marrying a Lakota mattered a good deal to Zitkala-sa.[11]

Gertrude Bonnin and Carlos Montezuma were both strong-

willed, stubborn people. They recognized these qualities in
themselves and in each other. They were probably attracted to
each other initially because of this similarity but in the end it
helped to dissolve their relationship. They had, she wrote,
"non-congenieal [sic] temperaments:" "I guess it seems odd to
you to find another as stiff-necked in old opinions as your
will-ful self." Her vacillating moods irritated him. When she
seemed to deny forever the possibility of their getting married,
he apparently responded angrily. "If you're so superior," she
retorted, "don't worry about losing such a worthless person."
Her loss of his engagement ring infuriated him. He wrote, she
thought, "cruelly, wickedly in the manner of some low Italian
day-go." But she proved equal to the task of a spirited response:
"I am proud—fearless and as independent as you are—man that
you pose to be . . . And now you fume about like a chicken
with its head cut off—knowing nothing of what you strike
against!" He demanded that she pay for the ring and a year later
threatened legal action against her for damages. A former colleague at Carlisle, Jessie W. Cook, wrote to Montezuma from
Sherman Institute:

. . . I know how devoted you were to her: I knew when she became
engaged to you, and I would have been glad to see that engagement
culminate in marriage but she is a girl of moods and many minds,
and you know all women have the privilege of changing their minds.
She wrote me when she lost your diamond and she was sick over
it. . . . I read your lawyer's letter to her . . . let the matter drop . . . the
moment it gets out you will be a laughing stock. So far no one knows
that you were engaged . . . The public won't be sympathetic. If you
need the money, the public will be surprised at that, too."[12]

And so it ended.

In addition to revealing something about why she did not
marry Montezuma, Gertrude Bonnin's letters tell us much
about her emerging values, views, and beliefs, presaging her
long career in national Indian concerns. Her letters show her
to be independent, a feminist, filled with misgivings about
white civilization and its proponents, and a firm believer in
the capability of Native Americans. "I raise both hands to the
great blue overhead and my spirit revels in a freedom no less
than the vast concave! I am free! I am proud! I am chosen! I

caper *[sic]* to no world of pigmies nor a pigmy God!" She advocated not only personal freedom but participation by Indian women in Indian matters. Montezuma told her about his idea of forming an organization of Indians, with membership limited to men. Zitkala-sa objected: "Why do you dare to leave us out? . . . Some time as I ponder the preponderous actions of men—which are so tremendously out of proportion with the small results—I laugh."[13]

She liked the idea of an organization but did not want to have to depend on charity—that is to say, white contributions. In general, she remained skeptical about white aid and assistance. Unlike Montezuma, she disliked Richard Pratt, whom she once labeled pig-headed. She thought Pratt ought to interest himself in giving college educations to Indians; instead he would make them slaves to the plow, and the plow was drudgery—"And drudgery is hell—not civilization." Gertrude Bonnin contested Pratt's claim that nonreservation schools were superior, for they removed Indian students from "the old folks." She would "never speak of the whites as elevating the Indian! . . . If the Indian race adapts itself to the commodity of the times in one century it won't be because of Carlisle, but because the Indian was not a degenerate in the first place! . . . If Carlisle expects the Indian to adapt himself perfectly to 'civilized' life in a century," she added, "she must admit that the Indian has powers which entitles him to a better name than Primitive!"

Zitkala-sa perceived contemporary American society as expecting little achievement of Native Americans, but she expected Indians to compete with the highest minds, for they were "spiritually superior to any race of savage, white or black . . . The Indian respects unwritten laws." To be the "master of circumstances," Indians must "claim our full heritage." One must compete, but one must learn from the old people, too, and "their treasured ideas of life." *American Indian Stories* and *Old Indian Legends* later would mirror her continuing respect for traditional life.[14]

Gertrude Bonnin had deeper, more continous ties to her heritage than did Montezuma. Montezuma did not believe in dwelling on the Indian past to the exclusion of and detriment of the Indian present. His writings at the turn of the century reflect the need, as he perceived it, for Indians to change and to be

seen as changing. Yet he and Bonnin were not poles apart, as
they could easily be portrayed. Zitkala-sa may have had something to do with the evolution of Montezuma's thought. They
shared ideas on many issues and cared about each other. It
seems reasonable that they could have caused one another to
reconsider their viewpoints on issues where they did not agree.
The dissolution of their engagement, moreover, came at the
time when Montezuma was reestablishing his ties to southern
Arizona, immediately preceding the creation of the Fort Mc-
Dowell reservation. Montezuma's relationship to McDowell,
as will be seen, would be the most fundamental factor in his
evolving and increasingly complex consideration of contemporary Native American life.

In large part because of his experiences in the West, at the
turn of the century Montezuma continued to despair of the impact of reservation life on American Indians. He did not think
the Native American condition was improving. His address to
Chicago's Fortnightly Club on February 10, 1898, for example,
revealed his sharp disagreement with the Bureau's diagnosis
of improving Indian well-being. Montezuma told the story of
a patient's friend who kept inquiring about the patient as the
physician passed each morning after calling on the patient. The
doctor would always say the patient was improving. Soon,
however, the patient died. When someone asked her what her
friend had died from, she replied that she guessed she died from
improvement. Montezuma felt it high time a red flag or some
other danger signal was hung on the present Indian policy lest
the Indians all die of "improvement."[15]

Montezuma emphasized that Native Americans were in a
transitional period. The Indians of today, he reminded his Chicago audience, were not the Indians of the past. They lacked
the advantages of their previous state and had yet to profit from
civilization—thus making "the Indians of the present more degraded than their forefathers ever were." Montezuma remembered the "strength, prosperity and happiness" of the people
of his childhood. But that old way was gone, and a new way of
merit had not taken its place. White Americans had "sent in
more vice than virtue" and "taken out more virtue than vice."

The reservation trapped and demoralized the Indian. It "is
not an earthly paradise, nor a land of milk and honey where

the pipe of peace is continually smoked. It is a demoralized prison; a barrier against enlightenment, a promoter of idleness, beggary, gambling, pauperism, ruin and death." The Native American situation could not be blamed solely on the victim. Writing in 1903 for a column in the editorial section of the Chicago *Tribune*, he charged that whites had abused their mission. "The great hindrance to the right road for the Indians comes from the sentimentalists and literature of the Indian question," he contended. Indians had to get away from reservations:

The first step towards civilization of the Indian is to place him geographically so that he can commingle with the conquering race, in the same manner and to the same extent that natives of foreign countries have become a part of the people in general in our country. Would anybody deny that whatever progress the negro has made has been due to the extent to which he has associated with those by whom he was once held as a chattel?[16]

The whites had cheated Indians of their birthright. "Maybe you have intoxicated us to sleep," he suggested, "and Rip Van Winkle like, we came back after many years and see the real as though after a dream." The whites had homes as tall as mountains, flew over old hunting grounds with the speed of the wind, dug into the earth for riches, could communicate instantly across hundreds of miles, had harnessed electricity. "Now we see why you have been so good to us," Montezuma said. "Tell me, is it not worse than robbery to make us blind and then take everything we possess?" He concluded in another phrase he would use insistently and incessantly: "Does not the Great Spirit say today, as of old, 'Let my people go'?"[17]

This must have been a discouraging time for Montezuma. His personal life certainly was troubled. After his engagement to Zitkala-sa ended, he proposed to another woman by the name of Lillian. Following the proper form of his day, Montezuma wrote to Lillian's parents, asking "for that sacred sanction to take her as my helpmate through life." She was a younger woman, and a non-Indian. Montezuma realized her parents might object because he was an Indian: "Even though I am an Indian, had I a loving daughter who was thinking of marrying an Indian, before knowing the man I would emphatically rebel

against such an outrageous idea. . . . Remember today there are
Indians and Indians," he added. "In my case it is so different,
it is an unusual exception—or I would not allow myself this
greatest request for my life happiness." Montezuma emphasized that he was known nationally on "the Indian question."
He had gained his degree against all odds and his "acquaintance is among the best and most influential." Montezuma
awaited "with loving suspense" the reply. It apparently was
negative, for we find no more mention of the woman. Montezuma would not get married until 1911, to a young Romanian-
American, Marie Keller.[18]

Pratt remained his loyal friend. Montezuma staunchly defended the Carlisle superintendent as the latter's position at
the school became increasingly uncertain. As "Your Apache
Whooper," he praised the exploits of the Carlisle football team
and accompanied it on a trip to Phoenix. He returned to the
Southwest on another occasion to try to recruit students for
the school. Montezuma wrote to Pratt about a proposed Indian
association's constitution (Pratt characteristically was skeptical of the organization, as he was of any body of people; individual effort would be more effective, he argued) and about
other matters. And when Pratt was finally dismissed as superintendent in 1904, Montezuma immediately offered him encouragement and support.[19]

Pratt's dismissal served as a reminder to Montezuma that
the Indian Bureau was incorrigible. The commissioner of Indian
affairs refused to explain the action against "the strongest and
best man in the Indian service."[20] In later years, Montezuma
would rail against the action and the subsequent step in World
War I of closing the school, which he termed the Indian's Gi-
braltar. The year 1904 thus marked another important step in
galvanizing the Yavapai physician toward active leadership in
Indian affairs. More particularly, it marked a hardening of his
position that the Indian Bureau had to be abolished before significant change for the better could take place in Native American life.

Given all the troubling things Montezuma experienced during the first few years of the century, it is tempting to portray
this period as essentially a negative time in his life, but this
would not be an accurate generalization, for it was also during

this time that Montezuma rediscovered his people and his heritage. This rediscovery would have an enormous effect upon his life and his opinions. He first traveled to the Southwest in January 1900, in conjunction with a western tour of the Carlisle football team. Montezuma visited Phoenix, Albuquerque, and Santa Fe, expressing skepticism to Pratt about the limited potential of the Indian schools in these cities. Phoenix Indian School's were impressive, he noted, "but I am afraid there is too much prejudice against the Indian, it being too near their homes to accomplish much good without any drawbacks." As Montezuma advanced eastward, he grew more hopeful; Haskell, while not up to Carlisle, was at least "located in the midst of a civilized community."[21] His return to Arizona had been a brief one, characterized primarily by his visit to the Phoenix school and his attendance at a somewhat one-sided football game, where Carlisle swamped Phoenix, 83–6.[22]

During the autumn of 1901, Montezuma returned to the places of his boyhood. He had been away for a long time, and as memories came back they were accompanied by powerful emotions. He realized he had been removed from camp life for a considerable period: "I ate their cooking and slept on the ground. The novelty of it is all right but to live and die like that is not comfortable. I endured five nights of sleeping on the ground quite well but I was really glad to get into bed last night." At Iron Mountain, everything seemed to have changed. The grass huts were gone; the trees had grown; the grass had been trampled under by cattle; even the mountain seemed to have grown.[23]

Montezuma, too, had grown and changed. The Globe *Silver Belt* noted his attire of canvas hunting garb, and commented that "he has the easy carriage and address of the refined easterner." The doctor reported that the Pimas received him "with wonder and gladness" for some remembered him being with Mr. Gentile. He visited nearby Florence and checked the records of the Catholic church. "Sure enough" he told Pratt, "there was the name and date, November 17, 1871. So you see I am insured for Heaven."[24] The visit to Adamsville stood out in his memory. Four years later, he sent some pictures of this trip to James H. McClintock of Phoenix and recalled that the first person he found in Adamsville was an old man. He could

not speak English, but summoned a younger man to interpret
for him. It turned out that the old man had lived in the area for
forty years. Montezuma asked him if he remembered a photographer from thirty-one or thirty-two years ago. He did. Did he
recall an Indian boy the photographer had purchased?

Before I finished the question, these sons of his were saying, "Montezuma! Montezuma!" He looked up at me and said "Yes." And I
smiled and pointing to myself, said, "I am that Indian boy." Quick
as a flash those boys and the gray headed father rushed forward with
extended hands and bid me welcome which was equal to a greeting
for a lost son's return after many years of absence.

The time in his home country confirmed loss of family but
created bonds with more distant relatives. Montezuma felt the
loss of his father, mother, and sisters all the more, having re-
traced their steps. He regained firsthand contact with Yavapai
relations, including Mike Burns and Charles Dickens. Burns
had quite a bit of knowledge about recent Yavapai history. He
had corresponded with Montezuma before the 1901 trip. Dickens and his brother, George, both would be important people
in Fort McDowell reservation affairs. They were first cousins
to Montezuma. Both Mike Burns and Charles Dickens also regarded Montezuma as a man sufficiently wealthy to help out
less affluent relatives. On November 2, 1901, for example,
Charles Dickens wrote to Montezuma: "... please Cousin Carlos will you please send me accordions only worth $3.25 just
look at in Montgomery Ward book no. 516—and I know how
to play accordians alright . . ."[26]
   By the time of Montezuma's excursions to the Southwest,
events were transpiring in the direction of making the Fort
McDowell reservation a reality. In the autumn of 1900, the Bureau of Indian Affairs had a report that eight of ten Mohave-
Apache families were living at the abandoned Camp McDowell
military reservation. Some of them formerly had lived along
the Verde River Valley, others at the San Carlos reservation.
An inspector from the Indian Office recommended that land
at McDowell that had not been taken by white settlers be reserved for the Indians, who could then, with a little help, take
care of themselves.[27]
   The Interior Department had been given the military reserve

of about twenty-five thousand acres on February 14, 1891, for disposal. The department directed the commissioner for the General Land Office on November 27, 1901, to reserve the lands for Indian purposes. White resentment helped to block a congressional bill at the end of 1901 and into 1902. In the summer of 1903, President Theodore Roosevelt dispatched Frank Mead to Camp McDowell to investigate the serious trouble threatened between the whites and the Indians there. Mead reported on September 4, 1903, that the Yavapais now numbered between 500 and 600 persons, including about 184 at McDowell and about 216 at Camp Verde. The Indian agent at San Carlos, Mead said, estimated there were 800 to 1,000 Yavapais at that reservation. The Indians assumed that returning to the Verde Valley was all right, as it was their home. They had left it twenty-nine years before at the request of General Crook. According to the Yavapais, Crook had promised them that when they had become civilized and were willing to live like white men, the government would allow them and assist them to return home. In part, this assistance was due because some of the Yavapais had served as army scouts, including participation in the Geronimo campaigns.[28]

The Yavapais appeared to Mead to be good prospects for aid. Though destitute, the Indians were "manly, honest, upright, would walk 50 and 60 miles to find work, were obedient and law abiding." Most of the men wore their hair short; all wore hats, shoes, overalls, and cotton shirts. Mead said he attended five councils at various camps and was met with the same request: "Give us land and a little help that we may be farmers and live and work like white men." The Yavapais said they did not want rations but wanted to support themselves.[29]

The irrigable land at Fort McDowell increased the possibility of greater self-sufficiency. Mead thought about two thousand acres were irrigable, with two-thirds of that amount already served by ditch irrigation. The irrigable land was capable of supporting 100 families (twenty acres per family). Deeming McDowell a good investment and the Indians worthy of assistance, Mead recommended the government allocate $25,000 to buy out settlers and an additional $3,000 to build necessary ditches. All settlers should be bought out, "especially as the influence of the existing white community, which maintained a flourishing saloon and gambling house, was very bad." On September 12, 1903, Mead submitted his report to Roosevelt. He concluded that the president should withdraw lands not legitimately claimed, in addition to buying out legal entries.[30]

With customary verve, Roosevelt immediately issued a presidential order on September 15, 1903. Land not legally settled or without valid claims were to be "set aside and reserved for the use and occupancy of such Mohave-Apache Indians as are now living thereon or in the vicinity and such other Indians as the Secretary of the Interior may hereafter deem necessary to place thereon." The Rev. W. H. Gill, a local missionary who had assisted the Yavapais, gained charge of the Indians and was told to get them settled on their new land.[31]

As might be expected, the transition could not be achieved without some problems. Mead secured peaceable possession of the reservation October 20, 1903, and opened a land office Octber 26–28. He decided that twenty-one settlers had valid claims, with fourteen residing on reserved lands containing government improvements. The latter were to vacate by December 1, 1903, with their improvements purchased. The homestead settlers held 2,275.18 acres of the total acreage of 24,971.11. Mead talked with Governor Brodie of Arizona Territory and Sheriff Cook of Maricopa County and instructed Gill to consult with Chief Yuma Frank and to keep the Yavapais separate until the land issue could be completed. In November, Mead submitted the options of the settlers. Congress appropriated $50,000 on April 21, 1904. On November 19, 1904, twenty-six quit claim deeds were paid for, with $48,281.04 being disbursed. Among the improvements were three irrigation ditches, the Jones and Shauver ditch (six miles in length), the Mazon ditch (three miles in length), and the Belasco ditch (four miles in length), with all their water rights.[32]

Despite the unhappiness of the settlers at having to move and their displeasure with the slowness of the government in paying their claims, and despite conflicting claims and problems of fraudulent entry, the Mohave-Apache or Yavapai reservation at Fort McDowell had become a reality. Gill wrote to Montezuma on October 26, 1903, datelining his letter *Mohave-Apache Indian Reservation*, and proclaiming that "this beautiful valley 10 miles long by 4 miles wide had been turned into an Indian reservation. . . . There is great joy here in our Indian camps."[33] Indeed, there should have been. When one considers the date and the era, the creation for the Yavapais of the Fort McDowell reservation was an impressive symbolic landmark. In a time when Indians all over the American West were losing their land, through cession and through sale of allotted lands, the Mohave-Apaches had gained rights to a homeland. In addition, unlike much of the remaining Native American land, it was promising land; it straddled the Verde River and already included irrigated acreage. The land was theirs. Now they would have to struggle to keep it.

Montezuma had just returned from his latest visit to southern Arizona. He had been in the Phoenix area in late July, accompanied by E. E. Witter of Des Moines. Described in the *Arizona Republican* as being quite well known throughout Arizona, Montezuma again journeyed to places of his boyhood, Adamsville and Florence, and the reservation at San Carlos. He pledged to help the missionary, Gill, in building a church. Even more important, Gill emphasized in October 1903, would be to take advantage of the property to be disposed of at very low prices. Houses, furniture, cows, hogs, goats, chickens, corn, wheat, and other items could be purchased inexpensively. Immediate cash could make a great difference. Gill pleaded with the Yavapai physician:

Now is the time, doctor, to put in your best blows for your people. God has been good to them, victory has been snatched from the very jaws of defeat and inaction now will be criminal suicide. Oh, help our fallen brother rise! *Help, Help, Help* and *now.* Think of our dear people, often hungry and cold, shivering in their wretched brush hovels on the barren hills. Shall we not bring comfort and cheer to these people now that it is in our power to do so? Move *heaven* and *earth.*[34]

Less than twenty years remained in the life of Montezuma. They would be two decades filled with remarkable activity and consuming energy, dedicated to the well-being of Native American people. In particular, he had now rediscovered his people. To bring them justice, to promote their vitality, and to ensure their future became his special crusade.

Yavapai woman and basket, Fort McDowell reservation, ca. 1910.
Arizona Collection, Hayden Library, Arizona State University.

Carlos Montezuma on the porch of the Carlisle Indian School hospital, 1902. Special Collections, Waidner-Spahr Library, Dickinson College.

Carlos Montezuma as a boy, 1873, after his adoption by Carlo
Gentile. Photo by Carlo Gentile; the adult in the photo is a friend
of his. Arizona Collection, Arizona State University.

Richard H. Pratt with recently arrived Navajo students at Carlisle Indian School. Pratt was an important influence on Montezuma, particularly during his early years as a national Indian leader. Photograph by J. N. Choate, 1880s. National Anthropological Archives, Smithsonian Institution.

Above left: Carlos Montezuma
sent this photograph of
himself to the commissioner
of Indian Affairs in 1889 from
Fort Stevenson, South Dakota.
National Archives RG 75, file
16867-1890. Arizona Collection, Arizona State University.

Above right: Carlos Montezuma, 1896. National An-
thropological Archives,
Smithsonian Institution.

Gertrude Bonnin, Zitkala-sa.
Yankton Sioux writer, mu-
sician, activist; engaged briefly
to Montezuma. Ella C. Deloria
Project, Institute of Indian
Studies, University of South
Dakota.

The Reverend Sherman
Coolidge, Northern Arapahoe,
was an important leader
within the Society of Amer-
ican Indians. Photograph by
DeLancey Gill, 1902. National
Anthropological Archives,
Smithsonian Institution.

Dr. Charles A. Eastman, Sioux,
a physician and writer, was a
prominent Indian spokesman
of his day. Eastman knew
Montezuma through the
Society of American Indians
and once participated with
him and Father Philip Gordon
in a speaking tour through
Native American communities
in Wisconsin. Photograph by
Wells M. Sawyer, April 1897.
National Anthropological Archives, Smithsonian Institution.

Carlos Montezuma and his wife,Mary, ca. 1920. Arizona
Collection, Arizona State University.

WASSAJA

INDIAN BUREAU

FREEDOM'S SIGNAL FOR THE INDIANS

Vol. 1., No. 1.   April, 1916.

INTRODUCTION

~~The WAR WHOOP having been abandoned on account of outside pressure~~ which was brought to bear, WASSAJA is taking its place. The name has been changed in the belief that the former name was not correctly understood.

The intent of the WAR WHOOP has been in the mind of the present editor for many years, and he believes that the time has now arrived to present the real conditions, for the public, and for those in power to consider and be in position to remedy the appalling slavery and handicap of the Indian race.

This monthly signal rays is to be published only so long as the Indian Bureau exists. Its sole purpose is Freedom for the Indians throughout the abolisment of the Indian Bureau.

It is supported by subscriptions and by private contributions from Redmen and everybody who has heart interest in the cause.

Its object is not to form a society, but to free the Indians by exposing the actual conditions of their imprisonment. If you want to help out on the expenses of printing and mailing, subscription is fifty cents a year.

We need your help if you are with us in this vital purpose.

ARROW POINTS.

Had the Indian been treated as a man, without discrimination, in the beginning of the pale-face invasion, today there would be no Indian Bureau and the word "Indian" would be only an obsolete name.

The Indian problem is a problem because the country has taken it and nursed it as a problem; otherwise it is not a problem at all.

What ye sow ye also reap. The Indian Bureau has sown, and it has brought forth nothing but pangs of sorrow and ruination to the Indian race.

It pays to make producers and wage-earners out of Indians rather than idlers and paupers. The Indian Bureau mill turns out the latter.

It does not cost much to feed and clothe the Indians, but the Indian

Wassaja, vol. 1, no. 1 (April 1916). The first issue of Montezuma's newspaper. Arizona Collection, Arizona State University.

Wassaja, vol. 2, no. 8 (November 1917). The second masthead shows Montezuma working with other Indians against the Bureau of Indian Affairs. Arizona Collection, Arizona State University.

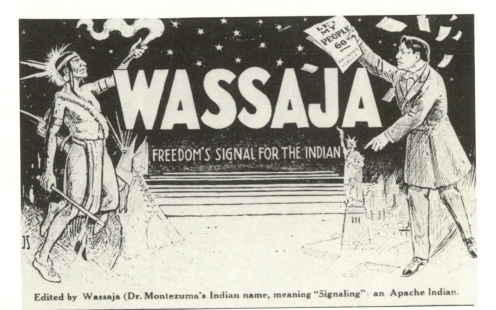

Edited by Wassaja (Dr. Montezuma's Indian name, meaning "Signaling") an Apache Indian.

Wassaja, vol. 5, no. 6 (September 1920). The third masthead reveals Montezuma with one of his essays, "Let My People Go," subtitled here "An Indian Classic." Arizona Collection, Arizona State University.

FREEDOM'S SIGNAL FOR THE INDIAN

THE WORK OF THE INDIAN OFFICE

WASSAJA

Edited by Wassaja (Dr. Montezuma's Indian name, meaning "Signaling") an Apache Indian

Vol. 7, No. 11   ISSUED MONTHLY   November, 1921

THE ONLY WAY TO GET THE INDIANS OUT OF THE CONTROL OF THE INDIAN BUREAU, IS TO GET THEM OUT OF THE CONTROL OF THE INDIAN BUREAU

THE SOCIETY OF AMERICAN INDIANS

Held Their Tenth Annual Conference in the Beautiful City of Detroit, Michigan

At the opening of the Conference the attendance was small, owing to the late hour when the notice was given where the Society was to hold their Tenth Annual Conference. The meeting was held in the auditorium of the Y. M. C. A. The Association was so kind and considerate of our welfare. They have a warm place in our hearts. We have heard of Detroit and we have seen Detroit. It is a lively city. The people and the automobiles seemed as though, they would run over each other, but they do not. The dynamo of industry was there. The display of electric lights at night surpass the dreams of fairyland. The people are young and full of life, and the city seems to have a great future. We shall keep in memory the warm reception given to us by the city and its churches.

The delegations from Canada voiced the same complaint, relative to their freedom and citizenship. They derived much benefit from their attendance at the Conference. It was too bad that some were compelled to leave before closing of the meeting. The Chippewas from the upper part of Michigan were there to get helpful ideas from the Conference. They were much interested and went home to interest their people, so that some of us may come among them and tell them of the vital object we are working for in the interest of our race.

On the last two days of the Conference, we had faithful workers arrive from long distances, which added much to our program. Several mornings and afternoons the handful of delegates met in the auditorium of vacant seats. We had a meeting to ourselves. The discussion was as lively as though the seats were fully occupied by listeners. Testimonies were heard from Indians and friends of the Indians. By the time we adjourned for dinner, or supper, we had learned much and felt that we were on the right road to enlighten each other.

Surprisingly, we were favored with two good afternoon audiences, which gave us much encouragement. Unusual enthusiasm was manifested at these meetings, and many friends were gained for the Indian people and their cause.

The night sessions were attended much better, and the last night was the climax. The auditorium was filled and the entertainment was equal to the occasion. Taking everything into consideration the Conference was a success—meaning that the Society of American Indians stood by their people and not by the Indian Bureau.

At one time, there being so few delegates, things looked precarious. We looked and asked each other: "What shall we do?" It appeared as though there was no way out. One said: "The Society is dead! let us go home." Another one said: "The Society is taken as a stench by the Indian Office and those who once had an interest in the Society." Some said: "We cannot afford to let it die." There was a little breeze "that I wish it would die." Those who were half-hearted in the Society proposed for better attendance the following: A change of officers and not be so radical. Let the next place of Conference be known many months before the time, and have some one do publicity work, at least, a month ahead. "Don't hurt everybody by abusive utterances. Stick to the principles and not be too personal." Let us

Wassaja, vol. 7, no. 11 (November 1921). This final masthead reflects Montezuma's despair with the impact of the Indian Bureau on Native Americans. Courtesy of Panhandle-Plains Historical Museum, Canyon, Texas.

The camp of George Dickens at Fort McDowell. It was to this area
that Montezuma came home to die in 1923. National
Anthropological Archives, Smithsonian Institution.

Charles Dickens, Richard Dickens, and Sam J. Dickens, Yavapais from Fort McDowell. Arizona Collection, Arizona State University.

Thomas Surrama, Yavapai, a relative of Montezuma's who succeeded Yuma Frank as the chosen leader of the people on the Fort McDowell reservation. Photograph by DeLancey Gill, June 1911. National Anthropological Archives, Smithsonian Institutions.

Charles Dickens, photograph by DeLancey Gill, June 1911. National Anthropological Archives, Smithsonian Institution.

Fort McDowell Presbyterian Church. Site of the second funeral service for Montezuma before his burial in the nearby cemetery. An initial service was held in Phoenix at a Baptist church. Arizona Collection, Arizona State University.

Grave of Carlos Montezuma, cemetery at Fort McDowell. The
tombstone reads: WASSAJA/CARLOS MONTEZUMA M.D. 1869–1923
MOHAVE APACHE INDIAN. Arizona Collection, Arizona State
University.

Carlos Montezuma – Fighter for Indian Rights

He waged a continuing struggle for Indian rights. He fought for the Indian right to vote, which was finally won in 1924. (Negroes won this right in 1888.) He fought for reforms in Indian health care, education, operation of the law. He was official representative for the Ft. McDowell Indians and others in government hearings. He fought also, against *Indian* traitors and opportunists. He died in poverty, of tuberculosis, among his own people. He will always be remembered with love and respect. We dedicate *Wassaja* to Carlos Montezuma. May his spirit live in all of us.

"Carlos Montezuma—Fighter for Indian Rights": The dedication of the contemporary *Wassaja* to the memory of Carlos Montezuma. *Wassaja*, vol. 1, no. 1. Arizona Collection, Arizona State University.

4

The Emergence of
a Native American Leader

Between 1905 and 1911, Carlos Montezuma emerged as a Native American leader of national significance. His participation centered in two areas: the movement toward an organization composed of Indians from across the United States and the affairs of the Fort McDowell reservation. In both these situations, Montezuma played strong roles. Both his allies and his opponents would recognize his willingness to express his beliefs and would confront the depth of those convictions. By 1911, Montezuma was well-known to officials of the Bureau of Indian Affairs, pan-Indian activists, and residents of southern Arizona. He clearly had become one of the most influential Indians in the United States.

MONTEZUMA AND THE SOCIETY OF AMERICAN INDIANS

The birth, growth, and decline of the Society of American Indians has been narrated in detail by Hazel Hertzberg in *The Search for an American Indian Identity*. Montezuma's participation in this century's first vital secular pan-Indian movement is not described in flattering terms: "Montezuma was by temperament and conviction a factionalist. He helped to

found the Society of American Indians and then spent most of
the rest of his life attacking it. Even as a Pan-Indian, he was
combative, without any gift for compromise."[1] As we shall see,
this is an incomplete perspective. A thorough review of Montezuma's papers, many of them unavailable to Hertzberg at
the time she completed her research, reveal a more complicated picture.

Recognizing the importance of this transitional era, Montezuma had advocated for some time the formation of a national
organization of American Indians, separate from the philanthropic organizations that had been dominant in Indian life.
Unlike groups such as the Indian Rights Association, Montezuma and others envisoned an association, composed of and
controlled by Native Americans. By the early twentieth century, a generation of well-educated American Indians had come
to the fore, ready to lead their people. They included Arthur
C. Parker, Seneca; Charles A. Eastman, Sioux; Sherman Coolidge, Arapahoe; Thomas L. Sloan, Omaha; and Charles Daganett, Peoria; as well as Montezuma and Zitkala-sa.

In addition to their educational training, these individuals
all had significant experience in the world of white America.
Originally from upstate New York, Parker was an archaeologist
and ethnologist with the New York State Museum. Eastman
was raised in Canada, returned to the United States, and graduated from Dartmouth and from Boston Medical School. Coolidge had been adopted by an army captain, raised in the East,
received a B.D. from Seabury Divinity School, and served as
an Episcopalian minister. Sloan graduated from Hampton Institute and became an attorney. Daganett, a Carlisle graduate, received a degree from Eastman College and was an Indian
Service employee. These men disagreed profoundly over many
matters. Sloan, for example, was a peyotist; Eastman and Zitkala-sa both detested the new faith. Daganett's employment
in the Bureau of Indian Affairs did not endear him to Montezuma. So basic differences of opinion would be built into the
organization from the outset. At the same time, and particularly during the first years of the organization, it appeared that
the commonalities would outweigh such differences. As Hertzberg has observed, just as reformers of the progressive era believed
in progress and established organizations to solve problems,

so, too, the "red progressives" of Indian America subscribed to the values of education and hard work. They believed in the future of the United States, and they believed in the possibility of a bright Indian future within the country. An association of well-educated Native Americans could contribute significantly to the prospect.[2]

The Society of American Indians held its first meeting in 1911. Several years of discussion and consideration preceded that initial gathering. The driving force behind getting Indian leaders together to organize such a society came from a non-Indian. Fayette McKenzie, professor of economics and sociology at Ohio State University, had received a Ph.D. in 1906 from the University of Pennsylvania, after completing a study of "The American Indian in Relation to the White Population of the United States." He was convinced that an association of educated Indians could do much to alleviate the Native American condition and he set about to do what he could in that direction.[3]

Montezuma was among those whom McKenzie first contacted. Why? Montezuma, of course, had earned an M.D., a distinctive accomplishment. He had worked at Carlisle and had cemented a close friendship with Richard H. Pratt, one of the most notable critics of contemporary Indian policy. In addition Montezuma had started to speak out and publish his views on a number of basic issues affecting American Indians. His growing stature at the national level definitely was linked to a widening circle of correspondents and an ever-increasing flood of columns and articles.

Among other things, Montezuma had established himself as one of the leading Native American critics of the current commissioner of Indian affairs, Francis Leupp. Leupp had succeeded W. A. Jones, the commissioner who had presided over Pratt's dismissal from Carlisle in 1904. Initially gaining experience in Indian affairs as Washington agent for the Indian Rights Association, Leupp had been critical of Pratt as early as 1896 because of the Carlisle head's philosophy and his denigration of the civil service system. As an associate of Theodore Roosevelt, he was a logical choice to follow Jones after the election of 1904. Leupp had traveled to many reservations and thus had seen many of the problems confronting Native Americans but he disagreed strongly with the prescriptions offered by Pratt and others.[4]

On April 9, 1905, the New York *Daily Tribune* had published a lengthy interview with Leupp on the Indians' future. Montezuma had printed a thirteen-page critique of Leupp's perspective. In addition to showing how the Yavapai physician disagreed with Leupp, it presented a clear statement of Montezuma's own judgment about the place of Native Americans in the United States. Not surprisingly, Montezuma devoted much of his piece to an analysis of reservation life and its effects. Leupp had been critical of the injustices that could take place in that locale. He had decried circumstances that kept "the administration at Washington busy all the time beating off human harpies of one race or the other." Montezuma applauded such an observation, but argued that what was needed was a "more radical treatment than the Administration at Washington has yet had the courage to prescribe, *viz:* the complete abolition of the reservation system, including of course, the Indian Bureau." Naturally, Montezuma commented, the commissioner had no such goal in mind: ". . . under his regime, it is to be, with a few amendments . . . the same old windmill, running the same old mill-stones, grinding out the same old results."[5]

Montezuma also quarreled with Leupp's approach to the education of young Indians. The commissioner had said he saw no point in Native American children reading about Paris and Peking when they had never seen a city. Rather, he suggested, "The young Indian should have for his reading something that 'hooks on' to his environment. Give him simple nature books— the life story of a wolf, a description of a family of prairie dogs, the wonderful adventures of Mr. Bear and Mrs. Bear and the three juvenile Bears. . . ." Montezuma protested, "If the object is to civilize the Indian, then the farther we remove him, bodily and mentally, from wolves, coyotes and the whole bear family, the more we are liable to make life attractive to him."

Finally, Montezuma lodged a strong protest against the transition he saw taking place at Carlisle. He complained, as he would continue to do, against the renewed emphasis on native arts and crafts, and the new military bent the school was taking. Even the school paper, formerly the *Redman and Helper*, had been rechristened *The Arrow,"* and had undergone a total editorial change that marked it as a "mouthpiece of 'the powers that be.' "

Montezuma's concluding paragraph presaged not only his participation but the movement of many Native Americans toward attempting to achieve meaningful reform of Indian affairs. He warned that it would be "a grave mistake for those in authority not to heed the signs of the times," for "a time of reaction is at hand." "Along with the intellectual development of this people there is an accompanying demand for larger freedom of action," noted the doctor. Indians were tired of being wards. As they realized their ability to take care of themselves, they were "bound to become more emphatic" in making themselves heard. Thus the Native American

is not content to remain silent. He knows what he wants and ought to have, and taken collectively, these demands of the large number of enlightened Indians in the natural order of things must bring about a change; and that change, to be effectual, can be nothing less than a complete overthrow of the system which is now more than ever intolerable.[6]

By 1905, Montezuma had become identified with a particular approach to solving "the Indian problem," as even then it was labeled. He believed that the fundamental step that had to be taken was to abolish the Indian Bureau. This radical step was not universally endorsed by other Indians. But Montezuma's belief in this course of action centrally influenced how he would relate to other pan-Indian advocates, why he would start his newsletter, *Wassaja,* and how he would deal with his people at Fort McDowell.

Given Carlisle's prominence, Montezuma's ardent championing of Pratt and his frequent lampooning of the contemporary situation at the school also served to bring him into the national limelight. He wrote to the editor of the Kansas City *Times* in March of 1905, commenting on "the Future of the Indian" and protesting the Carlisle situation. The edtor of the Boston *Herald* received a similar letter February 5, 1907. The *Public Ledger* of Philadelphia printed his critique and entitled it "Carlisle Indian School Drifting From Its Moorings." Montezuma spared few people on the subject, writing finally to William Howard Taft, president-elect of the United States, on December 24, 1908, recommending that the new head of state select Pratt as the next commissioner of Indian affairs. "We (educated Indians) are on the warpath to have Comm. Leupp relieved and have Gen. Pratt put in his place," he informed Ernest Robetail of Ardmore, Indian Territory.[7] Leupp, of course, eventually did have a successor, but it would not be Pratt, but Robert Valentine.

Clearly, it would have been difficult for Fayette McKenzie not to have heard of Carlos Montezuma by 1909. The Ohio State professor definitely thought the Chicago physician could make an important contribution toward the establishment of the fledgling Society of American Indians. Montezuma was to entertain intermittent hopes that this group was capable of making significant changes in Indian lives. He would sharply criticize Society leaders on a number of occasions, and he would question severely the value of the Society. Yet he frequently would support both the organization and its actions.

"In regard to the Indian Society and its effectiveness I am afraid unless there is real Yankee activity and 'ingin'-uity there will be not much come of it," wrote Pratt to Montezuma in July 1909. Despite that warning, Montezuma became actively engaged in the two years of planning that led up to the 1911 conference. He invited McKenzie to meet with him in Chicago in September. The two had a cordial session, with Montezuma giving McKenzie, as he left, a piece of pottery. McKenzie said he hoped other Indians "will soon express their approval of our plan for the salvation of Indians through the development of an Indian leadership of the highest type." He returned to Columbus, with spirits high:

The die is cast. The venture is great. The possibility of success rests now with the Indians of the country. If they respond in sufficient numbers and with sufficient enthusiasm success will be almost assured. If the response is too weak I suppose I shall have to drop the matter. But I am optimistic, not pessimistic. I shall appreciate your assistance.[8]

By October 11, 1909, McKenzie had received expressions of approval from eleven Native Americans of the plan for an Indian conference. He asked Montezuma for additional names that could be added to the list before he attended the annual conference at Lake Mohonk, beginning on October 20. The Mohonk conference dismayed McKenzie, as only one of three days included Indian matters and no consideration could be given the proposed meeting in Columbus, which he hoped could take place in 1910. Nonetheless, he and the Indians needed to push forward. What subjects should be considered? Who should discuss them?[9]

Montezuma forwarded to McKenzie a long list of possible topics for the conference. Dennison Wheelock suggested that a finances committee secure funds through subscriptions to pay for meeting expenses. He recommended Montezuma, along with Rev. F. H. Wright of Dallas and Howard Cansworth of Buffalo, New York, to chair the committee. Montezuma indicated an interest in assisting, apparently, but the other men proved less enthusiastic. On November 29, 1909, McKenzie acknowledged three letters from Montezuma, and urged him to persuade Rev. Sherman Coolidge "to share in this movement." Coolidge, at Fort Washakie on the Wind River reservation in Wyoming, had not responded to McKenzie's previous entreaties.[10]

McKenzie and Montezuma continued their correspondence in 1910, eventually looking toward a general conference in the following year. Increasingly McKenzie realized the diversity of opinion within the Indian ranks, but as he told Charles Daganett, the Columbus conference "could be neither a government conference nor an anti-government conference. It must be catholic in its inclusion of all. . . ." He asked Montezuma about issuing a letter with him signed by Montezuma, by Daganett, by Sloan, and possibly by the Cherokee writer John Oskison. Such a letter could assist in setting a date and a program ensuring adequate attendance to make a significant conference possible. Daganett and Montezuma both agreed to sign such a letter, and McKenzie suggested that four others join them as an executive committee; McKenzie recommended Sloan and Oskison as two of the four members, with Daganett and Montezuma each selecting an additional person. Daganett proposed Montezuma as chairman of the executive committee. As 1911 began, McKenzie must have been optimistic, indeed.[11]

Fall seemed to McKenzie the most auspicious time to sched-

ule the conference. Daganett had mentioned the summer, but
the professor, aware of the academic calendar, reminded him
that many people would be gone from Columbus during that
time. In January 1911, Daganett advised McKenzie that an executive committee meeting would be in order in the immediate future. He reminded McKenzie that a great obstacle to a
general conference was "that there is not now, and never has
been a unity of interests or feeling among the various tribes of
the North American Indian." How correct Daganett was about
potential factionalism McKenzie soon would discover.[12]

The temporary executive committee of the organization met
in April in Columbus, with Montezuma in attendance. Other
members of the committee were Daganett, who became the
chairman, Laura Cornelius (Oneida) who became the secretary, Sloan, Henry Standing Bear (Sioux), and Charles Eastman.
The addition of Eastman particularly pleased McKenzie, as the
Sioux physician had been slow to warm to the idea of the association; it was, McKenzie said to Montezuma, "a special advantage to secure his sympathy and cooperation." The group
slated October 12–15 as the dates for the conference. McKenzie gained the title "Local Representative." Rosa B. LaFlesche
was added as corresponding secretary and treasurer. The executive committee expanded to eighteeen members, among them
Henry Roe Cloud (Winnebago), Marie Baldwin (Ojibwa), and
Arthur C. Parker.[13]

As the conference drew nearer, Montezuma tried to sort out
his ideas about such an association and about the task of organizing Native Americans. He wrote to August Breuninger,
an Ojibwa, that he "hoped that the Indians would open their
eyes and see that we must organize and unite." Yet, Breuninger
chided Montezuma, the physician would "adhere to a theory
that is 'division' in itself." Montezuma believed deeply in the
necessity of Indians leaving the reservation and making their
way in the white world, but Montezuma's belief, he argued,
just could not work for many Indians:

Your theory is alright if the Indian did not have any physical property to look after and protect. Shall he let this go and jump in and
say, 'let me sink or swim?' I don't believe in it. I don't care to throw
away my property simply because I can go out into the world and

mingle with the masses, forget my home and folks and other things, but I believe in taking CARE of what I've got.

"You as well as myself know that there is need of an organization among us," Breuninger said. But the task ahead would be a formidable one:

To organize the Indian successfully is to show him 1ST that we CAN do something. We cannot make him BELIEVE that we are GOING to do something. He is a Missourian in that respect, that he must be "shown." You and all of the rest of the educated Indian leaders are GENERALS without an ARMY.[14]

As of April 1911, Pratt fully supported the evolving organization, suspicious though he might be of most such associations. The executive committee in April had gone out of its way to encourage that support, sending the general a joint letter expressing appreciation for his work and hope that his sympathy and aid would be given to the organization. Pratt liked the preliminary platform and pledged to "work for the accomplishment of the purposes you announce in any way I can." "You have only to indicate when and how I can help you and I shall act at once," he added. In another letter to Montezuma, Pratt wrote that he saw the committee of six as first rate. Even if Daganett were a government employee, for example, he had traveled among western Indians; he probably knew more intelligent Indians than anyone else on the committee.[15]

Pratt also cautioned Montezuma not to insist too dogmatically on a particular point to the disruption of the emerging organization. The head of the association should not be a government employee, he agreed. One needed to strike at the Bureau of Indian Affairs, but later on. Get the army together first, he counseled.[16]

Plans proceeded apace for the October conference. A conflict had developed with the annual Mohonk conference, so Temporary Chairman Daganett confirmed the dates as October 12–15. Pratt wrote to Sloan in April, informing him that he was going to help the association. In the same month, McKenzie optimistically expressed his feelings that he was receiving good cooperation from various people in Columbus. Thus six months before the conference, the outlook appeared bright for a well-organized, unified gathering.[17]

In May, however, signs of dissatisfaction emerged. McKenzie noted that *The Indian's Friend* would criticize the association for not making religion part of the platform. In addition, the Ohio State professor had agreed to do the Indian census for the federal government. "Hope you won't think I've deserted," he wrote Montezuma. Montezuma, of course, was not pleased. Although McKenzie reminded him in another letter that he would be working for the Census Bureau and not for the Bureau of Indian Affairs, new doubts had surfaced. Pratt agreed with Montezuma that McKenzie's employment would cost him necessary independence.[18]

Daganett called a meeting of the temporary executive committee of the American Indian Association for June. Montezuma did not attend, perhaps because of problems with mail delivery. He wrote to the organization's corresponding secretary, Rosa B. LaFlesche, expressing some questions about what had been happening. La Flesche tried to reassure him, emphasizing that McKenzie had tried his best to get money guaranteed by the city of Columbus, though without success. Once the association had become established, La Flesche believed, there would be no problem in attracting support from other cities.[19]

Montezuma was not reassured. Throughout the summer of 1911 he wrote to Indians around the country, raising questions about the proposed conference program, the conference site, and other matters. Such questions troubled McKenzie. "It would be distressing to me," he told Montezuma, "that the Conference had failed to meet its object and that it had failed to retain the hearty support of the man who first gave it support."[20]

Some of Montezuma's correspondents echoed his concerns. Russell White Bear called it an arduous task for the association to fulfill its stated purpose and yet work in harmony with the Indian Bureau. Noting the names of Bureau employees on the temporary executive committee, he asked: "How can these government employees on the committee list serve two masters?" How could they try to free the Indian and serve the government which was trying to keep him in bondage? August Breuninger said that "a shiver of disapproval ran all over me, it was uncontrollable." He could not see in the association's letters and purposes "any sign of your good intentions and I feel there is going to be a big fight on the floor of the convention." In another letter, he agreed with Montezuma's criticism of holding the convention in Columbus. Bids should have been issued, he argued. Breuninger asked if Montezuma would be a candidate for permanent chairman, labeling him the only one eligible. White Bear also added his sentiments that Columbus was not a good location, because of inadequate support and its distance from most Indians. McKenzie apparently told Breuninger that to hold the conference on a university campus would give it prestige. Un-a-qua countered: "It might among white people as a social affair, but not among Indians whom we are trying to reach." It would be better, he thought to meet somewhere like South Dakota, for "we must carry our methods to them, we cannot bring them to our methods."[21]

Pratt, too, had altered his views on the society. "My dear Monte," he wrote, "You are dead right in your estimate of your Indian Association program. . . . It is simply a skillful suppression of the vital needs of the Indians and a dilentante [sic] dancing attendance upon the Bureau's methods and supervision." Pratt's letter revealed that having Daganett as head of the association, even if temporarily, rankled Montezuma. And the general seconded such feelings. Montezuma, in his opinion, was the only "real Indian" not bought by Bureau employment or looking for Bureau favor.[22]

In August, Pratt again praised Montezuma's independent attitude. Nonetheless, he cautioned against boycotting the proceedings. It would be better to remain involved and make the gathering as big a success as possible.[23]

Despite Pratt's advice, Montezuma indicated in August that he would not attend the conference, forsaking the meeting for a trip to southern Arizona. Many people tried to dissuade him. Rosa La Flesche referred to "the organization you diligently helped to start." August Breuninger said he was really grieved at the possibility that Montezuma might not be at the meeting, while expressing the hope that he would be of great service to his people at Fort McDowell. Charles Daganett urged him to visit Arizona before or after the gathering: "By all means, Doctor, arrange to be with us and let us work together for the

common good whether we can agree on all points or not."
Henry Roe Cloud expressed regrets that he would miss the
pleasure of meeting him. Representative Charles D. Carter said
Montezuma should join him at Columbus and if his suspicions
were well founded, they should be prepared to defeat any such
attempts. In a last-ditch effort, Sloan, Eastman, Cornelius,
Daganett, and Henry Standing Bear telegrammed Montezuma
from Columbus on October 11: "5 of original committee of 6
are here and desire your presence with us in our first annual
conference others present also desire you be here."[24]

Montezuma did not yield to such entreaties. He not only
distinguished himself by his absence from Columbus, but he
resigned from the association, expressing "regret I had responsibility for the organizing of the Association of Educated
Indians." Why had he done so? He believed that an article on
officers of the association in the illustrated weekly magazine
of the Los Angeles Sunday *Times* had been inspired by some
one connected with the Bureau of Indian Affairs. This piece,
together with the conference program, confirmed his view that
the Bureau had attempted to usurp control of "our movement."
The article had painted a false portrait of Indian well-being,
even asserting that Native Americans were as well educated
as the whites. It is likely that Montezuma suspected that
Charles Daganett, a Bureau employee, was behind it all. And
Daganett was, at least temporarily, head of the organization.[25]

So Montezuma would forsake Columbus for Fort McDowell, for by this time his people had gained a central place in his
attention. He would not entirely give up hope in the association, to be renamed the Society of American Indians; indeed,
he would attend the very next meeting of the society. In 1911,
though, he had been very active in Yavapai concerns. Montezuma cited as proof of Bureau duplicity the recent investigation conducted by a congressional committee of expenditures
in the Department of the Interior. Documents from Bureau
files, Montezuma argued, disclosed "a persistent and well-laid
plan to deprive the Mojaves of their proper rights." In another
letter, written immediately before the conference, he spoke of
"persistent and wicked duplicity of management to rob the Mojaves." It was a time of crisis for the Yavapais and the Chicago
doctor had taken a main part in the unfolding drama.[26]

MONTEZUMA AND FORT MCDOWELL

The Yavapais had won their fight for a modern homeland with the creation of the Fort McDowell reservation. Now they had to attempt to take advantage of the resources of this newly established land base. They did not have a lengthy heritage of farming to fall back on. Before the 1870s, they had been primarily a hunting and gathering people, though farming on a limited scale had not been unknown to them. They had, however, gained valuable experience in tilling the soil during their years at Camp Verde and then at the San Carlos reservation. Now that the frontier had come to an end and there would be limits on the freedom of the old days, the Yavapais had to realize the agricultural potential of the land available to them if they were to survive.[27]

William H. Gill, the local missionary the Bureau had hired to assist the Yavapais with this transition, worked with his wife to build upon the previous experience of the tribe, the beginnings of clearing the land achieved by previous settlers, the tribe's determination to take care of itself, and to be sure, the access to the Verde River. Before they had to leave the reservation in 1907 because of an altercation over gambling during which the missionary had killed a Yavapai, the Gills (together with the Yavapais) had realized some success. Montezuma recalled in 1911 that his people had been instructed to be ". . . bee raisers, to raise domestic fowls (chickens and turkeys), cattle and horses; gardeners raised all kinds of vegetables, and did general farming; and then these good people, Mr. and Mrs. Gill, told the 'good old story' to them on Sunday."[28]

Given commitment and will, the key factor for the Yavapais had to be water. In the desert in which they lived, farming could only be successful on a sizable scale with adequate irrigation. At first glance, it would seem that irrigation should not have posed great difficulties. The Verde River providentially bisected the reserve. If the Yavapais could count on using significant quantities of the water from one of southern Arizona's major streams, they could look forward to a reasonably bright future. They had, for their numbers, a land base of sufficient size. They were situated near a growing market and trade center. Having survived the tribulations of the late nineteenth century, they were probably ready to breathe a sign of relief and assume that their worst problems were now behind them.

Of course it was not so simple. No sooner had the Yavapais been officially located on the Fort McDowell reservation than talk began about having them removed. Because they had desirable land and water, they would have to fight a determined battle to remain, for the Phoenix area had started its remarkable expansion. Ironically, as many observers have noted, Phoenix owed its beginnings to the need for a supply center for the old Fort McDowell military reservation. With the military departed, the developing Phoenix area needed water—from the Verde, from the Salt, from anywhere the precious resource could be found. People in the budding metropolis knew that the twentieth century could mean great prosperity for them if sufficient water could be obtained.

Passage of the Newlands Act, or Reclamation Act of 1902, augured well for the destiny of the arid West. This legislation, sponsored by a Nevada congressman, encouraged the federal government to take a more active role in reclaiming the desert for agricultural purposes. Experience had shown that private and state efforts, though philosophically pleasing, were inadequate. Lack of funds, insufficient technical expertise, and other problems plagued such attempts. As so often happened in the American West in the twentieth century, westerners complained about certain kinds of federal intrusions yet on other occasions asked Washington to bail them out. Reclamation was a case in point. Southern Arizona would be one of the areas directly affected by the new program, soon placed under the aegis of the Bureau of Reclamation.

At the beginning of the twentieth century, it had become quite clear that there would be a steadily growing demand for water in southern Arizona. Members of the Salt River Valley Water Users' Association—an organization founded in 1903—escalated the pressures on a finite supply. Personnel within the Bureau of Indian Affairs felt to an unprecedented extent the political and economic claims of such associations. In addition, irrigation on Indian reservations confronted Bureau employees. The 1906 report of the Commissioner of Indian Affairs, for example, commented on this situation. "Irrigation on Indian reservations, like most matters of importance connected with the

'Indian problem' was forced upon the service," it was noted, "and up to a comparatively recent date was without order or system." But "conditions rapidly changed. Irrigation by the white settlers who were continually crowding into the Indian country soon made the available water supply a consideration of the first importance."[29]

The commissioner's report stressed the role of the federal government in regard to Indian water rights:

The reclamation act of June 17, 1902, set aside the unappropriated waters of the public domain to be acquired thereafter in private ownership only under the doctrine of beneficial use, making a statutory change in the common-law doctrine of riparian right. Prior to that act there seems to be no instance of anyone denying the right and power of the General Government to appropriate sufficient water on an Indian reservation for the needs of the Indians.[30]

But times had changed:

Recently, however, these have been denied. Even where the Government has appropriated water under a clear implication of law, having specifically covenanted to protect the water rights of Indians and also, as trustee, expended many thousand dollars of their money in constructing irrigation systems, it has been urged before courts, the Congress, and the Department that the Indians had no such rights.[31]

"But surely," the report concluded:

if the Congress could appropriate all the unused waters of the public domain for the purposes of the reclamation act, it could appropriate waters in Indian reservations for the use and benefit of the Indian occupants of those reservations. Whenever the subject has been fairly presented to the Congress it has taken this view, and so far the courts also have sustained the rights of the Indians.[32]

Such matters became the focus of intense debate and discussion during the decade.

At about this time, Indian water rights had become an important issue in several regions of the American West. Nowhere would the issue develop more far-reaching significance than at the recently established Fort Belknap reservation in northern Montana. Created by executive agreement in 1888, the reservation for the Assiniboines and Gros Ventres was designed

to transform the Indians from hunters to ranchers and farmers. For such a conversion to be possible, irrigation would be
necessary. Lack of adequate irrigation caused repeated crop
failures in the first years of the reservation. By 1896 agents were
besieging Congress for funds to construct an irrigation system;
by 1905 the money allocated had already had a positive impact
in increasing the farming and ranching productivity of Fort
Belknap. During the same decade, however, white ranchers had
started to lease land on the reserve. The Amalgamated Sugar
Company joined such livestock concerns as the Matador Cattle Company in their use of Indian land. In addition, other
whites began appropriating water from sources near the reservation. Early in the twentieth century, such cattlemen as Henry
Winter and Mose Anderson had diverted enough of the Milk
River upstream from Fort Belknap to destroy the economic interests of both Indians and whites on the reservation.[33]

This situation forced the federal government into action on
behalf of both groups. It sued Henry Winter and his colleagues
and the famous *Winters v. U.S.* case began to make its way
through the court system. In 1908 the U.S. Supreme Court issued its landmark decision. The opinion of Chief Justice Joseph
McKenna noted: "When the Indians made the treaty, granting
rights to the United States, they reserved the right to use the
waters of Milk River, at least to an extent reasonably necessary to irrigate their land." McKenna concluded that the tribes
had rights established prior to other interests, but, more critically, he suggested that the standard of prior appropriation was
irrelevant because the Indians had reserved to them water rights
that could not be abrogated. Who had reserved the water, the
government or the Indians themselves, remained ambiguous,
but the reserved rights principle had been established. To the
Gros Ventre and the Assiniboines, as to the Yavapais of Fort
McDowell, McKenna's words rang clear: without adequate
water resources, their arid lands would be practically value-
less.[34] The decision, of course, was one thing, but its applica-
bility in the political and economic climate of the arid West
another. Indians, Bureau employees, state engineers, Anglo land
barons, and land speculators thus all wrestled with an extremely
complicated dilemma.

An intrepid figure in early twentieth-century water rights was William H. Code, an inspector and chief engineer for irrigation in the Indian Bureau. Code seemed to be everywhere in the American West during the beginning of the 1900s. He had a particular interest in irrigation in southern Arizona. Code had been involved in canal and lateral construction; he had been employed by the Consolidated Canal Company; and he had served with a local group interested in building a reservoir at Tonto Basin on the Salt River.[35] In general, here and elsewhere in the West, Code tried his best to cooperate and to avoid conflict with local non-Indians and with state authorities. In his zeal to keep from antagonizing non-Indian interests, Code sometimes appeared to compromise Native American concerns. The Fort McDowell reservation, in Montezuma's opinion, would be a case in point.

Water and land rights for southern Arizona Indians became one of the most important of Montezuma's causes during the final years of his life. While very much involved with these matters for the Yavapais of McDowell, he did not limit his attention solely to their affairs. Particularly during the period from about 1912 until his death, he concerned himself with conditions on other area reservations. The Pimas, the Maricopas, and the Papagos were among the other Native American peoples whom he tried to assist. As we shall see, Bureau personnel almost universally failed to appreciate Montezuma's endeavors. They generally regarded him as an outside agitator, an egocentric troublemaker, and, most ironically given his image, a supporter of the most conservative, unprogressive elements on a reservation.

Irrigated farming for the Yavapais at this time could be classified as problematic. The existing irrigation ditches continually needed repair. A letter from Code to the secretary of the Interior on April 20, 1906, indicated the difficulties the Yavapais kept encountering. Code had submitted the month before a report and recommendations for repairs of irrigation ditches on the reservation. He suggested $2,000 as an ample sum to accomplish these repairs, for there probably would be no further floods that winter. Inevitably, given such a bureaucratic prediction, the river flooded.

This view of the situation has proved to be unduly optimistic, since another heavy flood swept down the Verde River in the latter part of March, as I was leaving Arizona, changing conditions on the Reservation. . . . the river has again made inroads upon the irrigable lands. The last flood practically obliterated the Jones Heading, so that it would be most expensive to rebuild it. Under these conditions there is no recourse save to give the old Government Ditch a temporary heading and endeavor to obtain some water for summer crops.[36]

This kind of situation would be repeated on many reservations in the West. On the one hand, the federal government, through the Congress and the Bureau of Indian Affairs, expressed a strong desire to make Native Americans self-sufficient. On the other, the government had an equally intense wish to reduce expenditures on the Indians. The heyday of the Dawes or General Allotment Act found thousands upon thousands of Native Americans thrown on their own. Indians on unallotted reservations like McDowell frequently did not receive the kind of short-term assistance they needed to achieve the long-term goal of self-sufficiency. In the spirit of saving money, Code made several critical decisions and assumptions soon after the Yavapais were settled at Fort McDowell that would have a fundamental effect upon their future. He concluded that the acreage susceptible to irrigation on the reservation was limited. With a small population at Fort McDowell, Code believed that the Yavapais in their present location represented a poor investment. Temporary patchwork repairs would be made annually on the reservation; extensive, permanent repairs could not be justified. One is reminded of historian Richard Frost's description of repairs effected on the Rio Grande and the Pojoaque River by the Indian Service for the Indians of San Ildefonso Pueblo in New Mexico. The Service constructed an irrigation ditch, which was washed away. The Service brooded for eight years, made minor repairs, and the ditch washed away again. Then it started a project to pump water but abandoned it for economic reasons. Finally it sunk perforated casements in the Pojoaque and built a short ditch. "This solution," Frost noted, "was cheap, permanent, and ineffectual: there was not enough seepage in the Pojoaque to feed the Pueblo. There the matter rested."[37]

In spite of their unwillingness to invest in ditch repair, the government officials wanted as many Yavapais as possible to become farmers. What could be done? As Code informed the secretary of the interior on July 28, 1909, Fort McDowell was "but a few miles north of the area embraced within the boundaries of the Salt River reclamation project." He added:

It has been my belief for some years that the proper solution of the water problem at McDowell would be to move such Mohave Apache Indians as can be induced to farm, to a tract of land on the adjoining Salt River Valley Indian reservation, in order that they might also obtain the benefits of government reclamation.[38]

All these conclusions met with strenuous objection by many of the Yavapais. Montezuma soon became one of the most zealous complainants.

The proposal to move the Yavapais to the neighboring Salt River reservation, occupied primarily by the Pimas and also by some Maricopas, must be viewed in the context of contemporary economic development in the region. In 1904, the federal government encouraged the filing of a lawsuit in the third judicial district of Arizona. The suit involved the adjudication of the water rights to the Salt River. The timing of the filing obviously was influenced by the announced plans to construct the Tonto Reservoir, later to be known as Roosevelt Lake. With the creation of the Salt River Project, priority rights had to be established and those rights had to be quantified.

What part would the Indians of the area have in the definition of these rights? Here again Code took an active part in the process. He decided in 1905 that Indian lands on the Salt River reservation should be included in the Salt River project. As for Fort McDowell, he, together with Superintendent J. B. Alexander of the Salt River reservation and Superintendent Charles Goodman of the Fort McDowell reservation, arranged for Yavapai water rights to be specified through *Hurley* v. *Abbott*, the pending case involving Salt River water rights.

As Terrence Lamb has demonstrated in his recent dissertation, "Early Twentieth Century Efforts at Economic Development in Nigeria and Arizona," these decisions are open to severe question. They had pivotal importance for the Yavapais, as well as for other neighboring tribes. Code and others disregarded the Yavapais' longstanding claim to the use of the Verde

River, even though they were recent residents of Fort McDowell itself. In 1911, at hearings held by the House Committee
on Expenditures in the Interior Department (where Montezuma
and other Yavapais also would testify), Code contended that
the Winters Doctrine could not be extended to executive order
reservations such as Fort McDowell. In addition, he and others in the Indian Service determined that the Native American
peoples should be obligated to pay for benefits from the Salt
River project, just like anybody else.[39]

In 1909, for example, Code stated he could not see "why the
Apache Indian should escape paying for his proportion of the
reclamation cost any more than any other water user." He argued: "It would not be right for a white settler to obtain the
advantage of the Government's expenditures without paying
his annual assessments; and similarly the Mojave Apache Indians can claim no right in the Salt River project unless the
reclamation charge is met." Indians should be assessed the
same acreage charge as whites. Code did not reveal how the
Yavapais would be able to pay for these assessments.[40]

Code surely worked hand in glove with two of the other key
figures in the *Hurley* v. *Abbott* case: J. B. Kibbey and Chief
Justice Edward Kent. Kibbey had been governor of Arizona and
served as the principal attorney for the Salt River Valley Water
Users Association. Kent would issue the decree that adjudi-
cated the river's water rights and the rights of the Yavapais.
Not surprisingly, Kibbey endorsed the idea of involving the Indians in the Salt River Project and of increasing the support
for it by making them pay their "fair share." He also agreed
that there would be no problem in transferring the water rights
of the Yavapais from Fort McDowell to the Salt River reservation. According to Code, Kent stated that "as a general propo-
sition he could not endorse the policy of allowing water rights
which attach to a certain area of land to be subsequently transferred to other lands." On the other hand, Kent appreciated "the
advantages of allowing such an exchange in this particular instance." He insisted that if the Government were to make the
exchange, it should be accomplished before his decree. Kent
would not specify just how much water he would allow the
Yavapais, but said he "might be able to decree them between

200 and 300 inches, sufficient for the irrigation of from 800 to 1000 acres of land." Code thought this represented fair treatment. He recommended that arrangements be made for the Yavapais to be moved and a tract not exceeding 1,390 acres be selected on the Salt Reservation in sections 19, 20, 21, and 22, T. 2 N., R. 6 E.[41]

Thus not only were the Yavapais under pressure to move from Fort McDowell to the Salt River reservation, they were being compelled to move as soon as possible. Such an alteration of residence might be in the best interests of the government, the state of Arizona, and non-Indians of the region; it suited the needs of the Salt River project, and another use could always be found for 25,000 acres along the Verde River. But in the minds of most of the Yavapais it portended disaster. They did not like the idea of sharing a reservation with the Pimas, with whom, as we have seen, they had not always been on the best of terms. Moreover, they remained unconvinced that the land on the Salt River would be an improvement over the territory they already occupied. And finally, even in their few years of living at Fort McDowell, it had become home. It had what they wanted: water, farming and grazing land, and timber. It was theirs, and they saw no reason to leave.

In anticipation of the expected Kent Decree, the office of the commissioner of Indian affairs on November 20, 1909, directed the consolidation of the Fort McDowell Agency with that of the Salt River Reservation. During the following month, Superintendent J.B. Alexander at Sacaton on the Pima Reservation reported that water appropriated by and for the Yavapais would be ordered delivered to them through the Arizona Canal for the irrigation of certain lands on the Salt River Reservation, as Code had recommended. Alexander had been so informed by Kent, who had asked if the Yavapais had been removed to the Salt River reservation, "and said that they should settle on their lands on Salt River reservation at an early date, at once if possible."[42]

On March 1, 1910, Judge Kent issued his decree. The entire decision is beyond the scope of this study, but the details as they affected the Indians are most pertinent. Kent noted that for more than forty years Indians on the Salt River reservation had had 500 miners' inches of water delivered to them from the river for cultivation of their land. He declared that this land had acquired a prior right over and above all others to the amount of 500 inches. About twenty-five hundred acres of land had been irrigated with this sum, but to irrigate this acreage would require additional water. Therefore Kent increased the total to 700 miners' inches for the Indians to use upon these lands at all stages in the river, prior to disrupting and diverting the rest of the water in the river.[43]

The Yavapais of Fort McDowell, Kent observed, had cultivated approximately thirteen hundred acres. This land was entitled to a maximum of 390 miners' inches of constant flow. Proper irrigation had not been possible for some years owing to insufficient means of diverting water from the river "and for other causes." He concluded that the government intended within the next year to remove the Yavapais from their reservation to the Salt River Reservation, and to settle them on land within Salt River to be irrigated by their proportionate share of water from the Roosevelt Reservoir. Since this change of residence and the discontinuance of Yavapai use of water from the Verde was expected, the present diversion and use of water on the McDowell reservation could be maintained.[44]

In the month after the Kent Decree, Joe H. Norris, inspector for the Department of the Interior, visited Fort McDowell. He noted the rumors of removing the Yavapais to Salt River and allotting them lands there. Norris seconded the idea and urged that the process be begun at an early date. The inspector may have approved, but he realized after his journey to Fort McDowell that many of the Yavapais did not agree, particularly the more elderly members of the tribe. To move the Yavapais, he suggested, would require "much skill and tact to do so without creating much dissention." Norris recommended that the Indian Service proceed gradually, beginning with those who were willing to go. The Yavapais should be assured that they could keep Fort McDowell for pasture and wood.[45]

It did not take long for Norris to be proven formally correct about objections to removal. On May 7, 1910, some of the Yavapais assembled under the leadership of Chief Yuma Frank, a headman the people themselves had selected several years before. They stated that they had heard they would have to move to Salt River and wished to remain at McDowell. This noteworthy petition merits extended quotation:

We begged hard for this land for homes and the Government purchased it for us. We have been living here six years and think we are making improvement in our condition. We do not like to give up our homes and go to the Salt River reservation. We have some cattle and horses and would have no grazing for them at that place. We make a success of raising poultry. We have a good church here and all our children go to Sunday School and we are trying to have them grow up right. We appreciate the assistance the government has given us in our irrigating ditches but will undertake to keep them up in the future without any help. We have already told Mr. Inspector Norris, who visited our reservation a short time ago, these things. We therefore very respectfully petition you to be allowed to remain here in our old homes at Camp McDowell. We hereby appoint Carlos Montezuma as our representative in these matters.[46]

Charles E. Coe, superintendent at Salt River, forwarded the petition to the commissioner. According to Coe, when the Yavapais had the meeting to put together their protest, the younger men present would not sign the petition. Those who did sign, however, though Coe did not mention it, numbered among the most influential in the tribe. In addition to Yuma Frank, they included George Dickens, Thomas Surrama, Ovea Johnson, and Harry Mott. Nineteen signed the petition, and some others working off the reservation at the time, such as Charles Dickens, doubtless would have added their names to the document. Coe preferred to emphasize that Sam Kill and Steve Norton, whom he described as two of the most intelligent and progressive of the older men, did not sign; "with this nucleus to work with," he concluded, "we will get all the better class of Indians to see the advantage of such a move."[47]

As the year progressed, Coe grew less sanguine. By November 22, 1910, he informed the commissioner that a "large majority" were "very strongly opposed" to going to Salt River and that influential members of the tribe emphasized they would never accept any land there. A month later, Coe admitted that there was much "excellent" land on McDowell and that during the past year there had been "an abundance" of water in the reservation ditches. Recommendations for removal had been caused by the questions about the permanency of the

ditches. In any event, Coe's life was being made more complicated by unnamed individuals; he described them as mischief
makers who had advised the others not to accept allotments
at Salt River.[48]

Montezuma by this time had gained a reputation among Indian Service personnel as the leading mischief maker of them
all. The Chicago physician very firmly opposed the notion of
removal, and he advised his people in the strongest terms not
to agree to this action under any circumstances. Montezuma,
for one, was not impressed with the assurances of people such
as Code and Coe that the Yavapais could keep their land at
McDowell once they accepted allotments at Salt River. He was
convinced that once allotment had been achieved, McDowell
would be forfeited. Montezuma urged his tribesmen to work
hard, to regard McDowell as their home, and not to sign any
agreements until he saw them. He visited McDowell in the
fall of 1910 and would return a year later. Montezuma began
to sign his letters "Wassajah." Charles Dickens and other Yavapais wrote to assure him that they would not go to Salt River.[49]
As we have seen, Montezuma strongly objected to the reservation system. At the same time, he wanted the Yavapais to
keep what he regarded as their land. He desired for them to
have a good life. And he surely distrusted the motives, let alone
the actions, of people such as Code and Coe.

Code, Coe, and others in the Indian Service returned the
favor. Commissioner R. G. Valentine on December 23, 1910
sent a circular to all superintendents and agents, citing section
2103 of the revised statues of the United States. This section
provided "that no agreement shall be made by any person with
any tribe of Indians or any individual Indians not citizens of
the United States for certain purposes, except that it be exe-
cuted in a certain manner and receive approval of the Secretary of the Interior and the Commissioner of Indian Affairs."
Not only could the Indian Office disapprove of such agreements, it could even prohibit the negotiation of such contracts.
Indeed, the commissioner discouraged the process.[50] For people such as Montezuma, it meant that the Indian Bureau could
not merely deny him the power of attorney or power of representation, they could attempt to keep him from speaking to
Indian groups on the reservation. If Bureau officials decided that

Montezuma meant mischief, in other words, they could step in immediately to stop him from influencing Native Americans to think or act along improper lines. Such extraordinary police powers seem remarkable to modern observers, but they did characterize the turn-of-the-century reservation. Certainly they shed light on Montezuma's view of the reservation as a prison where one's rights could be violated.

Secretary of the Interior R. A. Ballinger responded on January 27, 1911, to a letter from Montezuma that protested the proposed removal of the Yavapais and requested that they be allotted at McDowell and that a new dam be built for them there. Ballinger argued it was in the best interests of the Yavapais to move, though his department did not want to move them against their wishes. Since over $9 million had been spent on the Salt River project, Ballinger said, it was extremely improbable that additional expenditures would be considered on a project benefiting a small number of people. Moreover, it was very unlikely that the government would agree to more money for repairs to the present dam and ditches in use at McDowell. Thus while the Yavapais who did not want to go to Salt River would not be compelled to do so they could expect little help in the future.[51]

Montezuma replied three days later, arguing that in his judgment it was not in the best interests of the Yavapais to move. "I positively know *it is not their wish to move,*" he emphasized. The proposed dam at McDowell would be cheaper than the $45,000 to have their water rights transferred to Salt River. The dam also would permit the people in a short time to become producers instead of wards. The Yavapais, he stressed, were not lazy, shiftless, and immoral but were industrious, pastoral people who had proven their loyalty to the United States. They had already made progress and would make still more.[52]

Bureau field investigator Carl Gunderson soon was dispatched to find out why the Yavapais generally refused to move. He reported that Montezuma had written a letter to Charles Dickens telling him that a bill has been introduced in Congress providing for the allotment of twenty acres of irrigable land for each Yavapai and that they would be permitted to use the remainder of the reservation for grazing purposes. Dickens reluctantly had given the letter to Gunderson when the latter demanded to see it. According to Gunderson, Montezuma had assured the people the bill would pass Congress soon, either this session or the next. Worst of all, the Yavapais "appear to have confidence in this man," he told his superior.[53]

Superintendent Coe notified the Commissioner that the Yavapais at a mass meeting had rejected all proposals. They requested they be allotted at McDowell and that a permanent dam and head works be built on the Verde. This request for assistance, Coe charged, "is the result of letters they have been receiving from Dr. Carlos Montezuma, who has been telling them to stick together in their determination to stay at McDowell, and that they could get a concrete dam, etc. in the Verde here by asking for it." Montezuma had sent Yuma Frank a copy of H.R. Bill 31920, introduced January 23, 1911, providing for allotment at McDowell. The bill, if nothing else, would stall matters considerably. Coe found encouragement in twenty-two young people who had accepted allotments at Salt River "in the face of the violent opposition of the rest of the tribe." Nonetheless, "owing to the outside influences," Coe thought it impossible to do anything at present with the majority of the Yavapais.[54]

The bill had been introduced in the House of Representatives by John Stephens. Montezuma wrote to Stephens on March 4, 1911, signing himself "authorized Representative of Mohave and Apache Indians." "In our good works fighting against odds and fulfilling the highest mission of our existence, we die and are forgotten," Montezuma said, but he hastened to tell the congressman that he was a true and noble friend of all Indians. He noted that the Yavapais asked only to remain on their own land.[55]

The Yavapais' representative had an exchange of letters in March with the commissioner of Indian affairs. Commissioner Valentine reiterated the Bureau's position to Montezuma— that careful investigation showed it not practicable to irrigate enough land on McDowell to allow allotments. Five acres with assured water rights could be promised the Yavapais at Salt River, with McDowell still being held in common. Once the people of McDowell had accepted allotments at Salt River, then the Office might consider the advisability of allotment at McDowell.[56]

Montezuma seized upon several of the details in Valentine's letter. He was glad the commissioner so closely agreed with their estimate of the irrigable acreage at McDowell; thirteen hundred acres at McDowell would be more than the Yavapais would be entitled to at Salt River. Montezuma contended that competent engineers had assured him that a dam at McDowell was amply practicable. He suggested there were selfish interests that encouraged the proposed removal and wondered why there was "this great haste to move these Indians." He concluded that a fair hearing would ensure that the Yavapais would not be removed from where they were "contented and where Nature assists them in their happiness and good, to a land of surroundings foreign to their every mode of life for generations, and peopled with other Indian tribes who for generations have been their sworn enemies."[57]

That hearing would not be long in coming. A committee to investigate expenditures in the Interior Department had been established in the House of Representatives. Montezuma had been in contact with the committee chairman, Congressman James Graham, and Graham had been impressed. Graham's committee invited Montezuma, together with several of the Yavapais from Fort McDowell, to come to Washington to testify. Yuma Frank, George Dickens, Charles Dickens, and Thomas Surrama all received summons to appear before the committee. Superintendent Coe telegramed and wrote to the commissioner, expressing his displeasure with the selection of "obstructionists." He suggested the substitution of "progressives" Sam Kill and Gilbert Davis and requested the office pay their way as well as his. Assistant Commissioner Hauke replied that as the committee had invited these people, the Office could not substitute others.[58]

Montezuma and the other Yavapais appeared in Washington before the committee in June. Coe and Code testified in July. While the testimony of these various individuals revealed little new information or perspectives that had not surfaced in private communication, the hearings afforded Montezuma and his allies a wonderful opportunity for national publicity and attention. Montezuma had recently retained an attorney, Joseph W. Latimer, to assist him. It marked the beginning of a lifelong association between the two. Latimer figured significantly in the ensuing, continuing debate over McDowell. From this point on, the Indian Service had to deal with persistent questioning from both men. At the hearings, the committee members even allowed Latimer to interrogate witnesses. The attorney had a pleasant time exposing the limited knowledge of some individuals, such as former commissioner Francis E. Leupp.[59]

On June 16, 1911, Montezuma testified before the committee. His testimony occupies nearly fifty pages of the hearings' record. Montezuma talked about a variety of topics, including his own life story. The occasion afforded him a splendid chance to expound on many subjects, ranging from Carlisle and Pratt to the Yavapais and Fort McDowell. Throughout, he stressed the lessons that could be learned from his own life experience, the problems that were inherent in the Indian Bureau, and the need for significant change in United States Indian policy. The Yavapais actually occupied a relatively minor part of his remarks, but his appearance on their behalf and the favorable remarks he made about their character combined to make it a significant day in tribal history. The other Fort McDowell representatives acquitted themselves well. Three years later, Congressman Graham wrote to Commissioner of Indian Affairs Cato Sells, telling him how impressive Charles Dickens and his colleagues had been.[60]

So the battle had been joined. Indian Service officials would never forget the kind of questioning and scrutiny to which Montezuma and his allies had had them subjected. Even with personnel changes in the field, local superintendents and other Bureau workers would pass along the word that Montezuma was an agitator—an outsider whose influence was significant and pernicious. Thus the highly educated Montezuma, one of the "red progressives" of his time, would be associated with the elements at McDowell and elsewhere in southern Arizona that Indian agents viewed as conservative or even reactionary—people who resisted Bureau plans. In Montezuma the Bureau had a scapegoat to blame when their plans could not be carried out.

By 1912, then, Montezuma had become a national figure of importance in American Indian Affairs. He had also established himself as a person to be reckoned with at Fort McDowell.

Other Indian peoples in southern Arizona were beginning to turn toward him because their problems in water rights and other matters were quite similar to those of the Yavapais. Soon he would establish his newsletter, *Wassaja*, dedicated to the abolition of the Indian Bureau. He would continue to defend the well-being of his people, who faced renewed threats of removal from their homeland. Montezuma had embarked upon the richest, most deeply committed period of his existence. He had slightly more than a decade to live.

5

"A Strong Warrior for Our Race"

The period from 1912 to 1918 marked the prime of Montezuma's life, the most productive time in his career as an Indian activist. Perhaps it was his happiest time. He married, finally, and the marriage seemed a good one. Within the Society of American Indians, he continued to be a central and controversial figure. To further his crusade against the Bureau of Indian Affairs, Montezuma began in 1916 his newsletter, *Wassaja.* His relations at this juncture with such key characters in pan-Indian activities as Arthur C. Parker reveal much about the strains attendant to developing a national Native American identity. On the Fort McDowell reservation, Montezuma maintained his fight to represent the interests of the Yavapais. He clashed, often bitterly, with Indian Service officials in southern Arizona and in Washington, D.C. During these years, Montezuma received a great deal of criticism. But he responded vigorously, sparing no one in his zealous efforts. Because information on this period is particularly rich and abundant, two chapters are devoted to it. Chapter 5 considers Montezuma's work at the national level, while Chapter 6 analyzes his involvement in southern Arizona.

"You have been a strong warrior for our race," wrote Charles Eastman to Carlos Montezuma. In his book, *The Indian To-*

day, published in 1915, Eastman acknowledged the stature
Montezuma had achieved. Chapter 8, "The Indian in College
and the Professions," included a section on "Some Noted Indians of To-day." "Perhaps the foremost of these," wrote Eastman, "is Dr. Carlos Montezuma of Chicago. . . . He stands
uncompromisingly for the total abolition of the reservation system and of the Indian Bureau, holding that the red man must
be allowed to work out his own salvation."[1]

The Dakota physician had chosen his words carefully and
accurately. Abolition of the Indian Bureau was Montezuma's
and *Wassaja's* battle cry. Attitudes toward the Bureau, as we
have seen, affected his view of the Society of American Indians.
Not only did the alleged influence of the Bureau upon the Society cause Montezuma to boycott the first annual meeting of
the Society, but the issue of the Bureau continued to pose problems for the Yavapai's relationship with the Association.

Despite Montezuma's sensitivity and reticence, other SAI
members still courted him. Secretary-Treasurer Arthur C. Parker persistently sought Montezuma's allegiance to the organization. The Seneca anthropologist wrote on March 4, 1912:

We stand in need of your continued interest and will be glad to have
your advice and suggestions on any point that you may care to mention. I was very much disappointed in not seeing you at Columbus
but I am hoping that our second Conference will be honored by your
presence. We need the true Indian spirit and I think that the distinguished Apache has it.[2]

Even Montezuma could not resist such an appeal. His flag-
ging commitment to the Society revived, and he responded to
Parker, offering him several suggestions. Upon receiving Montezuma's letter, Parker replied immediately. He attempted to
reassure Montezuma about the speech by the commissioner
of Indian affairs at the Society's meeting in Columbus: "Not
an address from the Bureau and far from being dictatorial it is
an appeal to you and I and every Indian to use his criticism
and offer his suggestions . . . a confession on the part of the
Bureau that it needed help and advice from the Indians." Parker continued in the most conciliatory terms about the issue
which bothered the doctor:

... the Indians have just cause for criticizing the Bureau ... our membership is about solid in its opinion that the Bureau is not all it should be. Our criticism of its actions is pronounced and I believe will quell any rumor that as a body we are in any way in sympathy with it. The sooner it is abolished the better my ideas will be suited. ...

He concluded with another invitation to rejoin the Society, which, Parker said, needed "your advice and your ability to express what you know to be true."[3]

Encouraged by Parker's seemingly strong stand in regard to the Bureau and heartened by Indian Service employee Charles Daganett's resignation from his temporary position as the top executive of the Society, Montezuma renewed his allegiance to the association. The fact that Richard H. Pratt had agreed to be present at the second annual conference in October doubtless further increased his interest. By August, he had committed himself to attendance at the gathering. Fayette McKenzie had written to Montezuma on August 17, 1912, expressing his delight that Pratt would be speaking during the conference and his hope that Montezuma would be present to hear him. Parker followed two days later, noting that with Pratt as a speaker "we seem to be getting the right element at the helm." He added that he felt "very deeply convinced that we shall be unable to get along rightly without you." Parker suggested that Montezuma could speak on the topic "The Status of the Indian of the United States." In addition, he forwarded Laura Cornelius Kellogg's idea that Montezuma could talk as well about public school education for the Indian. The reply from Chicago to Albany apparently was immediate and positive. By the end of the month, Parker notified Montezuma that the Yavapai's address on "Light on the American Indian Situation" would be the principal Indian speech Saturday evening.[4]

Others in the Society quickly welcomed Montezuma back to the fold. McKenzie expressed his pleasure that Montezuma was coming to Columbus. For good measure, the Ohio State professor enclosed a list of potential Indian members and urged Montezuma to persuade them to attend as well. Henry Standing Bear stated he would be glad to see Montezuma "get hold" of the organization. This year Montezuma arranged his trip to

Arizona for September so that he could return in time to attend the meeting.[5]

The Society of American Indians gathered in Columbus October 2–7, 1912. Montezuma made his presence felt, criticizing the reservation system, praising General Pratt, and speaking in favor of Indian attendance at public schools. Despite Montezuma's reputation as an archenemy of organizational unity, it was the "distinguished Apache" who suggested that Acting Commissioner of Indian Affairs F. A. Abbott be allowed to speak to the session. Moreover, McKenzie emerged from the conference with rejuvenated hope, greatly pleased with the conference, especially the presence of Montezuma and Pratt. "If the balance and harmony of views can be continued in the Society a great future may be predicted," he concluded.[6]

During the first few months after the conference, McKenzie's optimism seemed justified. Montezuma was even chastised by the Ojibwa August Breuninger for attending and participating in the meeting of the Society of American Indians. Breuninger charged that by his participation, Montezuma had gone over to the enemy and joined their ranks against his people.[7]

Early in 1913, Parker assured Montezuma that the Society was "doing some hustling you may be sure—and growing healthily." He invited him to serve as a contributing editor of the newly established quarterly journal of the association. Striking the right chord, Parker informed him that he had had a fine trip in Indian country; all over Oklahoma, he had preached Pratt's text and told the life stories of Montezuma, Eastman, and Sherman Coolidge as examples to the students, who "yelled themselves hoarse over the idea of Indians becoming independent and achieving the higher things."[8]

Montezuma agreed to serve as a contributing editor. The first issue of the *Quarterly Journal* appeared in March 1913. Pratt confessed he was "so much impressed by everything in it from cover to cover that Mrs. Pratt and I sent a goodly contribution to the Society." The general concurred with the idea of Denver as the site for the third annual conference. Among other things, meeting in Denver could help "discount in advance" the adverse impact of the Buffalo Bill show planned there for 1915. The city's western location would attract many Native Americans who had been unable to attend the first two meetings in Columbus. In addition, Denver promised the Society $2,000 to help cover expenses. The Society seemed to be on firm ground. Even Gus Beaulieu, an Ojibwa critical of many things, wrote in his newsletter, *The Tomahawk*, that the Society was a good organization and should receive the support of Indians throughout the United States.

Tranquility could not prevail for long. Pratt's daughter, Marion, sent him a copy of the April 24 edition of the Denver *News*, which suggested to him that the Society meeting would be used by the city of Denver to promote the forthcoming Buffalo Bill show. If there was one thing that could be counted on to make the old Philadelphian's blood boil, it was the spectre of some Wild West extravaganza. Pratt viewed such productions as totally contrary to the best interests of Indians, and any association with such a spectacle made him recoil in horror. Although he had just finished writing to some eighteen hundred former students praising the Society, he threatened to send another eighteen hundred letters to tell them he had been wrong. The fact that Bureau employee Charles Daganett happened to be stationed in Denver simply increased the odds for collusion.[10]

That summer Pratt encouraged Montezuma to drop all association with the Society of American Indians. The "very, very sporty" Daganett recently had taken Pratt for a ride in his $1,750 automobile; his appearance added to the general's suspicions. Pratt wrote to Parker in July asking the secretary-treasurer to delete his name and that of Mrs. Pratt from the list of associate members (only Indians were eligible for active membership in the organization). Despite Parker's efforts to convince him otherwise, Pratt remained obdurate.[11]

What should Montezuma do? He weighed his options during the summer of 1913, measuring his feelings about Wild West shows and his loyalty to Pratt against the potential of the Society. In addition, concerns over the Fort McDowell reservation continued to mount, and he needed to make a return visit to southern Arizona in the near future. A letter from Parker in mid-August forced him to decide. Parker wrote asking for suggestions and advice on how best to carry out the Society's conference program. He also expressed his sorrow that Pratt had resigned, adding that he feared the general did not

understand the Society's ideals and principles. "I think" said
Parker, "that General Pratt has an impression that every member should be compelled to submit to a rigid doctrine when
even that doctrine may be susceptible to some discussion."[12]

Addressing his reply to "My dear friend," Montezuma alleged
that the Society of American Indians was trapped in the cob-
webs of the Colorado Publicity League, formed to promote an
Indian show in 1915. He did not want to go to Denver to be
entertained by the league and he knew intuitively that the
league would take advantage of the Society's friendship. And
in no way could he be affiliated with Indian shows, which were
"simply a breeder of immorality and degeneracy to the Indians
who partake." Parker quickly replied that he could not see how
the Society was trapped. The best way to help was to stay: "I
think the Society can overcome anything and sail on."[14]

Given Montezuma's previous statements, Parker could not
help but be pleased with this last letter. He agreed with Montezuma's assessment of the Society's future, but "we can not
overcome unless men like you and Oskison stand like rocks
against the 'jingoism' that knocks at our doors." "When it
comes to solidity," he told Montezuma, "somehow I always
think of you." Parker expressed his wish to Pratt that the Doctor might be prevailed upon at the forthcoming conference to
assume the executive reins of the Society in the capacity of
president. He continued: "I could work with such a man as he
is and even if we do disagree in minor particulars, I could feel
that there was honesty on his side and I feel he would know
the sincerity of my position." To counter questions about government influence in the Society, Montezuma ought to "lead
his people through his ability and the confidence he inspires."
"Surely," Parker concluded, "Doctor Montezuma will never
be tricked by a Government Bureau scheme."[15]

Montezuma left for Arizona September 20 and did not go to
Denver for the conference. Having retreated from his strong
denunciation of the Society, he still could not bring himself to
be present and apparently endorse in any way the future Wild
West show. As we will see in the next chapter, he was devoting his attention to the serious situation facing his people.
Moreover, another vital matter claimed his attention—his en-

gagement to a young Romanian-American woman, Marie Keller. She was much younger than he, a non-Indian, and a quiet person who apparently lacked the crusading zeal of her fiance. A childhood friend, Elsie Severance, decades later recalled Marie Montezuma as one who perhaps did not fully appreciate the national importance of her husband, being a traditional European-American woman willing to remain in the background. Few of her letters from Montezuma are extant, but as Mrs. Montezuma had custody of her husband's papers for years after his death, it is quite possible that she chose not to save more personal epistles. In any event, it apparently was a marriage that worked. Given Montezuma's strong personality, it is perhaps not surprising that he married a "beautiful but demure" woman. Even if one accepts Elsie Severance's judgment that Marie Montezuma was "a faithful helpmate but did not quite understand his capabilities, his importance," one must also acknowledge her role in helping her husband to achieve the most productive period in his life.[16]

Nonetheless, Montezuma continued to have a life of his own after the Rev. W. H. Steadman married the couple. He and his wife helped to entertain many Indians who stopped in Chicago, but he almost always traveled on his own to carry on his crusades. Marie Montezuma, in fact, did not travel to Arizona with him until 1921. Even though he had just been married, Carlos Montezuma saw no compelling reason to postpone or cancel his planned visit to McDowell. Thus, he left for Arizona as scheduled, on September 20, 1913, having been married September 19. He was accompanied by some of his old hunting and social companions—but not by his wife. "My own Dutchie" received the following letter from Santa Fe:

We are here today.—The rest are uneasy that I do not write any more to you but we know best that if the folks do not know anything about us, the less letters to you will be better. You know we know each other and other people do not know. I feel good and happy that everything turned out all right. I hope you are still safe from the others finding out what happened. . . . Just keep brave heart and be happy. and don't cry too much.

                                                        Your *Husband*

don't blush[17]

We must conclude from the above that Marie Keller's parents were either not delighted about the prospect of their daughter marrying Montezuma, or were not informed about the marriage ceremony, or both. In spite of the couple's discretion, however, their wedding could not remain secret for very long. The Chicago *Record-Herald* printed a story about it in early October. McKenzie congratulated Montezuma later that month on his marriage. On November 7, 1913, the Pratts offered congratulations: "The fact that you have such a practical, home-making companion is a source of the greatest possible gratification to us . . . you can both feel assured of our continued fatherhood and motherhood. . . ."[18]

Montezuma may have missed the October conference of the Society of American Indians—his letter to his wife revealed that he had no plans of returning early from the Southwest to attend the meeting—but he did make a trip to Philadelphia the following February for a regional meeting of the Society. Pratt had promised Parker that he would be on hand. In turn, Parker invited Montezuma to speak at the session: "Nothing would please the General better and nothing would bring us greater pleasure than to see our unconquerable Apache friend, bringing with him his unbreakable principle that 'Segregation and reservation mean demoralization.' " Montezuma initially indicated he could not be present for financial reasons, but Pratt, writing on SAI stationery, urged him to change his mind. Commissioner of Indian Affairs Cato Sells would be there and he wanted particularly, Pratt assured Montezuma, "to see Indians who have gone out from the reservation and made a success of it." That was an opportunity Montezuma could not resist, and he traveled to Philadelphia for the February 14 banquet.[19]

His featured address, "The Reservation Is Fatal to the Development of Good Citizenship," earned high marks from Parker. "You hit the nail and the Commissioner listened with marked attention," he told Montezuma. "We are deeply indebted to you and I thank you from the bottom of my heart."[20] Later reprinted in the *Quarterly Journal*, the speech stressed familiar themes. Montezuma used the analogy of American policy toward foreign immigrants throughout his talk, suggesting that Indians must learn to speak English, attend public schools, and, in general, be placed in the surroundings of civilization. He also criticized the federal government for irrigation projects and forestry projects that had taken away Indian lands and timber and for locking up four Pima Indians at an agent's request and keeping them in the Phoenix jail without specific charges. Montezuma informed the commissioner that the Indian was generally still "an outlawed creature, with no rights that protect the ordinary human being," and that he was governed "by a machine whose agents have most despotic powers and whose unscrupulous actions in many instances 'smell to heaven.' "[21]

Having attended the Philadelphia meeting, Montezuma soon renewed his membership within the Society of American Indians. Parker continued to correspond with him in the first months of 1914, and in April, Sherman Coolidge expressed his hope that the Montezumas could come to the fourth annual conference, scheduled in Madison, Wisconsin, October 6–11. Coolidge said he would like others to meet Mrs. Montezuma as he had, "even if they do not have the benefit of her good cooking." Montezuma sent in his SAI membership dues in May. The corresponding secretary for the organization, Rosa La Flesche, in return enclosed a membership card showing him to be an active member in good standing. She could not resist adding: *Good standing*—isn't that wonderful for you? Ha! ha!" La Flesche added in a postscript: "Don't forget to bring your card to the Conference. I happen to know that you are in good standing with the Society but others might not know."[22]

With membership card in hand, Montezuma made the 150-mile trip from Chicago to Madison for the SAI conference. He had been invited to attend the Lake Mohonk conference, but he declined, saying to Mr. and Mrs. Daniel Smiley that as a Society member, he could not be in New York. Ironically, Parker and several other important people missed the Madison meeting. Apparently Montezuma was not a particularly divisive force at what proved to be a somewhat uneventful gathering. On December 10, 1914, many of the Society leaders met with President Woodrow Wilson to present their concerns in Indian affairs. Montezuma could not join them. He sent regrets to Parker, saying, "My spirit is with you. May God bless and guide you in the cause of our people."[23]

Instead Montezuma sent along an article, "What We Indians Must Do." Parker liked almost all of it but deleted passages critical of the commissioner of Indian affairs. The editor thought the cause best served by not directly antagonizing the head of the Bureau, even though he admitted what Montezuma said was "undoubtedly true."[24] Montezuma argued that the contemporary Indian must free himself by living off the reservation and obtaining a good education. The choice was a dramatic one: "Are we to disappear as the buffaloes or rise above the horizon of the twentieth century and respond, 'We are here!' " Indians had to stand together; factionalism had weakened the Society. They could not be too timid in regard to the Bureau. "There is nothing gained on this earth," he contended, "without a fight, without a struggle, without personal effort." And he knew from personal experience, as we shall see in the next chapter, that Indian agents would fight back against people such as himself: "It seems that an Indian can not speak to or for his people without being suspicioned. When such a thing occurs that Indian is pointed out as a grafter or troublemaker."[25]

Montezuma's conflicts with Bureau personnel, including the commissioner, over McDowell thus led him to be increasingly hostile to the relatively more conciliatory posture of Parker and other "moderates" within the Society. He initially entertained great hopes for Cato Sells to make significant improvement in Indian policy, but by the end of 1914 he had become quite discouraged. Sells merited criticism, just as the Bureau did. Working within the system, a procedure advocated by Parker, in the end could not be satisfactory if the system itself was fundamentally wrong. While Montezuma did not rescind permission for the *Quarterly Journal* to publish his piece, perhaps Parker's deletion of offending passages marked another transition in the Yavapai's feelings toward the Seneca editor, his journal, and the Society itself. If the magazine and the Society could not be totally forthright in their editorial policy, then another more candid journal was needed. Montezuma had not yet embarked upon this route, but he would soon; the first issue of his newsletter, *Wassaja*, would be published in 1916.

In the spring of 1915 another related matter further inflamed Montezuma's ire. Facing resistance from Indian Service agents in Arizona, Montezuma asked the Society to request permission for him to visit reservations in the state. Coolidge followed through on Montezuma's wish, but he met some resistance from Commissioner Sells, who indicated that a visit of this sort by an SAI representative might complicate matters. Montezuma did not care for Sells' response. "Is the Society dictated by the Indian Bureau what we must do?," he asked Coolidge. The Society must know what was going on on reservations, Montezuma asserted: "When I am working for the Indians, it is the duty of the Society to back me up." He repeated his request for a letter from the Society to obtain by the Commissioner's permission for him to speak to Indians on reservations in Arizona.[26]

Even though he had gained little satisfaction on this matter, Montezuma still looked forward to the 1915 annual meeting. He corresponded regularly with Parker about the upcoming conference. Parker invited Montezuma to participate in a debate on the topic of immediate abolition of the Indian Bureau, adding: "One thing is certain, under the paternal system of Bureau training independent responsibility has not been thoroughly developed." Montezuma renewed his membership in the Society at the end of April. He wished to assist in the process of promoting the conference: "We need to start the ball rolling for our next Conference in good earnest and have a large attendance. It is well to notify every member of the Society and get them to work. All of us must do something in order to make it successful."[27]

In June, Parker thanked Montezuma for another most encouraging letter. Without explaining why, he noted that no one had been willing to take the other side in the debate over abolition. Again Parker seemed sympathetic to the thrust of Montezuma's criticism of the Bureau, arguing that the Bureau had emphasized property "and not manhood and citizenship." The secretary-treasurer also acknowledged Montezuma's "standing clean for a united support of the Society despite occupation or employment on the part of some members by the Indian Bureau."[28]

Correspondence between the two men remained most cordial during the summer of 1915, giving no evidence of the rift that would soon develop. Parker appeared to be firm in his support of the essence of Montezuma's viewpoint. In one letter, he stated he did favor "the abolishment of the Indian Bureau as it stands, but I believe that the federal government cannot

be blind to the many laws and treaties and the human obligations of the country to a race which has been placed at disad-
vantage." The closing line of another letter read: "More power
to you, old soldier." Another said: "Good for you, Doctor. I
hope your speech will be a clarion call to freedom."[29]

At the same time, some storm signals began to fly. Henry
Standing Bear told Montezuma he did not know whether to
attend the next conference. He was losing interest, for the right
people did not head the organization. Standing Bear called the
Society a total failure, controlled by a few would-be great men.
Attorney Thomas Sloan labeled the Sells administration the
worst Indians had experienced, "so rotten that there is no excuse for its existence or continuance." "What has the Society
done?" asked Sloan. "Why it has stood with oppressors against
the Indians. . . . The Indian Office plans to control the Society of
American Indians and is doing so." Sloan said he would urge Indians who would do something to attend the annual meeting.[30]

The fifth annual conference, held September 28-October 3,
1915, in Lawrence, Kansas, featured conflicts over several basic
issues, including peyote and abolition of the Bureau. Parker had
feared that chaos and confusion would reign. Perhaps he had
been anxious over the role Montezuma might play. Writing to
him shortly before the meeting, Parker emphasized: "There
must be no attempt to cause a revolution or to stampede the
conference in a way that will destroy our effectiveness. Great
measures, if we are to accomplish them, will be brought forth
only by a logically cautious course of wise action."[31]

Montezuma spoke forthrightly and impressively at the conference. Even Parker agreed with him that the Indian office
should be eliminated as a special bureau. Later that autumn
the SAI treasurer, Marie L. B. Baldwin, asked Montezuma,
given his interest in the organization, to provide names of people to whom sample copies of the quarterly might be sent.
Thomas Sloan believed "we saved the Society some self respect
and made it considered by the Bureau." Newly elected an officer in the organization, Sloan proved quite pleased about the
outcome of the meeting: "Really, Doctor, we prevented the Indian Office making the Society of American Indians a laughing stock among the Indians and those who know something
of its affairs. We prevented the Society from kissing the hand

that strikes it. And to have raised its hands in self defense. Another punch like that will help put us on the map."[32]

Sloan's somewhat strident tone suggests the presence of considerable conflict in the Society over the abolition of the Bureau. Both privately and publicly, Parker and others chastized Montezuma for not providing a concrete alternative to the Bureau of Indian Affairs. "The fiery Apache wields a scalping knife in the sure hand of an experienced physician," wrote Parker in the Society's journal, but if the Bureau were to be abolished, who would look after unfinished business? To "fail to provide adequate laws and regulations for the conservation of his heritage would be poor wisdom," he admonished. In any event, Congress would never abolish the Bureau. Until Indians had learned to battle against adverse conditions in an imperfect civilization, the government would "have something pretty definite to say about Indian affairs."[33] Given some of the sentiments Parker had expressed in previous correspondence, his reaction perhaps annoyed Montezuma. However, Montezuma should have anticipated the mixed response to his speech in Lawrence, which was as vitriolic a condemnation of the Bureau as he had ever uttered. He also had been very critical of the way in which the Society had proceeded.

"Let My People Go," Montezuma entitled the address he read September 30, 1915. In it, he sharply attacked the unwillingness of the Society of American Indians to embrace his position of immediate abolition. "The Society of American Indians has met and met," Montezuma said. "This coming together every year has been the mere routine of shaking hands, appointing committees, listening to papers, hearing discussions, passing a few resolutions, electing officers, then reorganizing—and that has been the extent of our outlook and usefulness for our race." The Society members had been drilling in their uniforms, but not fighting; now they must fight or cease to exist. What was it good for? Dare it shy, run, cower, and hide? "The iron hand of the Indian Bureau has us in charge," he contended. "The slimy clutches of horrid greed and selfish interests are gripping the Indian's property. Little by little the Indian's land and everything else is fading into a dim and unknown realm." Thus the highest duty and greatest object of the Society must be to have a Congressional bill introduced to abolish the Bureau. There had to be unity on this matter, he concluded: "We must act as one. Our hearts must throb with love,—our souls must reach to God to guide us,—and our bodies and souls must be used to gain our peoples' freedom. In behalf of our people, with the spirit of Moses, I ask this,—THE UNITED STATES OF AMERICA,—'LET MY PEOPLE GO.' "[34]

Montezuma had come to a turning point in his life. He must speak out directly and strongly on the issue he believed to be so critical. "For many years I have looked on without saying anything," he wrote to L. V. McWhorter. Even though many people would have disagreed with this assessment, what mattered was that Montezuma evidently believed it. "I am criticized for being too harsh and too radical," Montezuma informed McWhorter. "If people will realize as I do they would be more so than I am." In his "feeble way," he had to "present the true position of the Indians."[35]

In *Wassaja,* inaugurated in April 1916, Montezuma found the ideal medium through which to carry out his crusade. He published this personal newsletter monthly until November 1922, by which time he was dying of tuberculosis. Here he was at his best. During the six and a half years of its existence, *Wassaja* carried on the good fight against the Bureau and for a place for Indians in the America of the twentieth century. It displayed his gift for polemic, his cutting sense of humor, and his dedication to the present and future of Native Americans. In his own publication, he could speak out freely, writing slashing editorials as well as printing news of Indian life from around the nation. A single copy of *Wassaja* cost a nickel; 100 copies set one back two dollars. A year's subscription was only fifty cents. Montezuma accepted no advertisements and had a difficult time finding the money to print what Elsie Severance termed "his chief obsession."[36] His financial records and *Wassaja* itself reveal what a struggle he had to publish the newsletter, but publish it he did, until almost the very end.

From the first issue, Montezuma made it clear why *Wassaja* had been created: "This monthly signal ray is to be published only so long as the Indian Bureau exists. Its sole purpose is Freedom for the Indians through the abolishment of the Indian Bureau." The first numbers featured a drawing of a Native American, pinned under a huge log labeled *Indian Bureau,* looking up at a ray of light labeled *Wassaja*, shining down toward him. The goal of the paper, Montezuma noted, was "not to form a society, but to free the Indians by exposing the actual condition of their imprisonment." And the editor believed that action must be taken immediately; gradualism on the question of abolition served no one but Bureau employees. Indian people living in the here and now deserved better:

It is too much to ask the Indian people that they give up two or three generations of existence before a state of things can be reached where future generations may come into their inheritance. The mere fact that in the course of time the brutal oppression of government, wherever it exists, will have passed away, is not a sufficient reason why the victims of misrule should supinely forego resistance.[37]

Montezuma would be the first to resist, and the Bureau of Indian Affairs would not be his only target. In the second issue of *Wassaja*, the Society of American Indians in general and Arthur C. Parker in particular found themselves targets of the Yavapai's pen. In "Arrow Points," Montezuma pricked Parker twice. First he criticized one of Parker's favorite notions, American Indian Day, a proposed annual observance in honor of Native Americans. Such an observance. Montezuma argued, was both a farce and a fad, as the Indian was not free. Second, Montezuma looked with disdain at the transformation of the *Quarterly Journal* of the Society into the *American Indian Magazine*, a publication which would "straddle" the issues. Buffalo Bill and P. T. Barnum had used the Indians, but now, Montezuma suggested, it was the turn of the *American Indian Magazine*.[38]

In addition, he characterized the Lawrence meeting of the Society in the most unflattering way:

The sky is clear and we meet only to discuss. It is so nice to meet and discuss. There is nothing wrong. We meet only to discuss. It is so nice to meet and discuss. We can meet and discuss as well as the Mohonk conference. . . . Meeting and discussing are so soothing and smoothing. Sh—! Sh—! Don't whisper about the Indian Bureau. . . .[39]

The Society of American Indians held its sixth annual meeting at Coe College, a small liberal arts institution situated in Cedar Rapids, Iowa. The conference selected *American Indian*

Magazine editor Arthur C. Parker as its president. Parker had recently taken the opportunity to respond in the pages of that journal to the first few issues of *Wassaja*. While agreeing that Montezuma was very earnest and had at heart the real uplift and freedom of his people, he suggested that the Apache doctor's view of the Indian Bureau as an agency of tyranny was worthy of a detailed psychological examination. Parker quoted the previously cited "arrow points" aimed at him and the Society and added: "Dr. Montezuma has a splendid sense of humor and luckily for the rest of us we have also." But he denied the charges leveled. Despite Parker's relative cordial rejoinder, it was clear that the friendship between the two men had cooled considerably.[40]

Montezuma enlivened a poorly attended conference by debating with SAI president Sherman Coolidge over the issue of Indian employees in the Indian Service. Coolidge strongly disagreed with Montezuma and, in order to confront Montezuma, stepped down from the chair, allowing Vice-President Henry Roe Cloud to become president. "It is about time we are setting you right," said the Arapahoe minister, "I think you can mix with the Indian Bureau." Marie Baldwin and Gertrude Bonnin sided with Coolidge; Philip Gordon, an Ojibwa Catholic priest, supported Montezuma. "I am an Apache," yelled Montezuma to Coolidge, "and you are an Arapahoe. I can lick you. My tribe has licked your tribe before." "I am from Missouri," retorted Coolidge, who stood inches taller than his Yavapai counterpart.[41]

Parker may have disagreed with Montezuma, but he reprinted the latter's address to the conference in his magazine. Montezuma renewed his attacks on the change of the journal's name, on American Indian Day, and on the Society's relationship with the Indian Bureau. Despite his confrontation with Coolidge, Montezuma said he did not want to fight and that he wished to see the Society grow. Still, Society members "must go right," that is, take a strong stand against the Bureau, which they refused to do: "When it comes to doing anything that radical, when it comes to the point of whether it is right or wrong they craw-fish, they duck. . . ."[42]

The October 1916 issue of *Wassaja* reflected Montezuma's extreme displeasure with the Cedar Rapids conference. "Ex-

President Coolidge of the Society of American Indian says that he can be loyal to the Indian race and at the same time serve the Indian Bureau," the issue began. "WASSAJA wonders if he serves God and the Devil the same way." Cedar Rapids had seen Indians "disagreeing, throttling each other, stirring up confusion and killing their organization." For good measure, he questioned the manner in which Parker had been elected.[43]

Nor in subsequent issues did Montezuma relent in his attack upon Parker. "The-man-behind the Pseudo-Indian Magazine deserves a blessing and reward from the Indian Office," he suggested. "No doubt a position is waiting for him." Montezuma compared the Society and its magazine to "a ship which is moving in a wrong direction. The ship is not at fault. What is the matter? The captain and the crew are steering it in the wrong direction or not steering it at all." He reaffirmed that the Society had good ideas for Native Americans, but charged that "the officers are all wrong" and "any good ideas can be killed by officers who have wrong notions of doing the best thing for the Indians." Montezuma continued:

WASSAJA most emphatically must say that the present officers are not for the best interest of the Indians, because their environment does not permit them to take right views of the welfare of their race. They have turned their ears, shut their eyes and ignored the freedom for their enslaved race.[44]

Not surprisingly, Parker dropped Montezuma from the roster of contributing editors to his magazine.

The Bureau of Indian Affairs, of course, remained the primary target of Montezuma's wrath. During its first year, *Wassaja* published two of his best salvos against the Bureau. Montezuma was fond of similes, and he liked to compare the Bureau and its personnel to various objects that either had outgrown their usefulness or had never had any utility in the first place:

The Indian Bureau is like an old, worn out horse, perhaps quite a nag in days gone by. The horse is now past his day. He limps, has the heaves, is blind, cannot hear a single sound, BUT HE CAN SMELL THE OATS. Some say: "Don't abolish good old horse. Brace him up, rather. Give him more oats ($12,000,000 is the present cost of the "feed"), rub his legs with arnice, give him a pill or two." Alas! Those of us who say: "Kill the brute and put him out of his misery," are often laughed at (by Indian Service employees) or rather humorously taken by the rest of mankind; it's so cruel to kill a poor suffering horse! OR MAYBE IT'S A DONKEY![45]

He often decried the incompetency of Bureau personnel. "On the Stage of Indian Affairs" starred a cast that included the following characters:

THE HONORABLE COMMISSIONER of Indian Affairs addressing his employees:
"Who says 'Freedom for the Indians' "
A BOLD GLADIATOR employee in the U.S. Indian Department . . .:
"Not I, for I work in the Indian Service. I got my job under Civil Service. Not I,—not I,—not I, my Lord!"
A VETERAN FEMALE employee in the Indian Service, testifies from her heart:
"Oh, how I love to work for the Indians. I could live and die doing what the Indians ought to do."
ONE ROYAL [sic] STAUNCH EMPLOYEE . . .:
"All these requirements of our Master we faithfully obey; we shut our mouths, see nothing and get our pay."[46]

Montezuma also used *Wassaja* as a forum in which to analyze the role of other institutions in Indian Affairs. He discussed the roles of the church and the schools. Montezuma particularly damned the churches, for he believed they had a special responsibility to minister to Native Americans, and they had not lived up to that charge. As a devout Baptist, he felt quite strongly about the matter: "The churches have acted as though the Indian race had the small-pox . . . If Christ came into the world He would tear down the barriers of the reservation." Given the frequency with which Christianity followed in the wake of disease among Indians, the reference was particularly telling. He had expected the most help and the most good from the churches, but had not received it. Church members had satisfied their conscience by saying: "The Indians are vanishing like the buffalo." "Ah," said *Wassaja's* editor, "be not deceived, they are here and will be to eternity."[47]

It is important to recognize that *Wassaja* did more than criticize the Bureau of Indian Affairs and chastise Arthur C. Parker. Often it looked to the future of Native Americans. Montezuma believed that Indians would endure, as the quotation in the preceding paragraph indicates. He thought that American Indians lived in a changing world. Indians of the present had an opportunity to create a better world for their children:

Fennimore Cooper's Indians do not exist today. We are their children's children. Things have changed and we have changed with them. We do not see things as our forefathers saw them nor do we live as they did. Let it be known that within the breast of every Indian there is a heart which throbs with the same yearnings that throb in all human kind.[48]

Montezuma expressed anger at both the individuals and the institutions that held Native Americans back or denied them their true potential. Therefore he lashed out at the Indian commissioner, the Board of Indian Commissioners, the Bureau, Bureau employees, the Indian Rights Association, and missionaries, who appeared to reject the notion that Native Americans could become self-sufficient.

As *Wassaja* entered its second year in 1917, Montezuma renewed his pledge to work for the abolition of the Indian Bureau. He viewed the present as a time "when the Indians are in a critical condition involving their life and liberty," when their rights were denied, and when their suffering continued. And he maintained the hope that the Society of American Indians could be vitally important. Montezuma made a distinction between writing against the Society and writing against its leaders; he had done the latter. He urged Indians from all tribes to attend the next conference of the Society, planned for Minneapolis.[49]

By June 1917, *Wassaja* had changed its cover drawing, though not its message. Now *Wassaja* shone on the door of a brick building, with the padlocked door labeled *Indian Office.* Montezuma and several other Native Americans were grasping a large battering ram of a log, emblazoned with the words *Freedom's Signal for the Indian.* The other Indians were in traditional and working clothes, while Montezuma was dressed nattily in a three-piece suit. The cartoon reflected not only the journal's continuing commitment to its initial purpose, but also Montezuma's strengthened ties with the people of McDowell and other reservation communities. The publication was devoting more and more space to the specific problems faced by the people at Fort Peck and the Crow reservations in Montana, and by other Native Americans, including those of southern Arizona.[50]

The site of the annual conference of the Society of American Indians was changed to Oklahoma City, and eventually the meeting was cancelled altogether. The officers blamed the cancellation on World War I. As Hertzberg has suggested, the officers probably feared defeat or dissension and preferred canceling the conference to losing control of the organization. Predictably, Montezuma was not at all pleased. He entitled his comment in the October 1917 *Wassaja* "Scalping the S.A.I. Again." He called postponing the meeting because of the war foolish and very silly. More likely, he suggested, the Indian Office had influenced the officers to cancel it, so the government would not be embarrassed during wartime. And most likely, in Montezuma's view, which was probably correct, the Society had had a very weak response from its Native American constituents.[51]

World War I itself inspired mixed feelings in Montezuma. He felt that because the United States had so mistreated the Indians, it should not be able to force Native Americans to fight on its behalf. Indians who wanted to serve in the war should do so; Indians who did not want to serve should not have to. Montezuma wrote several pieces on the subject for *Wassaja*. In April 1917, he wrote, "Steady, Indians, Steady!"; part of this work is reprinted here:

> The Ghost Craze has come and gone,
> The War Craze is on.
> If you want to fight—fight—
> But let no one force you in.
>   Steady Indians, Steady! . . .
> "Fight for your country and flag" is noble and grand,
> But have you a country? Is that your flag?
> If you do not know what you are fighting for, stay at home . . .
> They have taken your country,
> They have taken your manhood,
> They have imprisoned you,
> They have made you wards,
> They have stunted your faculties . . .
> You are not entitled to the rights of man.
> You are not an American citizen—

You are an Indian;
You are nothing and that is all . . .
Redskins, *true Americans*, you have a fight with
    those who you wish to fight for,
It is your birthright—*Freedom*;
Let them make good;
With better heart you will fight,
Side by side under the same flag,
    Steady, Indians, Steady![52]

Two months later, he noted that if the United States were fighting for democracy, then the Indians were holding out their
hands "for the same rights and freedom that the United States
is fighting for." Indian Bureauism," Montezuma contended, "is
the Kaiserism of America toward the Indians." In the autumn
of 1917, in "Drafting Indians and Justice," he again asked how,
if the Indians were not citizens, they could be drafted: "WASSAJA
believes that this drafting of the Indians into the army is another wrong perpetrated upon the Indian without FIRST bestow-
ing his just title—THE FIRST AMERICAN CITIZEN. Why not? He
was here before Columbus, he was here before Washington,
he was here before Lincoln and he was here and you came." A
cartoon in the same issue portrayed Sitting Bull looking out at
the awful carnage of World War I. The caption read: "Sitting
Bull: 'And They Called Us Savages!' "[53]

The year 1918 proved an eventful one in Indian affairs, and
Wassaja resounded with the issues of the day. Montezuma
clearly had encountered financial difficulties in publishing his
journal. His January issue opened with an appeal for financial
aid. February's number included a notice that "Let My People
Go" was available for sale; March's *Wassaja* advertised both
back issues and "Let My People Go." In July, Montezuma put
forth his strongest, most emotional plea for assistance. Every
Indian, every friend of the Indian cause, and every man interested in humanity should subscribe, he contended; no minister or school should be without the magazine, for it was "the
only paper that stands alone, that dares to fight, that is fearless to express the truth of the mistreatment of the Indian
as a man."[54]

As *Wassaja* began its third year, Montezuma reminded his
readers that his journal had not wavered from its mission. Let-

ters to the doctor reprinted in the journal encouraged him to continue the fight. One noteworthy letter came from Reserve, Wisconsin. Father Philip Gordon, the only Native American Catholic priest, praised *Wassaja* highly. Gordon, an Ojibwa, would play an important role in the upcoming meeting of the Society of American Indians. He said *Wassaja* was "doing an incalculable good." "You have taken the lead, Doctor," Gordon commented, "and I am most happy to think that your leadership has been an unqualified success." Montezuma's opponents were attacking his character, but this only indicated his influence. The letter concluded: "Doctor, for country's sake and for God's honor, keep up your fight. I, for one, am with you until the dawn of that new day of liberty for the Indian race."[55] An alliance with a Catholic priest would have seemed unlikely years before, but times had changed and Montezuma had changed with them.

Some things, of course, had not been altered. Gordon's "new day of liberty" had yet to be realized. A new development gave added impetus to Montezuma's campaign against the Indian Bureau. In the opinion of federal officials, the exigencies of World War I justified the closing of Carlisle Indian School. An army hospital would be housed in the school's facilities. Even though Montezuma had been highly critical of the school since Pratt's departure, the idea of Carlisle's termination sickened him. Its abolition was far worse than what Helen Hunt Jackson had portrayed in *Ramona* and *Century of Dishonor*; the blackest pages of American history still were to be written. How could the government "take away the cornerstone, the foundation of Indian uplift?" How could it close that "great sacred memorial monument," the "Indian's Gibralter [sic]?"[56]

The failure of the Bureau to oppose such an action earned Montezuma's continuing scorn. People who seemed willing to seek accommodation with the Bureau deserved continuing criticism. Through the pages of *Wassaja*, he railed against "the Kaiser of America," as he termed the Indian Office.[57] If the Society of American Indians was to fulfill its proper responsibility in representing Native Americans, then it must be led by individuals who agreed with his firm, unyielding position: the Bureau of Indian Affairs must be abolished. Indians in general had to unite on this one great issue. Throughout 1918, Montezuma persisted in his overriding theme, heralding the autumn meeting of the Society in Pierre, South Dakota.

Freedom and citizenship could only be gained through unity, harmony, and direct involvement. Taking a page from the recently successful drive for women's suffrage, Montezuma urged Indians to write their congressmen and senators to tell them to abolish the Indian Office; the "women of our country have gained their plea by going at it in the same way." Within the SAI, factionalism prevailed, with one side seeing no alternative to the Indian Office, and the other favoring abolition.[58] He hoped, obviously, that it was time for the abolitionists to gain the ascendancy. For that to happen, of course, the Society had to meet; the annual conference must not be canceled as it had been the previous year.

"Let Us Have A Pow-Wow," Montezuma headlined a piece in the July 1918 *Wassaja.* The Society of American Indians should meet every year, for there was an immediate need for a great Indian organization. Otherwise, Congress could never be persuaded to abolish the Bureau. The Society should meet in the West, "where there are Indians." If the organization expired, a new one could be formed. Montezuma encouraged Indians from around the country to write to him about this matter.[59]

By August, plans had been set for a meeting of the Society in late September. "Leave your ill-feelings at home and attend the Indian meeting," advised Montezuma. The September *Wassaja* again reminded Native Americans to attend.[60] Upon this occasion, there could be no doubt that the Yavapai physician would be on hand. He sensed, correctly, that the gathering in Pierre would mark a personal triumph and a victory for his cherished tenet.

The Society of American Indians would convene under the slogan "Indian Patriotism, Production, Progress." Gertrude Bonnin, SAI secretary, previously had expressed her sympathy to Montezuma for his strong sentiments about the closing of Carlisle. She was glad he would attend the meeting and asked him to present a paper on "Carlisle: The Leading Non-reservation School for Indians." Shortly before the meeting, she wrote again to Montezuma, thanking him for his assistance with the conference program. In addition, she requested him to respond to the welcoming addresses from the governor, mayor, and other South Dakotans. If the effort to have the Society vote to abolish the Bureau were to succeed, a bylaw must be passed to disqualify people in government service from holding office in the organization. Could Montezuma assist in this effort? It almost went without saying that he would be happy to do so.[61]

As the registration for the seventh conference of the Society of American Indians began at the St. Charles Hotel on September 25, 1918, the conference program indicated that Montezuma would be centrally involved in the proceedings. He alone would give two separate addresses: on Carlisle and on his life story. Other featured speakers included Sherman Coolidge ("Loyalty and Patriotism"), Clarence T. Starr, Sr. ("Citizenship for the Sioux"), Chauncey Y. Robe ("Indian Patriotism"), Matthew K. Sniffen ("Indian Work"), L. S. Bonnin ("The Indian Must Reserve His Birthright, a Portion of Land"), S. M. Brosius ("Peyote Menace"), Joseph Claymore ("Indian Welfare"), Gertrude Bonnin ("reading in a native costume," "Eulogy of Sitting Bull"), and Rev. Ben Brave ("The Dust of No Man's Land"). Chairman of the associates, Thomas C. Moffett, delivered the conference sermon, "The Blue Bird of Happiness."[62]

In the absence of President Arthur C. Parker, who along with fellow officers John Oskison and Margaret Frazier was serving in the military, Honorary President Sherman Coolidge chaired the meeting. According to the Pierre *Daily Capital Journal*, Montezuma quickly gained the spotlight during the first session, held in the hall of the House of Representatives. The local newspaper characterized him as "somewhat radical in his statements as to the governmental policy of Indian control which he says is the result of politics and patronage." Montezuma, of course, advocated abolition of the Indian Bureau and praised loyal Native Americans fighting voluntarily in the war, asking that Indians be given the rights held by other Americans. Later in the evening Gertrude Bonnin echoed many of his statements.[63]

Thursday, September 26, featured various reports and many addresses, including Montezuma's talk on Carlisle. But it was on Friday and Saturday that Montezuma and his allies would realize their crowning achievement: the Society of American Indians voted in favor of abolition of the Indian Bureau. The

October *Wassaja* soon celebrated the decision. The meeting had been held in Sioux country, and Montezuma noted that old Indians claimed that what the Sioux did was always decisive. He recalled the recent gathering emotionally and eloquently:

We Indians, and friends of the Indians, went there with a great object. While the world thought of war, we went there with the Indian race upon our minds. The wrongs perpetrated upon the Indian race was just as important as the Belgians; freedom of the Indian race was just as important as freedom of the seas, and that since an Indian is a man, he should have equal rights, treated humanely and justly. . . . We spoke of six thousand Indian boys fighting across the sea for freedom, and yet, the mothers and fathers, sisters and brothers of the six thousand are not enjoying freedom, but are caged up on the reservations. We spoke of equal rights; we could not go very far, because we have not given the Indian the rights of citizenship and protection under our laws. Democracy? The Indian Bureau is not democracy; it is the other way. As much as we try to justify it, it is autocracy . . . But our patriotism was not lessened, our hearts ached with loyalty and felt, if we are true patriots, it was our duty to righten the wrong. Never before in the history of the Society have we felt the great responsibility left upon our shoulders . . . The conference closed with the determination of having the Indian Bureau abolished, to set the Indian free, so that they may have the rights and privileges of citizenship.[64]

Now that the Society had concurred with his longstanding viewpoint, Montezuma sang its praises. He admitted that no Indian had criticized the association more than he had, but contended he had not tried to destroy it "but direct it aright." Montezuma had felt the Society could "be a power for the good of the Indian race" and had therefore renewed his membership after having once resigned. "In our crude, and often rude way, we tried to steer the Society in the right path that would lead the Indians into enlightenment, freedom and citizenship," he said. Now he could encourage one and all to join the Society. He lauded the new officers, President Charles Eastman, Vice-President Philip Gordon, Secretary Gertrude Bonnin, Henry Roe Cloud, De Witt Hare, Charles D. Carter, and Sherman Coolidge:

They are the most loyal of the Indian race. Who would hesitate to join the Society of American Indians with such a splendid corps of workers for the Indians? Indians, if you wish to help yourself and your race, join the Society of American Indians. Friends of the Indians, now is the time to show your sincerity by joining the Society of American Indians.[65]

The Society had embarked upon a new course. While Montezuma did not mention it specifically, he probably celebrated in private the downfall of Arthur C. Parker. Not only was Parker no longer president, but his days as editor of the society's journal were also numbered. Absent from the Pierre conference, Parker received notification of his reelection as editor, with the request that he reply immediately if he accepted. Gertrude Bonnin was eager to take on the task. She assured Montezuma: "When the time comes, I shall not be afraid to handle the magazine." Soon thereafter, in a letter responding to Montezuma's having enrolled his wife as an associate member of the Society, Bonnin noted that the executive council had acted on the matter of the editorship. Parker had responded on October 26 that he would continue, but the reply had come too late; the executive committee had already named Bonnin the new editor. She looked forward to her new responsibilities and to the prospect of Congress working out a bill abolishing the Bureau and improving Native American well-being. It did seem, she concluded, that there was "more hope for the emancipation of the Red Man in America than ever before."[66]

At the end of 1918, Montezuma, too, appeared more optimistic than ever that his long battle for abolition of the Bureau finally had begun to achieve important results. His spirits improved as he sensed new grounds for believing that whites and Indian Americans could achieve a better understanding of each other once abolition had been achieved. A war remained to be waged: "We Indians are going to strike out and fight for freedom, equal rights, democracy, humanity and justice for our race." He added:

The Indian's heart is crying for his rights in the sight of God and man. The moon is just right for a fight. In the shadow of justice, while the white man's cannon roar, the belching out of water, the shells bursting in the air and men are falling face to face, there is hope for us. These patriotic caucasians are feeling in their hearts what we have died and yearn for, for these many years. Their hearts and our hearts are coming together. They shall see us as we see them, and we shall know we are as one in God and that will make us free. IS NOT THAT WORTH FIGHTING FOR?[67]

In the meantime, the "brave warrior for our race" had been involved in an engagement in another arena. Back in his homeland of southern Arizona, the struggle for water rights and Indian rights had reached a new level of intensity. At McDowell and elsewhere in the region, Montezuma had been trying to safeguard the interests of Native Americans. This effort was undertaken in an area removed from Chicago and Washington, but it affected centrally how Montezuma viewed the Bureau and perceived contemporary Indian life. This aspect of his career occupied much of his heart and mind from 1912 to 1918. To understand properly the achievement of Carlos Montezuma, we must review in detail his endeavors in the Southwest during this period.

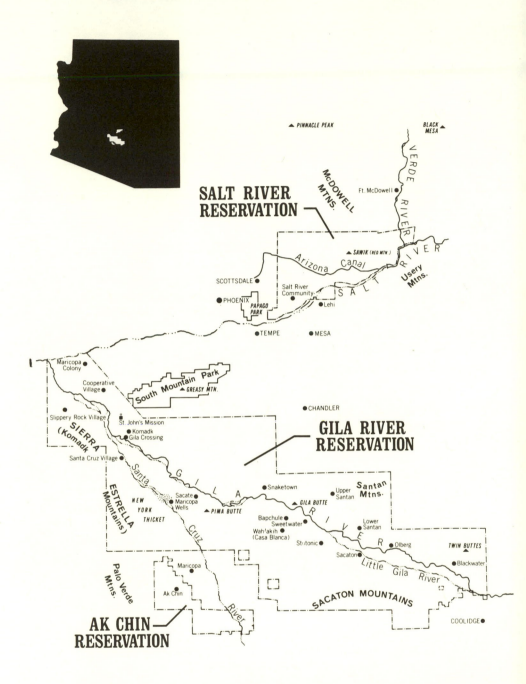

Map 2. The Salt River and Gila River reservations. By permission from *A Pima Past*, by Anna Moore Shaw, Tucson: University of Arizona Press, Copyright 1974.

6

Indian Rights and Water Rights in Southern Arizona

Yavapai leader George Dickens wrote to Montezuma in 1916: "We always do believe that you are the means of having us remain here at McDowell. And had it not been for your aid; we might have been down on the deserts; with Pimas; who are our dead[ly] enemies."[1] From 1912 to 1918, Montezuma waged a battle that became progressively more important to him. He fought to preserve the homeland of the Yavapais. He also challenged the Bureau of Indian Affairs and other interests in southern Arizona that opposed what Montezuma deemed to be proper rights for all Native Americans. Thus he transcended the usual tribal boundary to see the common concerns shared by differing Indian communities. The Pimas may have continued to be deadly enemies for George Dickens, but to Montezuma they became friends who needed his assistance.

Responding both to Montezuma's expressed interest and to the exigencies of their situation, the Salt River reservation Pimas and the Pimas and the Maricopas near the community of Lehi all appointed Montezuma as their representative during the first months of 1912. "I am interested in the Pimas as much as I am in the McDowell Indians," the Yavapai physician noted. "I want the Pimas and the Apaches always to be friends and brothers," he told a Pima leader. And to Pima Chief

Juan Andreas, he recalled that he had feared the Pimas as awful enemies, but now "40 years time has changed our thoughts for each other. Today we are brothers of the same blood. We are under the same cloud of trouble and we must help each other."[2]

Montezuma perceived a network of interests combining to take away Indian land and water rights. He told Herbert Marten, a British national and dissident Bureau employee on the Salt River reservation, that various branches of the government, including the Reclamation Service, had combined with realtors to force Native Americans to relinquish their lands, timber, and water rights. Montezuma warned that if the federal government did not "heed and do what is right now they will have litagators [sic] to contend with in the future because the next generation of Indians will be lawyers and men that have brains."[3]

"One good lawyer could have done everything for these Indians several years ago, and I still believe that can be done now," Montezuma told Marten in another letter. In Joseph W. Latimer, Montezuma had discovered an attorney who would vigorously press the Native American cause. In June 1912, Latimer forwarded to Commissioner of Indian Affairs R. H. Valentine copies of powers of attorney for Montezuma signed by Montezuma and the most prominent members of the three Indian groups. In addition, he requested an immediate accounting of the Indians' allotments, general condition, and "some intelligent idea of your departments plans to further the interest and care of these Indians." Latimer concluded by commenting that "Dr. Montezuma is entering into this matter with no fixed opinions, nor with any desire to in any manner antagonize or annoy your department, but as the representative of these Indians earnestly seeking, if possible, to cooperate with you for the betterment of their conditions."[4]

The officials in the Indian Service apparently thought cooperation neither possible nor desirable. They had no wish to see Montezuma serve in such a capacity and immediately so informed his attorney. Assistant Commissioner C. F. Hauke wrote Latimer a wonderfully bureaucratic reply, citing the provisions of Section 2103 of the Revised Statutes of the United States, regulations prescribed by the Department of the Interior, and circular number 497, also approved by the department. Unless proper authority had been granted, these contracts could not be negotiated; Montezuma had not been so authorized and thus not only could he not be recognized as a proper representative but the Bureau could not divulge the requested information. Latimer protested, of course, but to no avail.[5]

This kind of resistance continually characterized the relationship between Montezuma and the Bureau over matters at Fort McDowell. Latimer may have averred that Montezuma would avoid fixed opinions, but clearly his client had some rather set views. Each side mistrusted the other. The stakes in the region were high, and key Bureau officials were unaccustomed to public opposition from Native Americans. Even Montezuma admitted that the Indians had "been dominated for so long that they feel very shy to express themselves."[6] Despite persistent efforts to discredit him, Montezuma appeared to maintain the confidence of most Indians in the area. Not every individual welcomed Montezuma's efforts. Some young Pimas and Maricopas, according to the local Bureau superintendent, protested against having Montezuma as their attorney. Their complaint, however, seemed aimed as much against the power of older people in their communities as against Montezuma. Moreover, judging from available evidence, they were a distinct minority.[7]

The petition against Montezuma was composed by Calvin Emerson and some other returning students. Superintendent Coe labeled it "a protest against allowing an outsider to meddle in any way with the Indian affairs on their reservation . . . and to show their appreciation of the work the Government is trying to do for them and also as an appeal to the Indian Office to aid in preventing the old degraded dances which are bad for their people." Emerson and his associates called those who supported Montezuma "the leaders in pulling down progress on the Salt River Reservation." Montezuma had been appointed "to help them get back the ways of their ancestors"; his tribe was "still keeping up the old custom dances."[8] Thus by 1912 Montezuma had been identified as an ally of the conservatives on McDowell and Salt River. Far from being a white man's Indian, Montezuma emerged in Arizona to his opponents as an enemy of progress.

To be sure, the definition of progress varied. For Montezuma, progress in part meant justice for the Indians. With the resignation of W. H. Code in October 1911 as chief engineer of the U.S. Indian Irrigation Service, implementation of the Kent Decree adjudicating Indian use of the Verde and Salt rivers for irrigation had been stalled along with other matters. Debate over the decree and the general issue of Indian water rights continued unabated. Some Bureau of Indian Affairs employees argued for limited rights. Charles E. Roblin suggested to the commissioner of Indian affairs, for example, that the Kent Decree had been "*very* faulty" in its classification of Indian lands. Native Americans had been decreed an amount of water "far in excess of what they have ever used" and "far in excess of what they will ever beneficially use on such an area."[9]

Opinions continued to differ on many unanswered questions. The Yavapais could not be sure of the extent of their water rights, let alone where they would exercise them. Latimer and Montezuma spoke for most of them in insisting that Fort McDowell continue to be their home. If allotment would help in permitting them to stay, then so be it. Still, the Yavapais found themselves in somewhat of a no-man's-land. Their opposition to allotment anywhere except McDowell had delayed implementation of the plans to place them on the Salt River reservation. But Congress balked at providing them irrigation facilities on McDowell. The Department of the Interior hesitated to lobby Congress for authorization of additional irrigation works, for their officials believed that under the Kent Decree no additional acreage could be irrigated.[10]

In spite of something of a stalemate, limited recognition of both Montezuma and the homeland status of McDowell was achieved in the summer of 1912. While Montezuma could not be accorded the rank of authorized representative, Secretary of the Interior Walter L. Fisher expressed willingness to accept him as a "voluntary charitable worker." Under that classification, Montezuma and Latimer could receive some of the information they had been seeking. The doggedness of the Yavapais and their representatives, in addition, seemed finally to have paid off. On August 12, 1912, Fisher stated to Latimer:

... both the Department and the Indian Office consider the idea, in any form it may have taken either of plan or of action, of general allotment for the Camp McDowell Indians on the Salt River Reservation or on land adjacent to it rather than on the Camp McDowell Reservation, to have been a mistake. The Department now proposes to allot the Indians of the Camp McDowell Reservation on that reservation, and it believes that this should be done even before all the questions incident to the water situation are solved.[11]

While the department would retreat to some extent from this unequivocal statement, Montezuma and Latimer, not surprisingly, seized it and would not let it go. They had it in writing that the Yavapais should be able to stay at McDowell and should not be forcibly removed to Salt River or elsewhere. Moreover, Fisher had acknowledged that those who had accepted allotments at Salt River could still live on McDowell without water. Given this commitment to McDowell, Commissioner Valentine asked Superintendent Coe promptly to take a roll of the Yavapais on the reservation. On October 10, 1912, Coe submitted a roll based on a census taken in June. The total comprised 256 people, including thirty-six-year-old Charles Dickens and forty-year-old George Dickens—hardly elder statesmen by contemporary standards.[12]

Not everyone in Washington shared the department's commitment to McDowell. The commissioner of Indian affairs authorized Coe to allot the land on the Salt River reservation set aside for the McDowell Yavapais to Indians of the Pima and Maricopa tribes or to the Lehi Indians, but the new secretary of the interior, Samuel Adams, countermanded the order. Adams said he did not want to get the cart before the horse: "I certainly do not wish the Department to be put in the position of disposing of the Salt River lands reserved for the Camp McDowell Indians and then finding that the expense of irrigation on the Camp McDowell lands is prohibitive."[13]

The cost of irrigation at McDowell proved to be a perennial issue during the decade. Coe reported in November 1912 that the amount of land cultivated by the Yavapais had been gradually diminishing. Some land had simply been washed away during floods; some had become infested with Johnson grass. Certain tribesmen had abandoned labor-intensive farming when they saw prospects of wage work off the reservation.[14] If, in the end, the Yavapais were to be removed, then money spent on new irrigation works would be dollars wasted; until the money was invested, farming would continue to decline and land would continue to be unproductive.

Montezuma returned to the land of his birth in September 1912. The *Arizona Republican* noted his visit to Phoenix on September 15, labeling him "one of the leading medical practitioners in Chicago." The Phoenix newspaper observed that Montezuma had recently succeeded in inducing the government to permit the Yavapais to retain their holdings at McDowell. Before his departure from Chicago on September 10, Montezuma wrote to Lancisco Hill, saying he was coming out to Arizona "to see face to face those people or chiefs for whom I will endeavor to do something."[15]

Such visits undoubtedly reinforced Montezuma's influence among the Indians of the region. He followed his sojourn in September by writing many letters to various people, giving advice on a number of matters. Don't make trouble, stick together, be peaceable, he urged. He told William Johnson, Pedro Garcia, and John Allison that if the Pimas were allotted, they should take maximum advantage of the situation. They should have as much land as possible put at their disposal, and they must find out how long the government would supply them with water. "There are reasons," Montezuma emphasized, "why you Pimas should not dispose of your land. . . . Bye and bye there will be children. They will want land. You can be in a position to give them some. If you want more land to irrigate you can have more by paying water for the addition of lands. And if you want to sell in the future—you can sell and get more money than you can now—Remember the land now is worth $100 to $200 per acre in the Salt River Valley."[16] In another letter, written to Joe Ross, Montezuma sounded the same chord: ". . . you Pimas are not going to die out—You will grow more and more in the future—Your children will want land . . ."[17] This far-sighted advice would prove correct, but it ran counter to the popular wisdom of the era that Indians were a vanishing people.

In the minds of Bureau employees such as Coe, an essential component in the assimilationist program was the discouragement and ultimate elimination of traditional Indian customs. From 1912 to 1914, Coe carried on a concerted campaign to disallow the customary tribal dances. On July 10, 1912, he in-

formed the commissioner of Indian affairs that he had successfully prevented the dances the previous Christmas and on July
4. Coe contended he had the backing of all the more progressive Indians, who realized that the dances had immoral tend-
encies that produced a degrading effect on boys and girls. The
dances, he alleged, did more to prevent progress among these
Indians than the liquor traffic and all other evils combined.[18]
The current commissioner, F. A. Abbott, supported his superintendent, referring Coe to Paragraph 4, section 584 of the Indian Office regulations, which classified such dances as "Indian
offenses." His information showed that such ceremonies were
"orgies of savagery, the participants are half nude and the physical exertions are continued until many of the Indians fall from
exhaustion—some even dying. . . ."[19]

The issue surfaced again the following year prior to a planned
July 4 celebration. The popularity of dances on Independence
Day and Christmas should have been a commentary on the
flexibility of tradition, but Coe could not be deterred. He warned
the commissioner that the Yavapais might write to him asking for special permission to hold the dance. Apparently Richard Dickens recently had been convicted of concocting a batch
of tiswin (a fermented beverage) and his fine had been remit-
ted; Coe suggested to his new superior, Cato Sells, that now
the Indians believed all they had to do was to appeal to a higher
official and they could do as they pleased, "which means to
many of them the privilege of drinking, dancing and gambling;
the things we are trying so hard to stop."[20]

The July 4 dance apparently did not come to pass, but Montezuma wrote Sells in September to ask "an exceptional favor." He assured the commissioner that he, too, opposed Indian dances that took a week to prepare, a week to do, and a
week to recover from. But he had been asked to obtain permission for a one-night "dance of jubilee for my honor and
friends." There could be little harm in such limited fare. Sells
concurred, and the dance took place during Montezuma's visit
that month.[21]

For his indulgence, Sells earned the wrath not only of Coe
but of missionary George H. Gebby of Scottsdale. Coe apprised
the commissioner that such dances would "inflame the animal
passions and to my certain knowledge have lead [sic] to the

downfall of more than one Indian girl." Gebby argued that Montezuma's representation had been in error; when the dance had been permitted "among these unmoral and half-civilized people it was often accompanied or followed by fights, jealousies and domestic difficulties." The Presbyterian missionary said Montezuma had erred either from ignorance or through intention, but he believed that the Yavapai doctor had no better knowledge of local conditions than any other Chicago physician. Sells could only respond that if the dance were in fact harmful, then he had been misled.[22]

Sells had another opportunity to deal with dancing at McDowell when it surfaced like clockwork in June 1914. Several Pimas from Salt River had written to Montezuma on June 7 about their concerns, including a dance for July 4. Montezuma had petitioned Washington on their behalf, but this time Sells demurred. Sells reminded him that even innocent and harmless dances could sometimes be perverted with mischievous results, and such had been the case before the dances had been outlawed in 1912. The commissioner noted the adverse report made to him "by one in close contact with the Indians" as partial justification for his decision. In addition, the judgment of a superintendent should not be overruled without substantial reasons.[23] Sells's willingness to rely on an individual such as Gebby and his determination to support his personnel inevitably would lead him to direct conflict with Montezuma on other issues.

In this instance, the question had not been fully resolved. Coe wrote to Sells four days after the fateful July 4, telling him that a secret dance had been planned for Salt River. One of Montezuma's correspondents, Juan Andreas, had headed the forbidden foray. Coe had dispatched an Indian policeman and two deputies to break up the dance. They had tried to arrest Andreas and had encountered resistance, but Juan Andreas was eventually jailed. The superintendent blamed the fracas in part on Montezuma; the younger Indians, he thought, had been encouraged by the doctor's success the previous October in obtaining permission for a dance. On August 24, Coe complained additionally to E. B. Linnen, an inspector for the Indian Service, about the negative influence exercised by Montezuma in regard to dancing and other matters. Linnen, in turn, complained to

Sells. Coe wrote, as well, to Sells on September 5, advising him that the Yavapais were preparing to hold a dance the next time Montezuma visited the reservation. Here Coe specifically censured Montezuma for reviving the old-time ceremonies. "It seems strange," puzzled the superintendent, "that a man of his education and attainments should encourage the prepetuation *[sic]* of such practices if he knows how they retard the progress of the Indians."[24]

Responding to these complaints, the top men in the Indian Office expressed to the local Indians and to Montezuma their firm antagonism to the dances. Assistant Commissioner E. B. Meritt told Jose King and his colleagues at Salt River that such dances were "relics of the old-time customs" and "incompatible with the modern civilization which the Office desires to see the Indians accept." Coe, said Meritt, has been "fully instructed on the subject of dancing and you should be governed by his directions concerning it." Sells requested Montezuma to use his influence to dissuade the Indians from holding dances in his honor; the doctor's "hearty cooperation in keeping these Indians along the right road to good citizenship and morality is earnestly desired," he concluded. Finally, Sells reviewed for Coe his correspondence with Montezuma. His letter's last paragraph revealed the position he now embraced:

You may prohibit any of the old time barbarous dances from being held on your reservation, and by acquainting the Indians of this fact restrain them from being held. There is no doubt but what these old time dances are injurious to the moral welfare of the Indians, and retards them in the development which I am so earnestly aiming for. The sooner they are abolished the more rapid will be their development toward becoming model American citizens.[25]

Sells and Meritt obviously believed in a chain of command. As top officers in a sizable organization, they saw a natural utility in providing moral and philosophical support to their employees in the field. They disliked strongly the practice of Indians questioning either the authority or the wisdom of people such as Charles Coe; they found the habit of appealing over a superintendent to Washington equally distasteful. Sells and Meritt recognized that Bureau officials in Arizona and elsewhere worked in isolated locales generally at minimal salary, facing difficult questions and continual demands not only from Native Americans but from other Americans who had an economic or philanthropic interest in Indian lands and Indian societies. Such people often were not ill-intentioned, but they frequently were rigid in their approaches, defensive in their attitudes, and firm in their convictions. They tended not to be cultural pluralists. They generally advocated Christianity, private property, the work ethic, and assimilation. Coe and his colleagues could look to the growth of an Anglo-American population in southern Arizona with enthusiasm, for the Anglos' values and life-styles could influence those of the Indians in this transitional time.

In retrospect, it seems ironic that the Coes of Bureau officialdom should clash so bitterly and frequently with a man like Montezuma. Montezuma, after all, cherished many of the ideals they endorsed. But Montezuma had several strikes against him. Because he had not lived in the region for decades, local Bureau employees did not think he could understand daily life in southern Arizona. He was an easterner—a term traditionally reserved by westerners for anyone different and anyone living the slightest distance to the east (including all of the Midwest, for example). Montezuma, a physician and a resident of Chicago, had gained an education and had lived in an environment that made him unusual, indeed suspicious. One gathers that the Bureau did not object to education for the Indians per se but that there could be too much of a good thing in the Bureau's view. In addition, Montezuma possessed a personality that Bureau people found repugnant: he was forceful, aggressive, confident, and persistent. He clearly did not respect them or their policies. Better educated than Bureau agents, often more articulate, and more worldly, Montezuma threatened not only the self-esteem of the agents, but the work they saw themselves trying to accomplish under circumstances that were challenging at best. Montezuma gave voice and power to the misgivings and unhappiness of Indian people. He made life more difficult. He was in the way.

It is instructive, therefore, to review the series of confrontations that took place between various Bureau personnel and the Yavapai physician. The animosity reserved for Montezuma tells us not just about there employees but about life on the reservations. The limitations on freedom of speech and action are readily apparent. Also obvious are the uncertainties surrounding land ownership, land use, and water rights. The problems threatening Indians in southern Arizona bordered on the overwhelming; some were new and bewildering. In a small community such as the Fort McDowell reservation, few had had the education, the facility with English, or the experience to be able to cope confidently with these dilemmas. Montezuma thus proved more than useful to the Yavapais, as he proved more than a nuisance to some Bureau employees.

Montezuma bridled at the degree of authority exercised by the superintendent. He simply could not accept the unquestioning obedience that the Indian Office believed due that reservation figure. Meritt, for example, had responded to Pima complaints about Coe with the observation that the Indians' problems were due to their failure to cooperate with him. If the Pimas would listen to Coe's advice, said assistant commissioner, "and do as he directs, you will find that you will improve in many ways and you will recognize in the end that his advice has been good and a help to you." Meritt then clarified the ground rules.

You cannot expect to obtain help from your Superintendent without doing as he directs. If he were to accede to all your wishes, there would practically be no use of having him on the reservation. The Office aims to provide the Indians with Superintendents who are informed in the ways and customs of white people, and will therefore be in a position to assist the Indians to rise to the same plane that the white man occupies. The Indians would never succeed in doing this if they were to follow their own inclinations without the advice and directions of a Superintendent. I trust that you will hereafter listen to your Superintendent and that there will be no cause for complaint.[26]

Charles Coe was not the only local Bureau official with whom Montezuma collided. Indian Agent Frank A. Thackery opposed Montezuma's attempt to meet with a large number of Pimas in September 1913. Montezuma had arranged for a gathering without Thackery's knowledge. When Thackery heard of the meeting, he had the doctor brought to his office, where he did not receive a "satisfactory explanation" about the purpose of this session. The superintendent informed Montezuma—who, of course, had been enlightened on this score previously—about circular 497, and as Thackery put it, "the statue therein." According to the telegram Thackery sent to Sells, Montezuma insisted he sought justice; Thackery concluded he was trying to obtain power of attorney. How did he know that? The telegram states: "Letters received by Indians on this reservation show clearly . . ."[27] As on other reservations, the agent might demand to see a letter if he suspected that the contents were of a negative quality. On both Salt River and McDowell, friends of Montezuma had their letters demanded by Bureau officials. In this instance, Sells immediately supported Thackery. Given the opposition, Montezuma canceled his plans to meet with other Pimas at Gila Crossing.[28]

Thackery received backing from another party. John Baum had worked as an allotting agent on the Pima reservation during the winter of 1913–14. He told Cato Sells that Thackery had explained the project carefully and well and that there seemed to be little dissatisfaction among the Pimas; the opposition that later surfaced, according to Baum, had "been caused by one Dr. Montezuma, an Apache Indian of Chicago, who had appointed himself to act as guardian and adviser for the Pima tribe." Baum said Montezuma had a reputation as an agitator and fee gatherer. Denial of his application to represent the Pimas "would please the great majority of the Indians and releive [sic] the Superintendent of much future trouble."

A farmer stationed at McDowell also blamed Montezuma for a significant proportion of his problems. Thirty Yavapais had signed a petition on October 7, 1913, and Otis B. Goodall, supervisor of Indian schools, Riverside, California, eventually investigated their complaints. Goodall heard that John Shafer, the farmer employed by the Bureau to work with the Yavapais, had been absent too much and gained the unyielding antagonism of much of the tribe. While contending that the Yavapais were "hard to govern owing to the prevalent habits among them of indulging in 'tiswin' and gambling," Goodall concluded that Shafer had no more usefulness at the reservation and should be transferred. Following Goodall's report to Sells, Shafer responded angrily to the charges. The farmer argued that the petition and charges had not "originated in the mind of any of these Indians, but was conceived and born during the visit of Dr. Carlos Montezuma and his party of hunters (game vandals) to this reservation in October of last year." Shafer said he had told Montezuma of his opposition to Indian dances, gambling, medicine men, and the making and drinking of tiswin and would do all he could to suppress them. He also learned after the dance held in Montezuma's honor that the doctor promised to "kick Superintendent Coe and myself off the Reservation, of course, through his influence with the Indian Department." Montezuma's visits had promoted opposition to him. For the Indians to advance, the Department must "successfully combat the effect of this outside influence."[30]

The other superintendents at Salt River, of which McDowell formed a part of the jurisdiction, perhaps liked Montezuma least of all. C. T. Coggeshall expressed his hostility toward the Yavapai physician on many occasions. When *Wassaja* was first published in April 1916, Coggeshall quickly sent a copy of it to Sells, noting that he understood the commissioner was "somewhat familiar with the activities of one Dr. Carlos Montezuma in this section of the country and thought you would be interested in looking over some of his literary work that he had circulated amongst the Indians. . . ." Apparently Coggeshall would have liked the publication to be suppressed:

. . . that this man can and probably has done much to hinder the work among this people is unquestionably a fact and that if he is permitted to spread this sort of doctrine without let or hindrance will seriously interfere with law and order, Administrative control and the furtherance of the policies of the Administrative Office along all lines, is also a bare statement of fact. . . .[31]

Coggeshall remarked that he had but one difficult problem at McDowell and that centered on Montezuma. The plan to have the McDowell Yavapais take allotments on the Salt River reservation, he observed, did not meet with Montezuma's approval and "through his efforts and work . . . it appears that they will not peacefully and of their own free will make any such move." Later that year Coggeshall referred to opposition to settlement at Salt River as by "a handful of Indian malcontents or rather the so called 'Montezuma crowd.' "[32]

The dawning of the new year did not bring a better opinion. In January and March of 1917, Coggeshall again wrote angry letters to Sells about the insidious influence of Montezuma among his charges. One "very recent manifestation of the workings of his spirit among the Salt River Indians" involved four Native Americans whom the superintendent described in less than endearing terms:

Samuel Ludlow, one of the most pronounced Montezuma men of Salt River, Jacob Stepp, another of his followers and one of the few remaining long-haired Indians in this section, Jose King, another of his followers, a malcontent and thick-headed Indian, and Jose Eschief, a young Indian, an ex-Phoenix student, one of Montezuma's followers and a mischief maker with a reputation for being a worthless sort of fellow. . . .[33]

The eight-page typed letter defies adequate summation, but Coggeshall charged the four men with a variety of offenses, including calling a meeting without his permission and accepting the advice and teachings of outsiders. He threatened to jail for at least thirty days those "whose minds had been so poisoned by malicious influences from the outside that they refused to accept the authority of the Commissioner of Indian Affairs thru me, his agent at this post. . . ." Despite "all the moral suasion at my command," Coggeshall seemed unable to deal effectively "with the malcontent followers of this agitator, Dr. Carlos Montezuma."[34] The superintendent's letter in March echoed the rhetoric of his earlier harangue, describing "the agitation going on by one Dr. Carlos Montezuma directed against your Administration and our efforts in behalf of the Mohave-Apache Indians of the McDowell reservation. . . ."[35]

Byron Sharp, the last superintendent at Salt River during this period, inherited Coggeshall's perspective. His viewpoint will be delineated more fully in the next chapter, but one example of it is included here. Sharp wrote to the commissioner on August 3, 1917, discussing the closing of the school on McDowell. A new building could be constructed on the McDowell tract at Salt River, but this plan had encountered opposition from the "non-progressive crowd of malcontents" headed by the Dickens family. Sharp observed that a letter of complaint from McDowell residents had been forwarded by Montezuma and that fact was "in itself an explanation of everything it contained." The superintendent remarked:

Carlos Montezuma has been and still is a source of constant trouble breeding in this jurisdiction. This fact will be borne out by letters in the files of the Indian Office from former Superintendents C. E. Coe and C. T. Coggeshall. There never has been an effort made to benefit the McDowell Indians that has not been "knocked" by Carlos Montezuma through his henchmen, the Burns and the Dickens families, at McDowell.[36]

Had it not been for what Sharp termed "these conscientious objectors(?)," the superintendent believed there would have been no trouble in getting the Yavapais to accept allotments on the nearby Salt River reservation. Sharp's conclusion emphasizes one of the main efforts made by Montezuma during this period in regard to his people's well-being. Montezuma had become convinced that if the Yavapais were to agree to allotments on Salt River, they would then be susceptible to being moved off of McDowell entirely. Even though Bureau officials insisted that the two matters were not related, Montezuma could not be shaken from this belief. He worked hard to ensure that the Yavapais would not be swayed by the arguments utilized by Coe, Coggeshall, and Sharp, as well as their superiors.

The continuing battle over Yavapai land rights marked an interesting contrast in philosophies between Montezuma and Richard H. Pratt. Following his general dictum of "Kill the Indian and save the man," Pratt wrote to Montezuma in 1914 that he was "not so much concerned about lands or about those things that hold Indians together, and which constitute a good part of your interests." The former Carlisle head argued: "The land and property has been a mill stone about their necks all the time, and will continue to be. What value is it if they own vast property and are never going to be able to manage it?" Pratt agreed that the Yavapais were entitled to McDowell, but he believed the offer of irrigated acreage elsewhere was well worth considering.

In several letters to Montezuma, Pratt suggested that the Yavapai erred in this concern. On March 13, 1918, for example, he commented: "I feel quite sure you need to understand better the intention in regard to both the McDowell and the

Salt River Valley. You mistake when you keep on thinking the intention is to get away from the McDowell reservation by getting them to accept the allotment of ten acres each under the Salt River project."[38] Earlier, Pratt commended Montezuma for attacking Indian policy and treatment of the Yavapais, but added: "I think you ought by every possible way you can compel these Indians to give up their Indianisms. . . ." Pratt stressed the most important thing was not McDowell or Salt River, but the development of intelligence and ability to take care of one's self.[39] Montezuma hardly slighted the latter, but he knew that McDowell mattered. He also had been drawn to the people at McDowell and could not join in the onslaught against their "Indianisms." His experience at McDowell, then, was extremely important in his evolving perspective on modern Native American life.

Initially, Montezuma entertained hopes that the new commissioner of Indian affairs, Cato Sells, would be responsive to his ideas. Montezuma had toyed with the notion that Latimer might be commissioner, and it almost goes without saying that he would have liked to see Pratt in that post. But Pratt had visited with the new administrator and had been most favorably impressed. Sells seemed "a splendid fellow," thought Pratt; he obviously possessed good judgment, for he asked for Pratt's help and urged the old soldier to visit and write to him often. A late summer conference only heightened Pratt's enthusiasm. Sells was "by all odds the ablest and I think he is going to be by far the best Commissioner of Indian Affairs we have had within my knowledge, now running over 46 years." However, by the beginning of 1914, Pratt's ardor had cooled. He told Montezuma that he could not get Sells "down to good solid ground." Sells claimed sympathy with what Pratt had to say but showed no signs of acting on his recommendations. Pratt had seen this approach before, and he started to distrust the man he recently had praised so lavishly.[40]

Given his respect for Pratt's opinion, Montezuma surely wanted to give Sells every opportunity. The odds against a productive relationship between Montezuma and Sells, however, were formidable. What could Sells have thought of the doctor? Here was a man who advocated the abolition of the very bureau that he headed. According to the reports of his superintendents, Montezuma was a troublemaker of the first order. Seemingly the man epitomized reaction, obstinacy, and contrariness. While Montezuma had to be listened to as an influential and articulate Indian, one had to be wary of subscribing to his views and undermining the positions of his officials in the field.

Initially, the relationship between the two men was cordial. As we have seen, Montezuma submitted a special request to Sells, asking permission for a one-night dance to be held in his honor; the commissioner granted the favor. Pratt advised Montezuma to wait before criticizing the new administration publicly, despite the terrible problems the Pimas were facing. Montezuma did delay, uncharacteristically, in part perhaps because of Pratt's advice, and also because he had no desire to alienate an individual who could directly assist the Yavapais and other peoples in southern Arizona. As Sells grew less responsive to Montezuma's inquiries, the imposed honeymoon period started to draw to a close. Sells denied Montezuma's next entreaty in the summer of 1914. By the end of that summer, Sells had received a number of complaints about Montezuma from his personnel as well as a letter from Samuel M. Brosius of the Indian Rights Association damning Montezuma and his efforts in the region. Sells kept Montezuma at arm's length for the remainder of his tenure as commissioner, which lasted through the decade.

Brosius's letter is not lengthy, but could well have had an important effect on the Bureau's response to Montezuma. The Indian Rights Association agent insinuated that "visions of wealth" had inspired Montezuma's wish to represent the Pimas. Brosius had been "impressed with the valuable services" Superintendent Thackery was rendering. Montezuma should not be permitted to hold councils with the tribe—otherwise the Indians would become "disaffected" and it would be almost hopeless to try to build them up and advance them.[41] If Sells and Meritt needed additional support for their refusal to permit Montezuma to have meetings on the reservation, they now had it.

During 1913, residents of McDowell and Salt River flooded Montezuma with protests about administration of their affairs and with appeals for assistance. The Yavapai leader Yuma Frank, for example, wrote on February 15, in a manner that cried out for immediate aid. He chastised Coe and Shafer:

They rather impose laws and rule, then to advance us to progress of self-supporting. Every farmer and agent that had been sent here has been King. So we want you to take step, within your best judgment to consider it. Every Indian, from child to oldest age are looking upon you as our protector of our earthly rights.[42]

Yuma Frank denied that the Yavapai dancing smacked of superstition: "It is clean, gentlemanly and respectable." He noted that his people did not practice it often—mostly on national holidays. The chief also stated the need to practice "a song for prayer" in case of injury or sickness that over the ages had helped people; he could not see why it would harm the government for them to do so.[43]

Juan Andreas and Jose Easchief informed Montezuma on March 19 that one of their tribesmen had been jailed in Phoenix for removing posts that surveyors had placed in the ground. The man had been beaten when arrested. What were these "pipe posts" all about? Had the government authorized the survey?[44] In these and other letters, confusion, unhappiness, and at times despair poured out. The people hired by the federal government could not or would not help. The missionaries seemed unsympathetic to tradition. The white world was encroaching. Montezuma, they said, must speak out on their behalf.

Montezuma realized, of course, that Sells and his associates would not welcome beyond a fairly limited point his involvement in internal reservation issues. He suggested to the commissioner that the residents of these reservations would only turn to him when things were radically wrong. In an eight-page letter to Sells on May 12, 1914, Montezuma reminded him of the past prosperity of the Pimas and Maricopas, and how the diversion of the Gila River by white settlers had altered that prosperity. Now they lived "a mere existence of poverty and despair."

O that Cursed and damnable system! It has ruined that free and innocent people to an "Indian Bureau pecked creatures." They know no man but the Agent or Superintendent who frowns at them, rides around them in his automobile with a supernatural air and tells the Indians that he talks with Washington. It is sad and pitiful to see these sons and daughters of freedom bow to this man God in America.[45]

Montezuma charged that these people had been treated as though they were not human. They had suffered, been cheated, had their money misappropriated, and had their lands taken away. The Indian Bureau agents forced their charges to agree with them or be jailed. Surely Sells and his associates could chart a new course.[46]

The appeals from Arizona did not diminish. In 1915 Montezuma thought a visit by Sells to the McDowell reservation might enable the commissioner to understand why the Yavapais did not want to move to Salt River and why they needed a new dam at their present location. According to reports from his relatives, the commissioner did not arrive with an open mind. He immediately told the Yavapais that he wanted them to move to Salt River. Later, Charles Dickens wrote to Montezuma, saying they did not want to move. Dickens and friends said Sells argued a new dam would cost too much and that there was not enough land to justify the expenditure. "You want us to ask him and he never says anything to help us," the Yavapais observed. They instructed Montezuma: "We want you see Latimer and others and talk over this matter and through Congress for us and we have to say we don't want move to Salt River, then let us know."[47]

Sells's refusal to allow the Yavapais a new dam and his advocacy of their removal angered Montezuma. He had cautioned his friends to keep quiet, to work hard, and not to make trouble. He had told them that Sells would listen to them. It all appeared to have been for naught. Undoubtedly he remembered the letter written to him in November 1914 by the dying Yavapai leader Yuma Frank. "Dear Brother," he had written, "Remember me. You and me we help each other." Yuma Frank recalled how the government had wanted him to move and that he had said he could not. He had asked when testifying in Washington for a dam, and it had not been constructed. Now George Dickens would be chief and he would need help. Yuma Frank concluded:

Please alway saying to the Government: Build a dam for McDowell my peoples. Please, Brother, help all you can . . . Brother Montezuma, remember me and I always remember you too, and I am keeping my words in your book. Also tell my friends, Mr. Latimer, I am not able to live longer, so good-by and shake my hands with this letter . . .[48]

Such sentiments understandably touched Montezuma deeply. His response was one of the most eloquent statements he would ever make. Montezuma said, in part:

. . . No better man ever lived than you and I hope when this reaches you, you are better and that you have been cared for in the best way. We all have to die and if we face God, who made the mountains and all of us to live, know that we have been true and faithful to our people, He [God] will take care of us, when we leave this world for the home we are to have after we are dead. You have fought a good fight. You have seen the country taken away from your people now you have stood up as a brave man for the interest of your people . . . you have worked hard to be faithful as a chief to your people, and if you die, die happy, that we those who live, we will work just as faithful as ever to carry out what you had in your heart. But I hope that you will not die, but live long enough to see your people have a home on McDowell and that the Government will build a dam . . .[49]

Montezuma noted that Sells would soon come to McDowell, "and then you can ask him to construct the dam and see that your people are cared for after you are gone. . . . "He will listen to you," Montezuma promised, "because he is a good man. . . . I know he will do what you say to him."[50] Yuma Frank died the day Montezuma wrote his letter. The chief's words endured, we can be sure, inspiring Montezuma to greater efforts to maintain McDowell as the home for the Yavapais.

A lengthy memorandum from Meritt to Sells in the autumn of 1914 summarized the contemporary status of the McDowell debate. Meritt enclosed a file on what he termed Dr. Montezuma and the Camp McDowell case, admitting that there had been for some time a difference of views as to the best method of handling this situation. He noted that several years before, the Bureau had tried to remove the Yavapais to the Salt River reservation but that this attempt had been met by vigorous protest. The hearings in 1911 before a congressional committee publicized the Yavapai position. Such important congressmen as Stephens and Graham had concluded that the Yavapais should be provided for on McDowell. According to a recent estimate, a dam that would irrigate some thirteen hundred acres could be built on the Verde River for $75,000 or $80,000.[51]

From past experience, Meritt argued, it was apparent that it would be practically impossible to get the Yavapais to move to the Salt River reservation at this time. What should then be done? For once, Meritt and Montezuma agreed. The assistant commissioner contended that all of McDowell should be allotted to the Yavapais; the reservation should be fenced to keep Anglo livestock from grazing in timberland and from destroying Yavapai crops. In addition, Meritt continued, it might be desirable to provide the Yavapais with additional allotments of irrigable acreage, 10 acres each, on Salt River. In any event, the matter deserved immediate attention and definite and early action in fairness to the residents of McDowell.[52]

Despite Meritt's urgings, the controversy could not be resolved. N. W. Irsfeld, an assistant engineer for the Bureau, submitted a report in January 1915, discrediting the notion of satisfactory irrigated farming at McDowell. Irsfeld stated that fewer than 300 acres were being cultivated. The two ditches used were difficult to keep repaired and that discouraged the Yavapais from additional cultivation. The brush dams on the Verde washed out with every flood; the ditches could not contain the water brought in during storms through intersecting washes, so their banks were broken and the ditches filled with sand. Irsfeld determined that the only apparent solution of the problem was to transfer their water rights to the Salt River reservation, where there was much irrigable land without water. To stay at McDowell would mean being left to fight a losing fight; the Yavapais, good workers but poor farmers, would never advance.[53]

Based on Irsfeld's report, W. M. Reed, the chief engineer, disagreed with Superintendent Coe's belief that the McDowell ditch system should be repaired, contending it would only prolong the trouble and make it more difficult to deal with the Indians. As Sells would soon travel to the area, Reed advised that he should delay making a final decision. After the commissioner had had a first-hand look at local conditions, action could be taken.[54]

As has been described, Sells apparently went to McDowell in the spring of 1915 with his mind already made up. His visit did not result in any progress. The Yavapais had another guest that spring. At Montezuma's urgings, Fayette McKenzie went to McDowell in April. He told Montezuma that the government had "practically decided not to move the Indians and things are ready for a general forward movement." McKenzie had a good word for almost everyone, including Coe and the farmer; he complained only about Mike Burns, who had missed a meeting because, according to McKenzie, he had concluded the professor had no power. In his brief sojourn, McKenzie assured the Yavapais that the government would not move them and that it would be responsive to them, once officials recognized they were working and needed more water. George Dickens reported to Montezuma that the people were "very glad to hear his words and long talk" and reaffirmed their desire to stick together and not to "sign any papers as you told us."[55] Given the assurances of McKenzie, the Sells visit must have been all the more devastating for the Yavapais; the situation, obviously, was less secure than they had been told.

Despite the disappointment of Sells's visit, Montezuma took great pride in the Yavapais' responses to the commissioner. Some people—perhaps Coe or Valentine or Meritt or Phoenix residents—had convinced Sells beforehand, but he was unable to convince the residents of McDowell to move. George Dickens's response that if a dam could not be built, they would stay anyway must have taken the commissioner by surprise. Sells's argument that the dam would cost too much infuriated Montezuma, particularly given the price tag for Roosevelt Dam and other projects:

That will be worth millions for the white people. All the country once belonged to you Indians and all have been taken away from us and then when you as the children of those whom their fathers have murdered and owned all this rich country that they are blessed, this "costing too much" is a shameful expression. We will show Sells that it will not cost as much for this dam as he has been told by those who want McDowell. If a white man had McDowell he would build a dam to irrigate his land whether it be 1000 acres or 3000 or 5000 acres. He gave you poor excuse in order to have you move to Salt River.[56]

Montezuma cautioned the Yavapais not to accept the "too old" promise of allotments at Salt River with maintenance of McDowell as pasture land, for as soon as they moved to Salt River they would lose their rights to the Verde River. He noted the distinction between the government permitting the Yavapais to use McDowell and actual ownership of the land. "Do not be fooled," he admonished. "You stay on Mc-Dowell, use your brush dam and work the best you know how and Mr. Latimer and I will do all we can to guide you right." He closed: "Keep quiet, keep at work and know that McDowell is your home." Montezuma signed the letter, "Your relative 'Wassajah.' "[57]

The stalemate continued. Early in 1916, George Dickens, Charles Dickens, and other Yavapais went to see the governor of Arizona, George W. P. Hunt. The delegation expressed a number of concerns about its present situation, and Hunt forwarded questions to Sells. The commissioner had not budged. He continued to assert that the cost of constructing an irrigation system was prohibitive, given the limited area susceptible to irrigation. Even if an irrigation system were constructed, it would result in about five irrigable acres per person, and the Yavapais would remain somewhat isolated from their nearest market, Phoenix. Sells stressed that the Yavapais had been told that their best interests would be served by accepting allotments of irrigable land on the Salt River Reservation. He realized that relations between the "Apaches" and the Pimas had not been cordial and that "even today possibly that feeling is none too friendly." In addition, the commissioner gave credit for Montezuma's influence, without naming him directly: "Certain influences, all emanating from the same source, had also been at work with a view of leading them to believe that allotment on the Salt River Reservation is but an initial step in a deep laid plan to deprive them of their lands at Camp Mc-Dowell." Sells insisted that the Yavapais had no greater friend than himself and that he wanted to help them when they were willing to accept his offer of aid.[58]

George Dickens heard from Governor Hunt about Sells's

reply; Dickens told Montezuma that it made him feel pretty bad for the commissioner to be talking about moving the Yavapais from McDowell. The chief recalled that General Crook has promised they could return to their old home country if they worked hard enough and learned enough. Now Sells kept trying to remove them. "I say no and no," reported Dickens, "as you told us not to move to any other place. I don't wanted take two places. I rather stay here my old home."[59]

Pressure continued from local Bureau personnel to have the Yavapais move to Salt River. According to the Dickens brothers, the school teacher and the farmer wanted them to move. The brothers complained that the teacher had no right to do so. Richard Dickens and other Yavapais wrote to Montezuma, saying they had been told that most families had agreed to leave, and that they would then receive help from the government; if they stayed, they would get no help. If they moved, McDowell would be used to graze cattle and there would be no farming. Richard Dickens recalled that he had told Sells he could not make the desert country his home, because the water was poor and there were no shade trees; such country was good "for only the Papagoes and Pimas." McDowell was home. Their fathers and mothers had been born nearby. "We ask nothing from the Government," they said, "only to be let alone and to live here for the rest of our lives because the surrounding is our fathers and mothers homes. . . ."[60]

These letters prompted a series of exchanges between Montezuma and Meritt. Montezuma said he believed the Yavapais were being made to feel uneasy by those in charge of them; he labeled such action unfair and not right. He also inquired about the cattle. Meritt insisted that the Bureau was not trying to force removal. The cattle would be Yavapai property, subject to Office control, and would not affect farming. Montezuma fired off additional questions of clarification. Eventually Meritt conceded that the title to the cattle remained with the government until full repayment had been made by the tribe. The removal issue, of course, remained a standoff.[61]

In late 1916, as has been observed, Sells was receiving a steady stream of anti-Montezuma invective from Superintendent Coggeshall. The commissioner tried to bolster the superintendent's morale. Sells expressed his regret that outside influences were making trouble. He hoped that Coggeshall's prompt action in placing properly before the Indians matters concerning them would help when combined with the influence of the "more intelligent and progressive members of the tribe."[62] On another occasion, he told Coggeshall to tell the Yavapais that allotments at Salt River and cattle grazing at McDowell were in their best interests. He argued that the best way to ensure McDowell's retention was to use it to advantage; cattle grazing would work in that direction as successfully as it had elsewhere. Sells was certain all this would help the Yavapais and he could not understand how anyone concerned for their welfare could advise them differently. He wanted to help them, he insisted; anyone who suggested otherwise either did not know the facts or was a liar.[63]

It is reasonable to conclude that the amount of attention devoted by Sells, Coggeshall, and others to these nefarious "outside influences" represented a kind of grudging tribute. Had it not been for Montezuma's alliance with Indians on Salt River and McDowell, the Bureau administrators could have imposed their wishes. And there can be little question that Montezuma was essentially correct about the acceptance of allotments at Salt River. Had the Yavapais accepted the offer, they would have weakened their position at McDowell. Given the importance of the Verde River water, the proximity of McDowell to Phoenix, and the tremendous reduction of Indian landholdings during the first two decades of the twentieth century, the Yavapais must be judged fortunate to have retained their land base. One is reminded of the transition discussed by Frederick Hoxie in a recent analysis of the Cheyenne River reservation in South Dakota before World War I. The reservation, Hoxie contended, became progressively less of a prison and more of a homeland. It permitted the Indians a kind of boundary where their identity could be maintained.[64]

In the end, Montezuma still did not like the effect of the reservation on many Indians. He detested the kind of control exercised over Native Americans by superintendents, farmers, and other Bureau officials. These people, as Montezuma perceived it, had put Indians in bondage. He wrote in *Wassaja* (November 1918) about the current status of the Native American on a reservation: "He does not know whether he is an

American or what not. His life is permeated with fear. He lives by being ruled as cattle. The jail is always ready for him; with suspicion he roams the reservation cage...."[65]

Clearly Montezuma drew many of his lessons about the restrictions placed on reservation residents from his experiences in southern Arizona. The very language—cattle, jail—alludes to specific incidents of this era. He did not care for the impact of the reservation on some of its occupants, and he believed those people merited fairness rather than coercion. In *Wassaja* (September 1918) Montezuma lashed out at Cato Sells and his apparent efforts to have the Yavapais moved from McDowell. Montezuma cited "a powerful current working to have those McDowell Indian move to Salt River Reservation.... The undercurrent is so strong that Cato Sells has seen fit to go with the current. And he has allowed everything to be done in order to have those Apaches move to Salt River Reservation." He concluded: "Cato Sells is weak where he should stand up for the Indians." According to Montezuma, Sells had been guilty of a multitude of oversights, mistakes, and errors: not allotting McDowell, not building the dam, coercion, not asking for extra money for McDowell, driving cattle onto the reservation, taking away schools, and so forth. The commissioner, in sum, had "tried to smoke those McDowell Indians out and please his friends . . . but the Indians will not 'smoke out' worth a cent."[66]

In the remaining four years of his life, Montezuma finished his successful struggle against the forces that sought to remove his people from their home. He also continued to comment in *Wassaja* on important issues in Indian affairs, including the decline of the Society of American Indians. Yet by 1918, Arizona had become the focal point of his existence. One of the most interesting efforts of these years would be his attempt to become an enrolled member at the San Carlos reservation. Here the Bureau officials of whom he had been so critical would extract a small measure of revenge. Montezuma would be denied one goal he sought, but he would have the satisfaction of coming home.

7

The Circle Closes

Three concerns stand out in Carlos Montezuma's final years: his efforts in national Indian affairs, his attempt to become an enrolled member on the San Carlos reservation, and his work on continuing issues in southern Arizona. His journal, *Wassaja*, his letters, commentary from Bureau of Indian Affairs employees, and correspondence from Arizona Indians combine to provide a vivid picture of the period from 1919 to Montezuma's death in January 1923. This chapter on his last years is divided into three sections: national Indian life, application for enrollment, and Arizona land and water.

NATIONAL INDIAN LIFE

The prevailing principle for Montezuma remained abolition of the Indian Bureau. He had little patience with people like Arthur C. Parker who would ask, "But what would take its place?" In "Excuses to Abolish the Indian Bureau," printed in *Wassaja* (January 1919), Montezuma observed that immigrants to this country adapted and survived; so, too, had black people, freed only about fifty years previously. Citizenship for all Indians, freedom to advance, would solve this problem. The

January 1919 issue had a new cartoon gracing the masthead. It showed Montezuma on one side, pointing to the Statue of Liberty and holding the pages of "Let My People Go" (subtitled rather immodestly "An Indian Classic") with a traditionally clad Native American on the other side, holding a torch and reaching out; in between was emblazoned "Wassaja—Freedom's Signal for the Indian." The image, of course, dramatized Montezuma's belief that Indians must be treated with the same respect and given the same opportunities as all Americans.[1]

The Society of American Indians at its annual meeting in the autumn of 1918 had voted to abolish the Bureau of Indian Affairs. Montezuma remembered that "at the birth of the great Society of American Indians, a majority of the charter members thought that the society could harmonize and work with the Indian Bureau for one common cause." But in Pierre, South Dakota, "The REAL INDIANS of the S.A.I. turned the tide against the Indian Bureau." Montezuma eagerly reprinted a letter he had received from the Society's new president, Charles A. Eastman, which noted that with the new stance, people should no longer worry about the Bureau controlling the organization. Employing strong language, the president stated that Native Americans had "fallen into the clutches of a Bureau Machine, which controls our property, our money, our children and our personal rights." Now the ultimate object of the Society and its membership must be "THE FREEDOM OF THE INDIAN FROM BONDAGE." "We are not a 'dying race,' " Eastman emphasized. "We are alive and asking for our share of the LIBERTY AND DEMOCRACY THAT WE HAVE FOUGHT FOR."[2]

In Montezuma's view, 1919 would be the Society's greatest year. Under the vigorous leadership of President Eastman and Vice-President Father Philip Gordon, the Society campaigned actively for Indian freedom. In Eastman's words, Indians had allowed themselves "to be too long controlled by a political machine. . . . Our affairs have been mismanaged, and we have been deprived of our natural and ordinary privileges as citizens of a great and free country." Eastman argued that the Society had "rekindled our council fire."[3]

Montezuma assured his readers that he had met with Eastman and Gordon and that the Society was on the right road to face the foe. *Wassaja* called for unity and encouraged all Na-

tive Americans to attend the annual meeting, slated for Minneapolis; the Society expected it to be "the largest gathering
in the history of the Indian race, if not the greatest of importance." Montezuma, Eastman, and Gordon made a speaking
tour through Wisconsin in May. That month's *Wassaja* reported enthusiastically on the venture;[4] Gertrude Bonnin, in
an editorial comment printed in the Society journal, *The American Indian Magazine,* proved perhaps even more zealous. The
editor was particularly angry over the Bureau's refusal to let
the men speak on a reservation: "Though the riffraff of the
white people from the four corners of the earth may enter Indian lands and homestead them, thus permitting daily contact
with the very scum of other races, the educated, refined, and
patriotic Indian, teaching the highest ideals of democracy is
forbidden to meet with his own race, even for a day!"[5]

Bonnin corresponded frequently with Montezuma during
1919. As the Society's secretary and editor of its journal, she
remained excited about the new spirit and potential of the association. She praised *Wassaja,* talked about the growth in SAI
membership, and looked forward to a "humdinger" of a conference in Minneapolis. The only problem seemed to be time
and energy. "I am overrun by countless cases," she said to Montezuma. "I only wish I were more than one person with only
one pair of hands to take care of these matters . . ."[6]

The new decade, however, marked the rapid decline of the
Society of American Indians. Arthur C. Parker, already with-
drawing from the organization, did not attend the annual meeting in Minneapolis. Bonnin's husband ran unsuccessfully for
president; with his defeat, his spouse relinquished her commitment to the Society. Eastman, too, faded from view. The
American Indian Magazine published its final issue in 1920.
While Montezuma could be chastized for his earlier attacks
on the association, he remained faithful to it in difficult times.
He urged Indians to be loyal and to be present in thousands at
the annual conference in St. Louis in 1920. After the gathering, Montezuma acknowledged that attendance had declined,
but stressed that the Society had more representatives from
different reservations than previously. Most notably, *Wassaja*
reported, "We were of one mind, and . . . as an Indian organization we must stand together." Native Americans from Ari-

zona and elsewhere recounted problems faced on contemporary reservations.[7]

By this time the primary focus of Montezuma's attention had shifted to Arizona. He continued to urge people to attend the annual meetings and hoped to breathe some life into what obviously constituted an ailing body. "The S.A.I. Is Not Dead," read the headline of an article in *Wassaja* (July 1921). Those who labeled it as dead had not stuck by it. "A Society that stands for freedom and citizenship and the abolishment of the Indian Bureau cannot die," Montezuma stated. "You may as well get rid of God as to get rid of the Society of American Indians in its work for the Indians." Strong language, indeed, from the devout Baptist, but the times demanded it; even Montezuma admitted the Society had "gone through the valley of death." *Wassaja* regretted the absence of a journal and the criticism leveled at Society president, Tom Sloan. Native Americans must unite and stand by the Society, for it was "the greatest Indian organization in America," able to "help you, your tribe, your people, your country and the world."[8]

The Society held its tenth annual conference in Detroit. Attendance had dwindled again, and the future of the society appeared problematic, at best. Montezuma devoted nearly all of the November 1921 *Wassaja* to the organization. He observed that long distances, hard times, short notice, and illness all had combined to limit the assemblage. "Taking everything into consideration," he concluded stubbornly, "the Conference was a success—meaning that the Society of American Indians stood by their people and not by the Indian Bureau." Montezuma charged that Indians had a duty to stand by the Society and encouraged them to send in their membership dues to Thomas Bishop.[9]

In a second article in November 1921 entitled "Where Stands The Society of American Indians?" Montezuma applauded the Society's continued stance in favor of abolition of the Indian Bureau. "There is no faith like knowing you are right," he observed. Montezuma predicted that Indians "would be men and women and not wards, and that object would continue to be the goal of the association." Once again, he supported the group in the firmest terms: "If ever there was a society that was seeking God's will, endeavoring to help its fellowmen and stand-

ing true to its country, it is the Society of American Indians."
Privately, he admitted that attendance in Detroit had been poor
and some had come to see the death of the Society. Still, Montezuma wrote to Pratt, he gloried that the Society survived. It
was the one Indian organization opposing the Bureau. If the
"old" workers had fallen out, at least the "faithful" workers
still ran the Society.[10]

Such an affirmation proved to be as well something of a last
gasp. There essentially is no mention of the Society during
most of the next and final year of *Wassaja*, save a couple of
small advertisements for membership and brief boldface reminders in the September 1922 issue to attend the upcoming
annual meeting in Kansas City. This conference, held October
17–20, was a disappointment. Sloan seemed more interested
in perpetuating his presidency than in taking action; the Society appeared to be backing away from its strong stance against
the Bureau. People now talked of reorganization rather than
abolition. The Society had had a fine chance to regain its past
prestige but had muffed the opportunity. Montezuma had maintained at least intermittent hopes through the past decade for
the Society of American Indians, but by the autumn of 1922
he had become disillusioned. He must have realized that the
Society's life had nearly run its course. Ironically, one of its
last annual meetings took place in Chicago, in September 1923.
The site had been selected in large part because of Montezuma's residence in the city, but he did not live to see that session become a reality.[11]

If the Society had received a decreasing amount of attention
in the pages of *Wassaja* from 1919 to 1922, Montezuma sustained an assault against the Bureau and its leaders. Thus "Freedom's Signal for the Indian" remained true to its announced
primary purpose until its last issue, November 1922. Cato Sells,
still commissioner of Indian affairs at decade's end, received
continuing condemnations. Montezuma, for example, included
in the January 1919 *Wassaja* a poem by "J. W. F." on "Cato
Sells, He 'Heap' Big Man." The doggerel began:

> And Susie, dear, and did you hear
> The news from Washington?
> How Cato Sells sits around and tells

Of great things he has done!
And what he'll do for a poor old Lo,
And what hard work he does—
But Cato is just like the bee,
The most he's done is buzz . . .[12]

"Arrow Points" by "Junius" in the March 1919 *Wassaja* declared: "The general consensus of opinion among all Indian tribes is that Cato Sells is a great specimen of the 100 percent four flusher and hypocrite." Junius proposed that Sells "ought to be arrested for criminal negligence in his handling of Indians, defrauding the United States tax-payers by drawing a salary, and collecting money under false pretense."[13]

In April 1920, Montezuma summed up his outrage against Sells and his administration of eight years. His piece, "Hon. Cato Sells, 'Warden of Indian Penitentiaries,' " recalled the hopes that had initially been entertained for the commissioner and how that confidence had been abused. Montezuma pronounced Sells an ally of the lessors of Indian lands, a friend of the influential, a colleague of cattlemen, land buyers, irrigation project men, manipulators of mines and oils, and great promoters. Sells painted "Indians black who are working for the best interest of their race"; he poisoned "characters of those Indians who know about Indians better than he does." There can be no doubt that Montezuma numbered himself among those whom he believed the commissioner had slandered.[14]

Sells had come in and now departed with the Democrats; his successor, Charles H. Burke, arrived with the Republican triumph in the election of 1920. *Wassaja* would defer judgment on the man, but Montezuma noted that one did not have to know anything about Indians to become commissioner, as long as one were a brother Republican: "All he has to do is to take the oil can and grease the Indian machine faithfully; now and then tighten this and that loose screw; his main duty is to keep the machine [Indian Bureau] going." The odds favored following "the law of least resistance"—helping out old friends even if this harmed the Indians in matters of leasing of grazing or mineral lands, moving Indians from where they were, constructing dams on reservations, and so forth.[15] Burke would not personally be harpooned so frequently by Montezuma, but the pages of *Wassaja* showed no mercy for his position or for his agency. The final issues of the magazine featured a grim depiction of an Indian in stocks gazing at "Freedom's Signal for the Indian," with the stocks labeled "Work of the Indian Office."[16]

APPLICATION FOR ENROLLMENT

Montezuma would deal with Burke in regard to several issues, not the least of which would be the Yavapai's attempt to enroll at the San Carlos reservation. This effort revealed much about Montezuma's own feelings about his identity and the Bureau's response to him. This drama would be played out over seven years, beginning with an inquiry by Montezuma in the summer of 1915 and ending with Burke's denial of Montezuma's application in the summer of 1922.

On August 2, 1915, Montezuma wrote to Assistant Commissioner E. B. Meritt, inquiring about a treaty signed in the early 1870s and about his status as the legal heir of his relatives. Meritt asked for clarification. Was Montezuma applying for enrollment at San Carlos, where his relatives had been taken in 1871, or was he applying "as a survivor of a tribe or band of Apaches which was removed to said reservation?" If the former, Montezuma should present details of his Indian blood and family history and give the names of his relatives removed to San Carlos; then the Office would look into the matter.[17]

In fact, then, Meritt inaugurated the process. Whether he was merely trying to bait Montezuma or whether Montezuma eventually would have applied for enrollment is a matter of conjecture. In any case, Montezuma delayed for five years before making an additional formal inquiry. He told Meritt that his mother and brother had died at San Carlos in 1872 and that his father had died there in 1876. As he had been away from his people since 1871, he wished to be filed as a member of the San Carlos reservation. Montezuma stated he did not know what steps to take and asked for advice. If there were papers to be signed, they should be sent; or could the agent at San Carlos be authorized to register him as a member of the San Carlos reservation?[18]

It could not be that simple. Meritt informed Montezuma that

he must provide a sworn statement giving family history, Indian ancestry, place and date of birth, places and approximate dates of subsequent residence, whether a similar application had been made and what action had been taken on it, degree of Indian blood claimed, name of tribe to which each parent belonged, whether they were enrolled and recognized members of the tribes, and what benefits as Indians they received. Such a statement had to be supported by affidavits from two or more persons with knowledge of the facts of the case. Once the Office had received all this information, appropriate consideration would be given to his application.[19]

Montezuma decided to apply. In November 1920, he submitted papers that he trusted would comply with the instructions Meritt had outlined. Meritt promptly acknowledged receipt of the application for enrollment with the "Apache Indians" of the Salt River Agency. By return mail, Montezuma reminded the assistant commissioner that he had requested to be enrolled with the Apaches of San Carlos Agency. Meritt thanked him for the correction.[20]

The Indian Office then shifted its attention to San Carlos and its superintendent, A. H. Symons. From the outset, Symons seemed skeptical about the whole business. He told the commissioner that what he had did not seem to be a formal application. What kind of investigation did the Bureau have in mind? Meritt tried to explain. Eventually Symons responded on May 14, 1921, reporting he had been unable to find out anything very definite about Montezuma. Few actual facts could be established. The superintendent cited a precedent from the Fort Belknap reservation in Montana. Here, Secretary of the Interior Lane had ruled that Susie O'Brien, who had lived away from the tribe for much of her life and had been withdrawn from the tribal roll, could not be enrolled as she had lived separate and apart from the tribe for much of her life, she had gained citizenship, and she had therefore become independent and not entitled to tribal benefits from the reservation, although she was related to some of the Indians on the reservation. Symons suggested this precedent be applied in the case of Montezuma. Montezuma had gained citizenship on the outside, was perhaps a property holder in Chicago, and had made a living outside the tribe. Symons asserted that Montezuma wanted to be enrolled for "personal benefit as much as his feigned interest in the Apache Indians with whom he has never been associated."[21]

There happened to be another reason for Symons's recommendation that Montezuma be denied enrollment. Montezuma had visited the superintendent's office in the autumn of 1920, when heifers were being issued to some young Indian men on a reimbursable basis. A crowd of thirty Native Americans followed Montezuma into the office, as generally happened when the Yavapai traveled on the reservation. With these people "as spectators and listeners and absorbers of his false teachings," Montezuma "berated the Government in Washington and the management of this Reservation in particular for not giving these cattle to the Indian outright." His perspective made Symons's life more difficult, or at least more complicated, and that could not be forgiven:

He takes occasion to tell the Government employees in the presence of all Indians that he can get together, in a loud, important voice that the white man is simply on the Reservation for what he can get and is not interested in the Indian. That the Government of Washington is an Imposter. That the Indian people should be set free and that kind of talk. . . . I would therefore brand Dr. Montezuma as a trouble maker of the worst sort and would especially request that his application for enrollment be disregarded.[22]

Montezuma's application continued to be reviewed. Assistant Commissioner Hauke dispatched Salt River Agency Superintendent Byron Sharp to call on Montezuma's stepmother at McDowell and obtain her affidavit. Yu-co-dep-pah swore, as an Apache Indian woman, that she was Montezuma's stepmother, that he was born near where Roosevelt Dam had been constructed, that he had been captured by the Pimas, and that he belonged to the Pinal Apache tribe.[23]

Symons's replacement at San Carlos, Ernest Stecker, then provided the official response of the Business Committee to the question of Montezuma's enrollment. Business Committee members had been instructed by Stecker at a General Council meeting on October 22, 1921, to discuss the question in the districts with their constituents and then call for a vote on the matter. A week later, the Business Committee convened with

Stecker. San Carlos District and Bylas District had voted unanimously for enrollment; Rice District had voted for enrollment, with three negative ballots cast. The Business Committee then voted unanimously to enroll Montezuma at San Carlos. Oliver Belvodo, representative of San Carlos District, reported he knew the mother of Charles Dickens and all present said they knew Charles Dickens and Montezuma. Stecker concluded that, based on these statements and the vote taken, as well as the evidence in the affidavits, Montezuma was by right of birth entitled to enrollment with the San Carlos Indians, and he recommended that the request for enrollment be approved.[24]

Normally the Indian Office administrators in Washington supported the decision of their field people, but in this instance, they were willing to make an exception. Under other circumstances, when the applicant did not bear the label of troublemaker, the question of enrollment would presumably have been much more routine. Montezuma's application received an extraordinary amount of attention. Stecker's recommendation conflicted with that of his predecessor. Moreover, it must have been inconsistent with prevailing sentiments in Washington, for the investigation proceeded. Though the people of San Carlos and their superintendent had affirmed Montezuma's right to be enrolled on that reservation, their wishes would not be granted.

Commissioner of Indian Affairs Charles Burke turned to Charles L. Davis, superintendent of Fort Apache, which bordered San Carlos. Burke cited a need to acquire the facts and asked Davis, with his long experience in enrollment matters, to investigate the matters. The commissioner authorized Davis to visit McDowell and anywhere else necessary to conduct a more complete investigation. He wanted to find out how much hearsay testimony had been collected and stressed the importance of talking to the most reliable people. Significantly, Burke called Davis's attention to Symons's letters, but not to the Stecker letter.

Davis accepted the assignment, of course. He reviewed the record and talked with Stecker and Superintendent Virtue at McDowell before responding to the commissioner. He contended that Montezuma should be interrogated under oath, in order that the Yavapai's application be in proper form, so that his full life's history could be brought out, and "to present his attitude toward the government."[26] While Davis disavowed any desire "to apply the so-called 'Third Degree,' " or to give any indication of bias or unfriendliness, his letter would not have made Montezuma feel more optimistic about his chances.

On March 7, 1922, David conducted a hearing at San Carlos, in which he questioned certain witnesses in regard to the application. Eben Beads, Ernest Ewing, Arthur Kichiyan, Charles Baslee, Hiram Ward, and Sarah Carlos testified, with Kichiyan and Ward particularly providing supportive details and clarifying the distinction between Mohave Apache and Apache. Davis then left for McDowell to secure additional details.[27]

On March 10, 1922, Little Jack, Sam Axe, Sugeathe, and Yumedeppah provided testimony for Davis at McDowell. They emphasized the events surrounding Montezuma's capture and reviewed again the identities of his nearest relatives. Their recollections indicate that Montezuma may have been about the age of six rather than four, as he later suggested, at the time of his kidnaping. Davis did additional research in Phoenix before returning to Whiteriver on the Fort Apache reservation.[28]

From Whiteriver, Davis wrote to the commissioner on March 20, summarizing his investigation. He noted tht he had been surprised to learn that Montezuma was not an Apache and that his band or tribe did not belong to the Athapascan family; rather his band was part of the Yuman family, and "the 'Apache' which has since attached to it is a misnomer." Davis assumed, correctly, that Montezuma had not tried to deceive anyone on this score, but had merely been confused, as many others had been.[29]

In the meantime, an anxious Montezuma wondered why his application was receiving such a lengthy examination and whether the matter had been overlooked or disregarded. He had not heard anything from the Indian Office, and so he inquired of Meritt. Burke responded immediately, on March 25, noting that the application was being considered and that Montezuma would be advised as soon as the case was settled.[30] Thus, in other words, the investigation had entered its final stages, and a ruling could be anticipated within the relatively near future.

To be sure, Burke awaited Davis's final report, which arrived in mid-April. In a single-spaced typewritten letter of nearly eight full pages, the superintendent presented an analysis along the lines of ten interrogatories he had prepared. Though they were never made, because Burke was anxious to conclude the case as expeditiously as possible, these questions reveal some of Davis's main misgivings about Montezuma's application.

In addition to the distinction between Mohave-Apache and Apache, Davis also drew attention to the improbability of the age at which Montezuma had reached certain educational levels. He wondered if Montezuma claimed to be a U.S. citizen and an Illinois citizen. Had he voted? If his application were approved, would he reside on San Carlos? If the purpose of federal guardianship was to prepare Indians for assimilation into American life, then why did he seek enrollment? Did he still adhere to the principles he outlined in his speech in Lawrence in 1915 at the meeting of the Society of American Indians? If his application were approved, would he assume the status of other Yavapais? If he did still adhere to the principles or if he would assume that status, or both, then he should explain why he had applied for tribal membership.[31] Davis's queries are based on certain assumptions about the role of the federal government, the place of an Indian on a reservation, and the degree to which self-sufficiency and tribal enrollment were incompatible. In his view, Montezuma's application must have appeared contradictory and paradoxical. Why would Montezuma apply?

Davis drew several interesting conclusions about Montezuma, his life, and career. His distinction between Apache and Mohave-Apache, and his awareness that the two spoke different languages, led Davis to be distrustful of the evidence he had gathered at San Carlos; he would discard that testimony, as he believed it was based on details learned from Montezuma himself. The superintendent also questioned the testimony of people from McDowell. He doubted that Sugeathe was Montezuma's mother's sister and he again felt that much of the testimony was based on information initiated by Montezuma. In addition, Davis found that Montezuma was more than four years old, and even more than six years old, at the time of his capture; he thought Montezuma was at least ten years of age, or probably twelve. Davis even believed the baptismal certificate at Florence must be disallowed since it did not confirm that Montezuma was an Indian.[32] In retrospect, some of Davis's conclusions seem justified. Obviously, Montezuma was not an Apache. It seems likely that he was more than four years of age when kidnaped. Some of the testimony Davis gathered probably amounted to hearsay. In any case the dismissal of the baptismal certificate appears extreme. Davis's nearly total skepticism of what his Indian informants told him does not seem proper. The superintendent wanted to challenge Montezuma at every possible point. If the Yavapai could not be proven wrong, Davis spoke of "conceding" that Montezuma was right.

The investigator's perspective, above all, was governed by a desire to deny Montezuma's application and by dislike of the man. He assumed that only Indians who needed governmental assistance should be enrolled members of any tribe. A decade before, he had complained about allotment clerk Herbert Marten fomenting the Pimas and charged that Marten was being secretly aided by others. Davis in 1922 had risen from supervisor of farming to superintendent, but his basic views had not been altered. His letter concluded on an antagonistic note:

If he is seeking enrollment that he may share in the tribal wealth of the San Carlos Indians his application should be rejected on the grounds that he is not entitled thereto. We know that his past attitude has not only been one of opposition to efforts of the government, but that it has been almost entirely hostile, seemingly for the sake of hostility alone. The questions of the propriety of giving him recognition as a member of any tribe is, therefore, an important one. . . .[33]

Thanks to Davis's report and the prevailing attitudes about Montezuma within the Bureau of Indian Affairs, Commissioner Burke's recommendation to the secretary of the interior must have been negative. On June 12, 1922, Burke wrote to the Secretary, summarizing many of Davis's findings. He concluded that the facts did not warrant Montezuma's enrollment at San Carlos.[34] Assistant Secretary of the Interior F. M. Goodwin three days later certified that the application had been denied and returned it to the Indian Office. Burke notified Montezuma that he could not be enrolled at San Carlos; Montezuma tersely acknowledged to the commissioner that his letter had been duly received.[35]

Though he would not admit it to Burke, Montezuma was deeply troubled not only by the decision but also by the rather confusing information about his tribal identity. The day after he wrote his one-sentence letter to the commissioner, Montezuma wrote to Latimer, observing that at the time had had been captured there had not been a tribe called the Mohave Apaches. In July, he wrote to Pratt, remarking that he had once thought of applying at McDowell, but had decided to apply at San Carlos, because his father and mother had lived and died there.[36] Perhaps it would have been more advisable for Montezuma to have attempted to enroll at McDowell, as it had become the home of his relatives. Undoubtedly, however, different obstacles would have been placed in his way there. Though he wondered aloud to Latimer if his attorney might help in some way, Montezuma was not about to repeat the ordeal of application. He must have known that his chances would have been no better at McDowell, particularly since he would have been subjected to the same review process by the same reviewers.

In any event, he remained upset about the issue of tribe. He wrote to Frederick Webb Hodge at the Smithsonian Institution in Washington, D.C. to ask about the classification of his people. "In what year were the Apaches of Arizona classified?" he queried. "Why were the Mohave Apaches called so, when they were enemies of the Mohave Indians who lived on the Colorado river?" Montezuma referred to the Mohave-Apaches as misnamed Indians and briefly traced for Hodge their demographic history in recent times. He labeled the Mohave-Apache appellation "absurd, when the Apaches had no use for the Mohave."[37]

H. W. Dorsey and J. N. B. Hewitt responded to the inquiry. Montezuma wrote one final letter to the anthropologists, commenting that he was in a "controversy relative to my status as an Apache." He summarized his family history, saying his father "knew nothing of Mohave Indians." "I believe I belong to *Pinal Apache*," Montezuma argued. He concluded by pleading, "I wish you would help me out in this matter."[38] Dorsey and Hewitt, no doubt, replied, but their letter is not available, and it probably did not satisfy a man who had seen himself all his life as Apache.

ARIZONA: LAND AND WATER

However disturbed this episode may have left Montezuma, it did not deter him from a continuing commitment to the Yavapais at McDowell throughout the final years of his life.

Wassaja and Montezuma's correspondence demonstrate that McDowell had become his primary concern in Indian affairs. His unyielding opposition to Yavapai removal, his loyalty to his tribe, and his clashes with Bureau field personnel all continued through this period. They reflected the degree of importance that his people's concerns had assumed and help us to understand why Montezuma would decide to return home to die.

On February 21, 1919, Bureau Inspector E. N. Sweet, Jr. submitted a memorandum on the subject of Yavapai allotment. The inspector noted that Montezuma had represented to the Yavapais that if they accepted allotments under the Salt River Reclamation Project, they would be driven from McDowell and their home would be given to white men. The commissioner's statements to the contrary notwithstanding, the Yavapais were not satisfied. The answer, Sweet believed, was to allot McDowell to allay Native American fears. The inspector contended that the Yavapai attitude must be understood in the context of Indian history, Indian removals, and unresolved questions about water rights.

Sweet had some grasp of the Yavapai resistance to removal. He may have been inclined to be sympathetic to the Yavapais, but not to Montezuma personally. In another memorandum on law and order, also dated February 21, 1919, he observed that there had been no drunkenness among the Indians on Salt River and McDowell for more than a year and added that the better he knew the Yavapais, the more sympathy he had for them, considering Montezuma's influence, doubts about water rights, and the location of their homes.[40] Sweet's comments are noteworthy. They give additional credence to the notion that Montezuma exercised considerable influence at McDowell. In addition, they speak to the uncertainty over water rights and the attractiveness of the Yavapais' current locale: both vital factors in the firm resistance to Salt River.

Of course, it was Sweet who previously had praised the Bureau farmer, Thomas Little Bison, for his good work at McDowell. That good work, in Sweet's judgment, had consisted in significant measure in overcoming the effect of Montezuma. Little Bison had been the source of many complaints by the Yavapais. Despite support from his immediate superiors, he eventually fell from grace. As an Indian, he had been welcomed initially. But his advocacy of removal to Salt River caused his decline in popularity. Eventually, according to Mike Burns, Little Bison was convicted of larceny and dismissed from his position.[41]

Burns, Charles Dickens, and other Yavapais continued to write to Montezuma in this period. Their letters mirrored the conditions at McDowell. They wrote about problems: illness, removal, and individual personalities. They spoke to Montezuma as one of them and yet as one who lived apart. Montezuma represented an ability to counteract the forces that threatened them and against which they did not always know how to proceed. He also could still be a source for funds and clothing. Charles Dickens, particularly, leaned on Montezuma to help out. After inquiring about when Montezuma would be visiting again, assuring him that all were eager to see him, Dickens would follow with reminders about the obligations of kinship:

. . . One of our best friend Name if Yuma Dick he is here at my camps today while I am writing these letter and he said to me and he ask you have you got old hat and He wants you if you got one sented to him, and Adress me. Also my old mother she ask to send her 15 yards of Calicos. She say she close relation to you. If you please dear Cousin hunt up $4 per of old Shoes for my Childrens and sented to us by Express. No 5 1/2 and No. 4 and No. baby shoes 2 years old, and one girl shoes No. 3. As I told you I have no money to buy shoes for them. . . .[42]

George Dickens's letter to Montezuma of September 8, 1919, is another example of a McDowell individual's request for advice and assistance. A surveyor had come to McDowell. Why was he there? Why had he chopped down trees? Montezuma wrote to Meritt, who in turn wrote to Superintendent Sharp. Sharp responded, and then Meritt told Montezuma that a windstorm had blown down several trees. The surveyor had come from Phoenix, which had requested permission to reestablish a survey initially made in 1915 for a right-of-way for a pipeline through McDowell and Salt River. The surveyor was authorized but he symbolized another intrusion on the reservation and a possible threat to Yavapai water rights. Sharp, incidentally, took this occasion to denigrate Dickens as "an old Indian

who can neither read nor write but is considered by the Mc-
Dowell Indians as their chief, and being a relative of Montezuma is strongly under his influence. . . ." According to Sharp,
indeed, Dickens had written in part because of his relative's
power over him. Dickens and his associates still were swayed
by Montezuma's teachings "which are to the effect that the
Indian Bureau is holding them in slavery and oppression and
is only waiting for a good opportunity to take their reservation
from them."[43]

With progress being achieved on irrigation works at Salt
River, government officials again hoped to convince the Yavapais to take advantage of the land reserved for them there. Now
that the headgate in the Arizona canal from which water was
to be diverted had been finished, perhaps the opportunity might
appear more attractive. What were the chances of changing the
Yavapais' mind? Sharp, for one, predicted it would be "impossible" to get the Yavapais to move to Salt River, as they were
under Montezuma's influence.[44]

Sharp clashed with Montezuma over internal Salt River matters as well. Samuel Ladlow and Santiago Baptisto had written
to Montezuma inquiring about money that had been collected
three years earlier for sheep-grazing fees. Perhaps "the agent
that was here before Mr. Sharpe enjoyed it himself," they suggested. Montezuma asked Meritt about it, and again, Sharp had
to respond. The superintendent did not find the matter amus-
ing. He recorded that $106 had been collected and that with
these and other receipts a corral solely for Indian use had been
constructed, "but it appears that Ladlow, Baptisto and several
others comprising the 'bolsheviki' element among the Indians
under this jurisdiction and who are under the pernicious influence of Doctor Carlos Montezuma are ready under the least
pretense to pour their tales of woe into his willing ear." Sharp
believed that Montezuma's influence was "gradually being
eliminated from among the Indians here but there are still a
few of the older people who believe in his wonderful powers."[45]

Montezuma gave his quarrels with Sharp national publicity
through the pages of *Wassaja*. More than half of the October
1920 issue detailed a confrontation that had occurred during
his latest visit to Arizona. Montezuma had been summoned
by Sharp from a horseback trip in the mountains near McDow-

ell. He returned to the reservation, where an automobile waited to take him to the agency headquarters. Montezuma took along his wife, George Dickens, and Nellie Davis, a Yavapai interpreter. In front of these associates, Sharp accused Montezuma of being a bad influence, of being an undesirable person. He alleged that the Yavapais did not own McDowell; Montezuma alleged Sharp was working for the interest of Phoenix people and not for the Indians. McDowell had been maladministered. No new school had been built, stock raising had replaced farming as a Bureau priority, and a water pipe was going through the reserve without the Indians' permission. Sharp threatened to remove Montezuma from the reservation if he continued to agitate his people.[46]

The January 1921 *Wassaja* finished the episode. The Montezumas, by prior arrangement, met some Pimas at Mesa and traveled north of the town to a Mormon mission church, devoted to the Pimas and Maricopas of Lehi. Ellick Sorensen, Agency farmer for Lehi, informed Montezuma that the Mormon bishop had forbidden the Yavapai to speak in the church. So the meeting was held about two miles away in an Indian home. In the midst of the gathering, Sorensen reappeared. He ordered the Montezumas to go with him immediately to see Sharp. Montezuma replied that he could not be arrested, as "a citizen and not a reservation Indian," but he could of course be removed from the reservation. He told the assemblage not to make any trouble. Then, he said, his wife—"a woman who did no wrong and who should be handled with due consideration, in her righteous protest, she was brutally and shamefully forced into the automobile," and they were driven off the reservation. The next day, outside the reserve, the interrupted meeting finally was concluded.[47]

This treatment of his wife, "for whom he would die," and the impunity in general of the superintendent understandably infuriated Montezuma. "Indian Has No Rights Whatsoever" he headlined his lead story in the March 1921 *Wassaja:* "The position of the Indian is a nonentity. They are not counted as anything in the human scale. They are used as tools, and not treated as God's creatures. . . ." As a specific example of the absence of Indian rights, Montezuma cited the laying of a pipeline through McDowell. When he accused Sharp of working for the interest of Phoenix people, he was referring to this issue. Montezuma quoted Meritt as arguing that there could not be any infringement of Indian rights by the pipeline, because the Act of February 15, 1901 (31 Stats., 790) authorized the secretary of the interior to permit right of way through Indian reservations for pipelines and the like for domestic, public, or any other beneficial uses. Native American approval was not required and not sought. Non-Indian interests could be dominant.[48]

Piping water for Phoenix residents through McDowell simply increased Montezuma's suspicion that the Bureau and the city were allied and that they both wanted the Yavapais off McDowell. In fact, the papers of Carl Hayden reveal a degree not only of communication but of collusion between metropolitan and federal interests. Hayden then served as a congressional representative from the new state of Arizona but, since he came from the Phoenix area, was most responsive to its needs. As an Arizona representative, he also, inevitably, took an active role in Indian affairs. He had submitted, for example, a citizenship bill for Indians several years before. Montezuma had not been impressed with the legislation. He wrote to Charles D. Carter, chairman of the Indian Committee of the House of Representatives, calling the bill "pervertive good will for the Indians." Hayden obtained the letter in some fashion and no doubt was displeased with the assessment.[49]

The May 1921 *Wassaja* reprinted correspondence from Latimer to Commissioner Burke, which in part called on the latter to help stop the pipe laying and digging now taking place on the reservation for the benefit of an Arizona water company. On May 23, 1921, Hayden sent a copy of this *Wassaja* to Avery Thompson, the Phoenix city manager. Hayden suggested Thompson write to Latimer and present the facts of the case. The city, not a company, was putting in the pipeline and it would not, he argued, interfere with any water rights the Yavapais might have. Thompson immediately wrote Latimer to that effect.[50]

The permit, issued in September 1919, stipulated that Phoenix would pay to the secretary of the interior on demand damages that might result to the Indians of Salt River and McDowell because of the construction, operation, and maintenance of this pipeline. Commissioner Burke informed the city commissioners of Phoenix that in 1921 the Yavapais had been prevented by the pipeline from irrigating and cultivating their lands. He claimed $450 damage, for 45 acres at $10 per acre. The city officials balked. Burke suggested he might recommend to the secretary of the interior that the permit be revoked.[51]

This seemed like rather uncharacteristic behavior on the part of the commissioner, and Hayden decided to determine the cause. After his third conference with Burke, Hayden finally discovered the reason. According to Hayden, the main reason for Burke's desire to settle this matter promptly was his desire to leave no cause for complaint on the part of Dr. Carlos Montezuma. Montezuma, it turned out, had appealed to the highest officer in the land. According to Hayden, President Warren G. Harding had directed Burke to ensure that no injustice was done to the Yavapais; the commissioner wanted to give a satisfactory report to the president and was eager to settle the controversy.[52]

Montezuma's letter to Harding had been only one letter in a barrage he and Latimer had fired in the direction of Washington. Their primary concerns had been the old ones: the threat of removal from McDowell and the construction of a dam at McDowell. Things seemingly had reached another crisis point. As Montezuma explained to Pratt, in February 1921 Allotting Agent John Baum had tried to force the Yavapais to take the acres of irrigble land allotted for each at Salt River, while McDowell was allotted as grazing land only. Baum held a meeting to urge the residents of McDowell to take allotments at Salt River first. Nellie Davis wrote to Montezuma informing him that George Dickens almost agreed, but then, after Montezuma's latest letter was read to him, the Yavapais left the meeting. These maneuvers by Baum, Montezuma asserted, merely indicated again that Phoenix was after the Verde River. It is worth noting, as another point of divergence, that Pratt did not entirely side with his former employee. Pratt agreed that "the permanent forces of the Bureau, led by Mr. Hauke, are in sympathy, if not in direct cooperation, with the water users Association of Phoenix and the valley." But if the Verde water as it appeared, was "preeminently the best," then, Pratt argued, "it is to my mind clearly their right to have it." The Indians should give their consent and be compensated. They should not be "obstinate against it" or "unduly exhorbitant in their demands" or they would have no voice in the matter. Pratt concluded: "No man, or group of men can under our system be allowed to stand in the way of the best interests of the whole people." Montezuma could not accept that opinion.[53]

On May 25, 1920, President Wilson had, indeed, authorized allotments as Montezuma outlined it. Meritt had instructed Baum that it was important to allot the Yavapais as early as possible. What Meritt termed necessary arrangements had been made to transfer the Yavapais' water rights to the Verde to the Salt River reservation. The assistant commissioner told Baum, however, to allot McDowell before Salt River. As usual, the agent could make selection for minor orphans and Indians who refused to participate.[54]

Meritt reaffirmed traditional department positions in a letter to Montezuma on April 1, 1921. He said it would be in the best interests of the Yavapais to allot them on Salt River and that from an engineering standpoint irrigation at McDowell could not be carried out. There was no ulterior motive in allotment at Salt River; instead the irrigable acreage should be seen as "an additional gratuity." Latimer and Montezuma protested strongly that the executive order by President Wilson not only had been obtained secretively—they had but recently discovered its existence—but that the order ran counter to the expressed opinions of former Secretary of the Interior Fisher.[55]

Montezuma's first letter to President Harding was referred to the Department of the Interior, for response by its new head, Albert B. Fall of New Mexico. Fall, of course, was sympathetic to non-Indian interests, and his response is hardly surprising. He reiterated the department's stance that Fisher's plan to irrigate McDowell could not be realized, as "a more thorough investigation . . . disclosed that the turbulent nature of the Verde River being subject to violent and unexpected floods is such as to make the cost of the project prohibitive." Hearings were not needed; the matter should be seen as closed. Fall said he would see it as a kindness if Montezuma would use his influence to persuade the Yavapais to accept the arrangements.[56]

Montezuma and Latimer were in no mood for kindness. Latimer responded to Fall on May 12, asserting that the facts of removal had indeed been contemplated by the Bureau. The term itself had been employed many times in 1910 and 1911 by Bureau personnel; Latimer quoted from five separate documents to that effect. He also suggested that the language of the Kent decree only became mandatory when the Yavapais were removed. The allotment on Salt River under these circumstances could hardly be considered a gratuity.[57]

Montezuma followed with a letter to President Harding. He attempted to refute the idea that the Verde was turbulent and ridiculed the notion that the Yavapais somehow would be better off on Salt River. Montezuma declared that interested parties were seeking the removal of the Yavapais. As president, Harding must see that right and justice prevailed, with God as his guide.[58]

During the next month, a series of exchanges took place, with the principal parties reiterating familiar stances. Burke said no public good would be served by further discussions. Fall maintained that a dam at McDowell would not have solid foundation, that flooding was a real danger, and that maintenance costs would be prohibitive. Given these continuing responses, Montezuma decided a trip to Washington was in order. He traveled to the nation's capital to try to talk with the commissioner of Indian affairs.[59]

On June 23, Montezuma wrote to his wife, telling her that he had made an appointment to talk with Commissioner Burke. He planned to adhere to his position and to be on guard. The next day, he had a long talk with Burke, tracing the history of the case and his own involvement in it. The commissioner also inquired about his views on the Bureau:

He squirmed and spoke of "sedition." Then that stirred my ire up. I could see a flag out of the window. I pointed to the flag and said, that I am only upholding that flag that speaks of freedom, equality, democracy, humanity, and justice, if that is sedition then I am guilty and then I landed into him as I did at Mr. Sharp at Salt River reservation. I had him spell bound for 15 minutes. . . .[60]

In all, the two spoke for over an hour, and Montezuma felt hopeful about the outcome. Burke emphasized that the Yavapais would not be moved, that he wanted to hear more about the matter, and that $35,000 could be allocated for a dam, though for $90,000 he needed an additional appropriation from

Congress. The commissioner also wrote to Latimer, who was then visiting the city, that he had "had an extended and full statement from Dr. Montezuma in person" and hoped to hear soon from the attorney.[61]

Latimer promptly visited Burke, encouraged by his conciliatory tone and his expressed desire to adjudicate the matter in a satisfactory manner. During their forty-five-minute encounter, however, the commissioner lambasted Latimer for the language employed in his newly minted summary of the case, entitled "The Rape of Fort McDowell." Burke accused Latimer of only being interested in exploiting the situation. Latimer reported on the meeting to Harding, reminding the chief executive of the government's responsibility as trustee and its obligation to live up to the decision of Secretary Fisher.[62]

Before returning home to Chicago, Montezuma wrote several additional letters to his wife about his experiences in Washington. He told his "Dovey Dovie" that he and another Yavapai, Gilbert Davis from McDowell, had been busy visiting members of the Indian committees in the House and Senate. Latimer, now in New York, had encouraged them: "The only way is publicity." In some ways, what he had encountered had been discouraging, for Fall, Burke, and others were trying to defeat him. Some of the congressmen seemed educable but many were influenced by the Bureau, whose leaders believed Indians were not prepared to protect themselves and thus needed governmental help.[63]

Despite this attitude, Montezuma remained determined to fight. "My claim for my people is that much stronger, and the Indians are with me," he wrote Marie.[64] Montezuma thus no longer spoke of "you Indians"; he was an Indian. His letters to his wife are signed "Wassaja."

In August, Marie Montezuma left alone for a trip to the Southwest. Montezuma had wanted to accompany her, but nagging financial problems made him decide to stay in Chicago. He wrote a series of affectionate letters to her, talking about both serious and light subjects. Here was the domestic side of the man that one seldom observed. He related his attempts to make jam, for example. At the beginning of one letter he informed her that he was waiting for his grape juice "to boil down to a consistency for jam. I bought for 5 cents spoiled grapes and I am going to make jam out of them. I will get 4 glasses." But the confidence faded by letter's end. "I do not think my jam is a success—does not harden." Or he wrote of mundane, urban tasks. He had to drown a litter of kittens. Or: "I am everlastingly killing cockroaches—I take one hour every night. Good exercise."[65]

His letters show a real fondness for his wife; a rare letter from Marie reflects the love they shared. He worried about her catching cold, and he obviously missed her. "To-night," he wrote, "I can imagine you are asleep, and maybe, dreaming of Chicago, and when you are awake, you are at McDowell, many miles from home. But you must think you are at home with those blood relatives of mine." She closed her letter: "I could write to you for ever I have so much to tell you remember me to all and send you my Love and Kisses I longing for you and hope you can come yours Marie."[66] He wanted to join her, but could not justify the expenses when they needed the money at home. Montezuma estimated that he had on hand only $350 and concluded it would be foolish to spend most of it on the trip.[67]

His letters reflect a contemplative mood about life and his work. He told Marie that although her trip had been rough, it had been very instructive, and only thus could she have gained a sense of the country. She could look back on it in later life with pleasure. That was what made life "so good." He also spoke of her feeling restful "to be at home," again mirroring the fact that McDowell, too, had become home. And while despairing of the contemporary situation facing the Yavapais and the uncertainty that surrounded his work on their behalf, ultimately he could not be pessimistic:

... You and I know the work for the Indians is discouraging. There is no great work that is not discouraging. That is the time we need to forget ourselves and go right on. If we think upon the dark side too much we will give up and efforts have been wasted and disappear. It is by going on under difficulties and discouragements that wins in the long run.[68]

And so he kept going during the final months of his life. As we have seen, he pursued the matter of enrollment at San Carlos until he was rejected in the summer of 1922. He continued to publish *Wassaja* and continued to fight for what he believed right for Indians in southern Arizona. His relations with Bureau personnel, as one would expect, did not improve.

Byron Sharp's successor, Frank A. Virtue, was the last of a series of Salt River superintendents who were hostile to Montezuma. For example, in April 1922, Virtue responded to a letter from the commissioner that had enclosed various letters of complaint from the Indians at Lehi. Virtue dismissed the validity of their grievances: "All these Indians belong to what the good Indians call the 'Montezuma bunch' and all have been punished for violations of the rules. They do not represent the progressive class of the Indians. I have the confidence and respect of all the good Indians and the respect of the bad ones."[69]

Two of the bad ones, clearly, were Pete Vest and Sandy Eldridge, whom Virtue identified as leaders of the "old-time" Maricopas. "They are too old to be reasoned with," the Superintendent observed, "but have a certain following." And these members of the Montezuma bunch wanted "the old order of things . . . no supervision, no law, no morals." Why didn't the Maricopas like Virtue? The main grudge of the complaining Indians was a prohibition against singing and dancing all night and a total prohibition against women and girls participating in the dances. But generally, the Indians were "opposed to all that Government does."[70]

Such a dialogue sounds familiar; the Indian Office response also remained constant. One of the petitioners was Charley George from Mesa; Assistant Commissioner Meritt told George that his objection was not justified and that he should not make unfair complaints against the superintendent, who had Indian interests at heart.[71]

In the summer of 1922, Montezuma began to complain about his health. He told Pratt in late May that he had the flu and had been in bed for two weeks. His wife had been uneasy over his condition. Montezuma was trying to get back to his usual work. Their recent move to 2720 Michigan Avenue had been arduous. They had, he admitted, "more old things than I ever thought of." Moreover, life on such a main thoroughfare proved unpleasant, as there was too much noise from automobile traffic. Even if he and Marie were "making the best of it," he declared, "for a doctor to get sick does sound strange but they do get sick and die."[72]

As a physician, Montezuma knew he was ill and knew he was not likely to get better. He had contracted tuberculosis, a disease that claimed many Indian lives during this time. He attempted to keep up his old routine in Chicago, but it was difficult. Latimer wrote most of the articles in the September issue of *Wassaja*.[73] In the October issue, the Yavapai conceded he was in failing health. "Dr. Montezuma Is Not Well," read the headline.

No time in the history of Wassaja had he to slow down upon his work. For many years he thought he was made of cast iron physically, but for a year, he found out that he was a mere flesh, bone and blood. Since publishing "Wassaja" he did his work between 12 and 2 a.m., while Chicago was asleep. He devoted all day to his profession. But for two months Wassaja was down and out.[74]

Montezuma said he had been just strong enough to attend the Society of American Indians conference in Kansas City in early October. That he went at all, indeed, represented a kind of last tribute to his concern for the organization—to give the Society a last opportunity.

Since his return, Montezuma claimed he was improving slowly and hoped that in time he would regain his health, provided that he took care of himself. Perhaps "camp life" could "regain him his health." However, financial considerations dictated that he stay in Chicago, "do his best and see what the Lord will do."[75]

Montezuma published his last issue of *Wassaja* in November 1922, in two parts. The first provided excerpts from a paper read at the Society's conference by Robert Hamilton, an Indian from Montana. The second piece, written by Montezuma, also dealt with the Society and its future. It was entitled "The Indian Bureau—the Slaughter House of the Indian People." The editor had not entirely given up on the Society, as long as it would maintain the abolition of the Bureau as its central credo. Montezuma argued that the Society must be more "fightingly organized" and the journal must be revived to "give light and spirit to the cause with which we are entrusted."[76] The fight, in sum, must go on.

"It is a coward that speaks of death," wrote Montezuma to a sick friend in Detroit. "Medicine will help you, but the most important thing is to control yourself. Cheer up! There is no use of looking at things darkly."[77] This philosophy guided Montezuma during the remaining months of his life. Except for the public announcement of his poor health in the October *Wassaja*, there is very little evidence of outcry or fanfare surrounding his declining physical well-being. Maybe it was part of being "a man," that ideal that he always sought. Perhaps, too, it signaled an acceptance that little could be done.

In December 1922, Montezuma decided to complete his life's circle. He boarded a train in Chicago and returned to McDowell to be with and to die with his people. Before going out to the reserve, he stopped in Phoenix and bought six woolen blankets and six comforters. Montezuma had the Dickens family construct him a kind of brush shelter near their dwellings. A friend brought him a good spring bed, but Montezuma took the spring away. He stayed in bed or on the dirt floor most of the time. The weather had turned uncharacteristically cold. George Dickens kept a fire going. Montezuma's two extant letters to his wife indicate that he did not lack for company; both Yavapais and outsiders came to see him. A Tempe physician encouraged him to go to a sanitarium, but he refused, saying he wanted to die in the land of his forefathers. "Be a brave girl and let us hope for the best," he wrote to his wife. Yet he weakened and finally died on January 31, 1923, at 3 P.M. Marie had made the journey to Arizona and was with him when he died. At his request, he was buried at a simple gravesite on McDowell.[78]

In the final paragraph of the last article he wrote in *Wassaja*, Carlos Montezuma spoke about the battle that remained for the Society of American Indians. We may be sure that he was writing as well about his own remarkable struggle. The words serve as a proper epitaph for his life and his career:

. . . if the world be against us, let us not be dismayed, let us not be discouraged, let us look up and go ahead, and fight on for freedom and citizenship of our people. If it means death, let us die on the pathway that leads to the emancipation of our race; keeping in our hearts that our children will pass over our graves to victory.[79]

8

Epilogue: Carlos Montezuma and the Changing World of American Indians

"Dr. Montezuma Dies at Home of His Fathers At Fort Mc-Dowell" said the headline in the *Arizona Republican*.[1] And so he had. In coming home to die, the Yavapai physician made a statement about himself that remains vivid in the memory of Native American peoples in southern Arizona. His funeral symbolically again bridged the worlds in which he had lived. The Rev. W. B. Percival led services in the First Baptist Church in Phoenix, with the pallbearers being chosen from students at the Phoenix Indian School.[2] A second service took place at the Presbyterian Church at McDowell before burial on the reserve. As Anna Moore Shaw, a Pima, later recalled: "Carlos Montezuma spent most of his life in the white man's world, but his heart was always with his people. He came home to us in his dying days."[3]

In his tribute to Montezuma, Percival observed: "His life links together in a marvelous way the past and the present of our country."[4] Carlos Montezuma lived little more than half a century. During his lifetime, however, the world of American Indians had changed enormously. At the time of his birth, in the 1860s, whites had not yet populated all of the West, and Native Americans in many parts of the West had not been defeated by the Anglo-Americans. For many Indians, in the

175

Southwest and elsewhere, the reservation world loomed at most as a distant reality. With resistance, and with a minimal Anglo-American population, perhaps the old world could be maintained.

By the early 1870s, when the Pimas captured young Wassaja, the world of Native Americans had begun to change rapidly. In 1871 Congress decided that no additional treaties with Indian tribes would be signed. That decision formalized the change in Indian-white relations that had been evolving during the nineteenth century. For policymakers in Washington, Indians were still in the way, but they seemed generally less than equal powers. Five years later, the battle of the Little Big Horn shocked a country about to observe its centennial; Geronimo and other Native Americans continued to battle the Anglo-American encroachment into the 1880s. But the overwhelming tide of American migrants to the American West could not be denied.

In 1890 the tragedy of Wounded Knee coincided with the closing of the frontier. With the conclusion of warfare, a new era dawned. The reservation was seen as an environment in which Indians could be made over in the image of the dominant society. Missionaries, school teachers, and government agents all combined forces to attempt to transform tribal cultures. Popular wisdom held that Native Americans were a vanishing race. Indians did not speak the proper language, did not use their lands properly, and did not worship the proper God.

At the same time, with the passage of the Reclamation Act of 1902, the federal government made a new commitment to the arid West. Even desert lands, such as those of Arizona, took on new value. The potential of a region that knew no winter began to be tapped. The greater Phoenix area was one such place; its future was bright if a reliable water supply could be guaranteed.

By the turn of the century, Montezuma had completed medical school, finished his stint with the Bureau of Indian Affairs, and returned to Chicago to start his medical practice. His life mirrored his determination to demonstrate to the white world that Indians could achieve great things, if given the opportunity to do so. Even in Chicago, even as a successful physician, Montezuma remained an Indian. He began to speak and write about the contemporary status of Native Americans.

In common with other well-educated Indians, Montezuma realized that Native Americans were not vanishing, but changing. The world in which they found themselves demanded that they adapt—that they learn new skills and learn to understand Anglo-American society. Such an understanding did not demand a complete renunciation of the Indian heritage, nor a thoroughgoing conversion to the Anglo-American culture. Montezuma and other progressive Native Americans looked to a different future for Indians and wanted to work hard to improve the chances for each Indian to develop his or her potential skills and talents.

Between the 1880s and the 1920s, Native Americans lost millions of acres of land. Some of this decrease in Indian landholdings may be traced to the Dawes or General Allotment Act of 1887, which encouraged the division of the tribal estate into individual plots and the sale of surplus land to outsiders. The tremendous pressure on all land in the West for agricultural, industrial, and residential development meant additional reductions. The creation, let alone the maintenance, of a land base such as the Yavapais' Fort McDowell thus ran fully against the current of this period.

Montezuma obviously viewed an entity such as McDowell with considerably mixed feelings. His earlier experiences as a Bureau physician on several western reservations strongly influenced his perspective. He tended to see reservations as prisons, whose inhabitants had minimal rights. Montezuma's later involvement in Arizona, to be sure, confirmed his suspicions. Yet much as he hated the institution of a reservation, he wanted justice. He knew that non-Indians desired the Yavapais' land, and he did not believe they were entitled to it. If the reservation had not been so thoroughly dominated by Bureau personnel, and if Indians had not been so isolated and controlled on it, Montezuma would have had a different attitude. In other words, his conception in many ways presaged the less oppressive reservation world that exists today.

The Bureau of Indian Affairs would not be abolished, but it could change significantly. In Montezuma's last days, a movement began in the Southwest that would have a dramatic impact in Indian Affairs. John Collier and others led a reform movement that helped to usher in the end of the Americanization era. Collier became Commissioner of Indian Affairs in

1933 and during his tenure essentially halted the erosion of the Native American land base. In addition, a year after Montezuma's death, Congress passed legislation making all American Indians citizens of the United States. That act certainly expressed a goal very dear to Montezuma.

Carlos Montezuma cannot be seen as a typical Indian of his day. But as has been described, his activities involved him with the basic concerns shared by average, rural Native Americans of his time. Through his writings, his lobbying, his speeches, and his stubbornness, he increased the odds that their lands and their rights would not be further harmed. One must not see his relations with other Indians as thoroughly one-sided, for they gave him something as well. They helped him to achieve a fuller understanding of their world. In so doing, they changed his.

When one reviews the life and career of Carlos Montezuma, one is struck first by the man's personal qualities. He was an individual who clearly realized his own importance and his own place in history. Montezuma cannot be seen as a humble man. To the contrary, he was egotistical, and, like many egotists, he proved sensitive to the smallest slight and the tiniest wound. While his pride in his achievements was understandable, his quickness to be insulted and injured did not always serve him well. The form of Montezuma's tirades unfortunately often obscured and limited the vital points he was attempting to make.

Like many crusaders, Montezuma always seemed to be convinced that he was right. He appeared to many of his contemporaries, friend and foe, as one who would not budge from his opinions. Once he had decided that the Bureau of Indian Affairs should be abolished, that was it. While Montezuma occasionally showed a willingness to compromise, often he would not. Those who admired him but who did not necessarily agree with him, such as Arthur C. Parker, frequently bore the brunt of severe editorial retaliation, in the pages of *Wassaja*, the meetings of the Society of American Indians, and elsewhere. Had Montezuma been more willing to acknowledge the possibility, for example, that even a severe critic of the Bureau could justifiably be hesitant about its abolition, his campaign might have been more persuasive.

The kind of campaign Montezuma waged made him a target for criticism during his lifetime and a relatively easy mark for later critics. Because he did not offer a definite alternative to the Bureau of Indian Affairs, he could be labeled as irresponsible by those who feared that the demise of the Bureau would be worse than its continuation. In short, his criticism was not constructive. In fact, he was not the most pragmatic of men, and at times he seemed more interested in making an immediate point than in eventually winning a convert. While he was an important figure within the Society of American Indians, he could have been more influential with some of its members had he been willing to take a more moderate stance. Had he presented a less extreme message in *Wassaja*, the struggling publication might well have enjoyed a greater readership than the few thousand copies that circulated each month. If Montezuma had not been so unyielding in his lambasting of Bureau field personnel in southern Arizona, they might have felt less threatened and responded to him in a less vindictive manner.

Having noted the limitations of Montezuma's style, method, and substance, it is also useful to remember his influence within the Society, the impact of his journal, and the nature of Montezuma's opposition in the Southwest. Because he was willing to take a stand on the Bureau and because of his energy and conviction, Society members had to pay attention to him. If he had been less extreme in voicing his opinions, would he have achieved more results? Had *Wassaja* been more middle-of-the-road, would it have accomplished anything? If he had been more acceptable to the combined governmental and non-Indian interests in the vicinity of Fort McDowell, what would that have said about what he was espousing? The kind of reactions and responses that Montezuma inspired cannot simply be attributed to his style. The substance of his crusade is worth noting, and it is not surprising that Montezuma's critics were so vehement and vociferous. The Bureau of Indian Affairs merited censure during this era both for what it did and for what it did not do. Montezuma correctly attacked the ways in which the Bureau could be influenced by the politics and economy of non-Indian America. He properly noted the incompetence and insensitivity of many people who worked for the Bureau. He accurately observed the occasions when its personnel did not look after Indian well-being. Moreover, Montezuma had his allies and his sympathizers. He was not a completely isolated voice. Perhaps the most interesting of these cohorts were the traditionalists among the Yavapais and other southern Arizona tribes who turned to him in an era of desperate need. They were hardly the "bolsheviki element" portrayed by beleaguered Indian reservation superintendents, but rather people with limited experience in the world beyond their own community, who feared the intentions of those superintendents and who saw them quite perceptively as agents of forced acculturation and change. The allegiance of Yuma Frank and others to Montezuma represented as telling a tribute as the Yavapai physician could have wanted.

Today, Montezuma perhaps is best remembered by students of Native American history for his iconoclastic role within the Society of American Indians. He is recalled as a proud, contrary man who gave voice to his feelings through the Society and through the pages of his journal, *Wassaja*. That image of Montezuma is less incorrect than incomplete. Had he lived longer, and had he been involved with a larger community of Native Americans than he was in southern Arizona, the picture might be less fragmentary and more accurate.

The legacy of Montezuma is difficult to measure. He was a man of considerable stature and influence within his lifetime. During the first years after his death, his perspectives continued to affect the thinkings of many Indians, including some with whom he had not had much contact. Later was largely forgotten, except by the residents of Fort McDowell, where his memory remained the strongest. Today, partly because of the emergence of new collections of his papers, partly because of the growing interest in Indian life, Montezuma appears to be regaining much of his former prominence. His colorful, unusual life cannot help but attract some popular interest. An appreciation of his true importance is something that may come only when we move beyond the more sensational and extraordinary elements of his existence.

The Society of American Indians officially honored Montezuma after his death by a poem and a prose tribute, both written anonymously. The poem is not a literary masterpiece, but its feelings merit reprinting:

Montezuma!
Montezuma!
Spirit potent and immortal,
   From this land of crowding shadows.
We, as brothers, praise and bless you,
   As we trail through many sorrows.

We have called you Brave Was-sa-ja,
   Mighty signal—for the people.
As you stood a flashing beacon,
   Lifted from a lofty steeple.

Sad the days, O! Montezuma,
   Greatly do we mourn your passing
We shall miss your honest counsel,
   Magic voice with wisdom ringing.

Rest Was-sa-ja—"It is finished"
   Tribe to tribe shall tell your story.
Hoary braves to youth relate it,
   Mon-te-zu-ma's fame and glory![5]

"To An Indian Leader," published by the Society just a few days after Montezuma died, hails him as "one of its greatest leaders":

. . . Doctor Montezuma was one of the outstanding figures in the public life of this country, so far as Indians are concerned. He was present at the inception of this Society, and ever afterward took a keen interest in the complicated affairs of the Society. There probably has never lived a full-blood Indian who so effectively demonstrated the capabilities of the Indian race to high culture, and a life of real usefulness than Doctor Montezuma. With a most remarkable personal history that reads more like fiction, than actual occurrence, his life was one of unique success. He became a most competent physician and successfully practiced in the midst of fiercest competition in Chicago, winning for himself fame and distinction.

There probably never has been an Indian that burned with patriotism, with greater ardor than Doctor Montezuma. Like many great historical figures, he was often misunderstood, and sometimes almost persecuted, because of honest political and economic opinions. All were not expected to be in accord, it is true. With the Doctor's conclusions, nevertheless, none can be found who doubt the utmost sincerity of the great and good man now in eternity. Doctor Montezuma was a great and good man, an intense patriot, a lover of freedom, a hater of deceit and hypocrisy, and a natural-born orator. His voice was ever raised in defense of oppressed peoples of any race or color.

Many think of Doctor Montezuma as a ruthless opponent, but a kinder man never lived. He loved the little ones, and nothing so pleased him, than a romp with children.

The Society of American Indians has lost one of its greatest leaders, and the Indian race, its greatest lover and greatest benefactor.[6]

This passage has been quoted extensively because it speaks strikingly to the esteem that Montezuma had earned, despite his firm convictions and outspoken manner. Here one sees the sources of his influence: achievement, demonstration of Indian capability, oratorical skills, dedication to freedom, and loyalty to Indian people. To describe Montezuma as a great lover and benefactor of Native Americans is far more accurate than to term him a "white man's Indian."

In *Cycles of Conquest*, anthropologist Edward H. Spicer noted the influence wielded by Montezuma not only during his lifetime but also after his death. Spicer observed that Montezuma's "appeal had been based chiefly on the dignity and worth of the Indian racial and cultural heritage." His ideas cannot be considered unique, but Montezuma had a unique influence because he personally dealt with Native Americans and because he had accepted the white man's way but had returned "to the clear view of the worth of the Indian way." Some of the older Pimas continued to be known as "Montezumas" for their traditional views and their hostility toward the local superintendent. Moreover, on the Papago reservation, Montezuma's ideas affected the League of Papago Chiefs, whose leaders in the 1930s also acted in the manner of their Pima counterparts. Some of these headmen even believed for a time that Montezuma had some supernatural quality; he "would one day return and restore better times and good moral behavior." Apaches on the San Carlos reservation also drew inspiration from his life and career.[7]

Montezuma's influence, however, was not limited to the Southwest nor to his own time. Following Montezuma's death, his attorney, Joseph Latimer, continued to publish a newsletter, *Bureaucracy a la Mode*, in which he expressed opposition to the Bureau. Among the backers for Latimer's unsuccessful attempt to gain the commissionership of the Bureau was Seneca political activist Alice Lee Jemison. Laurence Hauptman recently noted the impact of Montezuma's ideas on Jemison and others of her generation; reform of the Bureau could only strengthen rather than reduce its control over the lives of Native Americans. She and other Indians active in the American Indian Federation quoted Montezuma in their assaults on the Bureau. Thomas L. Sloan also played an important role in the federation, and he, of course, had had direct association with Montezuma. The American Indian Federation proved a curious entity, with its ties to far-right critics of the New Deal. However, as Hauptman and other contemporary historians have observed, such members as Jemison were nonetheless important for their understanding of Indian diversity and their comprehension of Commissioner John Collier's limited experience with Indians outside New Mexico.[9]

When Indian editors Rupert Costo and Jeannette Henry decided to publish a national Native American newspaper in the early 1970s, they turned to Montezuma's *Wassaja* as a name for their journal and as a model. "Let My People Know" replaced "Let My People Go" on the new *Wassaja*'s masthead. Costo and Henry admired the combative Yavapai who showed the world "that Indians can become doctors, engineers, scholars, and who demanded self-determination for the Native Americans." Their newspaper became an important source for news about Indian America and a forum for Native American viewpoints.[9]

Within the Yavapai community at Fort McDowell, not only do people remember Montezuma, but his forthright defense of their land continues to be an inspiration. In *The Yavapai of Fort McDowell*, a seventy-page publication recently compiled by anthropologist Sigrid Khera, Montezuma emerges as a major figure. Khera concludes, for example, "Thanks to their courage and persistence and thanks to the help of Dr. Montezuma and other friends the Yavapai have held their reservation, the last portion of their ancestral land to today."[10]

Interviews on the reserve confirm the legacy of Montezuma. Tom Surrama's son, John Williams, said, "He said don't move out, so that's why we didn't move out." Mike Burns's son-in-law, John Smith, knew Montezuma during the physician's last years, when Smith was a teen-ager. Montezuma would come down on vacation, he recalled, and liked to dress "sloppy" and go hunting. He would enjoy talking about a lot of things. Montezuma would go to Smith and say, "Hey, boy, come on, let's take a walk." So they would walk for a mile or so, get up on a ridge and look down at McDowell and out at Four Peaks. "Sometimes he would take a rock and pound on another rock. 'Boy, you tear down these reservation fences and get out into the world.' He'd talk like he's talking to 1,000 people, but I'm the only one there."[11]

Smith noted that Dr. Stroud had asked him to go to a sanitarium where he might be cured, but Montezuma said: "No, I want to die like my ancestors died." "I used to take care of his fire and bring him water," Smith remembered. "He'd say, 'I'm cold! I'm going to die of cold in here!' " The funeral was well attended. "People were pretty well attached to him. Everybody I knew liked him well. He seemed to love it here. That's why he came back here to die."[12]

The Yavapai people still live on McDowell. Today they face yet another challenge to their right to reside on their homeland. The gigantic Central Arizona Project includes the proposed Orme Dam, which, if completed, will flood the reservation. Since 1972, when they learned of the plans to inundate their land, most Yavapais, along with active allies such as Carolina Butler of Paradise Valley, have battled against the idea. John Williams, Minnie Williams, Pamela Mott, Ralph Bear, Andrew Johnson, Emma Johnson, Mr. and Mrs. Tom Mike, Mike Harrison, Virginia Mott, Hiawatha Hood, Dixie Lee Davis, Lola Dickson, and others wrote letters, circulated petitions, and generally organized opposition to Orme Dam. In 1976, the people voted 144 to 57 against the sale of their land, despite the sizable financial gain they stood to realize from such a transaction.[13] Despite this firm position, the Yavapais may still be separated from McDowell. Interests not unlike those against which Montezuma contended earlier in the century favor the dam. Flooding problems in the Phoenix area in the late 1970s heightened pressures on the federal government to proceed with the project.

As of this writing, although the future of the Yavapais at McDowell remains very much in doubt, one believes that they will somehow triumph. Dixie Lee Davis, John Williams, and others have cited Montezuma as a significant influence in their ongoing campaign to save their home. "I don't want to see the land where Montezuma is buried covered by water," said John Williams, echoing the sentiments of many of his people.[14] Such a tribute undoubtedly would please the man who fought so vigorously for the future of his people.

Carlos Montezuma looked to a changing world in which Native Americans would adapt, survive, and flourish. The combativeness and determination which have characterized the Yavapais and other Indian peoples represent a continuing legacy of Wassaja, who knew Indians would endure. As he once wrote:

> Who says the Indian race is vanishing?
> The Indians will not vanish.
> The feathers, paint and moccasin will vanish, but
>   the Indians,—never!
> Just as long as there is a drop of human blood in
>   America, the Indians will not vanish.
> His spirit is everywhere; the American Indian will not vanish.
> He has changed externally but he is not vanished.
> He is an industrial and commercial man, competing
>   with the world; he has not vanished.
> Whenever you see an Indian upholding the standard of
>   his race, there you see the Indian man—he has not vanished.
> The man part of the Indian is here, there and everywhere.
> The Indian race vanishing? No, never! The race will
>   live on and prosper forever.[15]

Notes

CHAPTER ONE

1. These generalizations are based on E. W. Gifford, "The Southeastern Yavapai" and "Northeastern and Western Yavapai." See also Albert H. Schroeder, "A Study of Yavapai History."

2. Gifford, "Northeastern and Western Yavapai," pp. 247–55, 303–5, 321–23; Schroeder, "Yavapai History," pp. 256–63. Sigrid Khera, in *The Yavapai of Fort McDowell*, a seventy-page outline of Yavapai history and culture published by the Fort McDowell Mohave–Apache Community in 1979, says bluntly, "Calling the Yavapai 'Apache' was a very convenient excuse for the English speaking Americans to kill the Yavapai and take over their land" (p. 2).

3. Edward H. Spicer, *Cycles of Conquest: The Impact of Spain, Mexico, and the United States on the Indians of the Southwest, 1533–1960*. See, for example, pp. 245–52, 267–72.

4. Ibid., p. 148. The date of this attack is sometimes given as 1872, but given the date of Montezuma's baptism, it must have occurred during the previous year. The site of the attack generally is set at Iron Top Mountain. Anna Moore Shaw, a Pima, in her book, *A Pima Past*, describes it as "a place called Black Mesa under the shadow of Four Peaks" (p. 238).

5. Shaw, *A Pima Past*, p. 239.

6. George Webb, *A Pima Remembers*, p. 31; for details about Montezuma's family, see the testimony acquired by Agent Charles Davis in his investigation in 1922, conducted in connection with the

187

application by Montezuma for enrollment at the San Carlos reservation. National Archives and Records Services Record Group 75, Bureau of Indian Affairs, San Carlos Central Classified Files, 1907–39, 45642-20-053 (hereafter NARS, RG 75, BIA).

7. A copy of the baptismal certificate is in the collection of the Arizona Historical Society. Among the sources for this paragraph is a letter from G. M. Ingalls to the president of the Y.M.C.A. for the Illinois Industrial University, October 16, 1878, Montezuma biographical file, Chicago Historical Society. Ingalls was the Baptist representative who entrusted the care of Montezuma to W. H. Steadman.

8. Testimony of Carlos Montezuma, Hearings before the Committee on Expenditures in the Interior Department of the House of Representatives on House Resolution No. 103 To Investigate the Expenditures in the Interior Department, June 16, 1911, pp. 351–53; Ingalls to Y.M.C.A. president, October 16, 1878; "To the Students of Carlisle Indian School" (n.d., ca. 1888), Papers of Carlos Montezuma, Arizona State University Library.

9. Ingalls to Y.M.C.A. president, October 16, 1878.

10. The thesis and the newspaper account are both in the University of Illinois Library.

11. Montezuma testimony, 1911, pp. 356–57.

12. This paragraph is based upon two Ph.D. dissertations, Everett Gilcreast, "Richard Henry Pratt and American Indian Policy, 1877-1906: A Study of the Assimilation Movement" (Yale, 1967), and Carmelita Ryan, "Carlisle Indian Industrial School" (Georgetown, 1962), as well as Robert H. Utley's edited version of Pratt's memoirs, *Battlefield and Classroom.*

13. Richard H. Pratt to Carlos Montezuma, January 21, 1887. Richard H. Pratt Papers, Beinecke Library, Yale University.

14. Pratt to Montezuma, August 20, 1887, Pratt Papers; Montezuma to the Secretary of the Interior, June 14, 1887, National Archives, RG 75, BIA, Letters Received, 1881–1907, no. 15604-1887; J. D. C. Atkins to Montezuma, June 28, 1887, NARS, RG 75, BIA, Letters Sent, 1870-1908, volume 81 (lands), 400; Montezuma to Atkins, July 22, 1887, NARS, RG 75 BIA, LR, 1881-1907, no. 19288-1887.

15. Pratt to Montezuma, February 25, 1888; Pratt to Montezuma, March 8, 1888; Pratt to Montezuma, March 21, 1888; Montezuma to Pratt, March 26, 1888; Montezuma to Pratt, March 26, 1888; all in Pratt Papers.

16. Pratt to Montezuma, March 28, 1888, ibid.

17. Montezuma to Pratt, August 14, 1888; Montezuma to Pratt, February 19, 1889; ibid.

18. Montezuma testimony, Hearings on Expenditures, 1911, p. 357; Thomas J. Morgan to Montezuma, August 3, 1889, NARS, RG 75, BIA; LS, 1870–1908, vol. 103 (accounts), 356-366.

19. Montezuma to Morgan, August 12, 1889, NARS, RG 75, BIA; LR, 1881-1907, no. 22772-1889.

20. Ibid.

21. Francis Paul Prucha, "Thomas Jefferson Morgan," in Robert H. Kvasnicka and Herman J. Viola, eds., *The Commissioners of Indian Affairs, 1824-1977*, p. 193.

22. Montezuma testimony, Hearings on Expenditures, 1911, p. 358; Montezuma to Morgan, September 6, 1889, NARS, RG 75, BIA; LR, 1881–1907, no. 25499-1889.

23. Montezuma, "The Indian of Yesterday", June 18, 1888, Carlos Montezuma Papers, Wisconsin State Historical Society, Box 5.

CHAPTER TWO

1. Carlos Montezuma to George W. Ingalls (?), ca. 1896–1901. Ruth Underhill Papers, University of Oregon.

2. Richard H. Pratt to Montezuma, October 29, 1889. Richard H. Pratt Papers, Beinecke Library, Yale University.

3. Montezuma to Mrs. A. S. Quinton, November 14, 1889. *The Indian's Friend* (monthly publication of The Women's National Indian Association), January 1890, vol. 2, no. 5.

4. Ibid.

5. Address to the Students of Fort Stevenson School, n.d. Carlos Montezuma Papers, Arizona State University, Box 6, File Folder 2.

6. Ibid.

7. Montezuma to Thomas J. Morgan, May 14, 1890; National Archives and Records Services (NARS), Record Group (RG) 75, Bureau of Indian Affairs (BIA), Letters Received (LR), 1881–1907; 20376-1890.

8. Morgan to Montezuma, June 17, 1890; NARS, RG 75, BIA, Letters Sent (LS), 1870–1908; vol. 24 (education), 303; Montezuma to Morgan, June 27, 1890; NARS, RG 75, BIA, LR, 1881–1907; 20376-1890.

9. Montezuma to Morgan, June 27, 1890, ibid.

10. Morgan to Montezuma, July 1, 1890, NARS, RG 75, BIA, LS, 1870–1908; vol. 112 (accounts), 338; Montezuma to Morgan, July 30, 1890, NARS, RG 75, BIA, LR, 1881–1907; Montezuma to Pratt, July 20, 1892, Pratt Papers.

11. Montezuma to William J. Plumb (Indian Agent, Western Shoshone), July 30, 1890, NARS, RG 75, BIA, LR, 25715-1890; Montezuma to Plumb, November 28, 1890, ibid., 37768-1890; Montezuma to Plumb, June 20, 1891, ibid., 22864-1891; Montezuma to Plumb, September 8, 1891, ibid., 34219-1891; Montezuma to Plumb, October 6, 1891, ibid., 37073-1891.

12. Montezuma to Plumb, March 3, 1891, NARS, RG 75, BIA, LR, 13647-1891.

13. Morgan to H. L. Dawes, April 23, 1892, NARS, RG 75, BIA, LS, 1890–1892, 440.

14. See, for example, Thomas J. Morgan, "Supplemental Report on Indian Education," submitted to the secretary of the interior on December 1, 1889, reprinted in Francis Paul Prucha, ed., *American-*

*izing the American Indian: Writings of "Friends of the Indians,"
1880–1900*, pp. 221–38. The quotation is on page 228. Perspectives
on Pratt and Carlisle may be found in two Ph.D. dissertations: Carmelita Ryan, "Carlisle Indian Industrial School" (Georgetown, 1962)
and Everett Arthur Gilcreast, "Richard Henry Pratt and American
Indian Policy, 1877–1906: A Study of the Assimilation Movement"
(Yale, 1967). For Pratt's early educational career, see the dissertation
of Pamela Oestreicher, being completed in anthropology at Michigan
State University.

15. Montezuma to Horatio N. Rust, U.S. Indian Agent, Colton,
California, September 5, 1892, Huntington Library; John Fosher to
Montezuma, September 26, 1892, Carlos Montezuma Papers, Wis-
consin State Historical Society, Box 1; Indian Agent at Sac and Fox–
Shawnee Agency, Misc. Correspondence, Letters Sent, August 31,
1892–June 27, 1893, vol. 8, p. 29, microfilm.

16. Montezuma to Pratt, March 15, 1892, Pratt Papers.

17. Ibid.

18. Ibid. See also Richard H. Pratt, "The Advantage of Mingling
Indians with Whites," in Prucha, *Americanizing the American Indian*, pp. 260–71, which comprises remarks given in this year at a
conference in Denver. An excellent summary on Morgan and the
Church controversy may be found in the second chapter, "Commissioner Morgan and Father Stephan," of Prucha, *The Churches and
the Indian Schools, 1888-1912*, pp. 10-25.

19. Montezuma to Major Hal J. Cole, January 27, 1893, NARS, RG
75, BIA, LR, 1881–1907, 6892-1893; Morgan to Montezuma, November 19, 1892, ibid., LS, 1870–1908, vol. 135 (accounts), 217; Montezuma, telegram to Commissioner, December 2, 1892; ibid., LR, 1881–
1907, 42972-1892. Morgan to Montezuma, LS, 1870–1908, vol. 136
(accounts), 66.

20. Montezuma to Cole, January 27, 1893, ibid., LR, 1881–1907,
6892-1893; Montezuma to Morgan, January 27, 1893, ibid., 5872-1893.

21. Prucha, *The Churches and the Indian Schools*, pp. 27-28; R.
V. Belt to Montezuma, February 24, 1893, NARS, RG 75, BIA, LS, 1870–
1908, vol. 137 (accounts), 386; Montezuma to Cole, February 1, 1893,
Federal Archives and Records Center, Seattle, RG 75, Colville, Miscellaneous Letters Received, 1879–1904, Box 31.

22. Montezuma to Cole, June 15, 1893; NARS, RG 75, BIA, LS, 1870–
1908, 24037-1893.

23. Montezuma to Pratt, April 18, 1893, Pratt Papers.

24. Ibid.

25. Montezuma to Cole, July 3, 1893, FARC, Seattle, RG 75, BIA,
Colville Miscellaneous Letters Received, 1879–1904, Box 31; Mon-
tezuma to Commissioner of Indian Affairs, November 18, 1893, NARS,
RG 75, BIA, LR, 1881–1907, 43306-1893; Montezuma to Y.P.S.C.E. and
E.W.M.B., n.d. (from Nespilem, ca. 1893), Montezuma File, Univer-
sity of Arizona, Box 1, Folder 7.

26. Montezuma to Pratt, with covering remarks by Pratt forwarded

to Commissioner of Indian Affairs, November 22, 1895, NARS, RG 75, BIA, LR, 1881–1907, 47781-1895.

27. This paragraph is based primarily on Gilcreast, "Richard Henry Pratt," passim.

28. Ibid., pp. 303–5; Montezuma to Pratt, December 23, 1896, Pratt Papers.

29. F. S. Livingstone, "The New American" (n.d.), pp. 664–65, Papers of Carlos Montezuma, Arizona State University.

30. Ibid., pp. 664.

31. Montezuma, remarks recorded in *Proceedings of the Eleventh Annual Meeting of the Lake Mohonk Conference of Friends of the Indian* (1893), pp. 90-91; Herbert Welsh to Montezuma, January 27, 1894, Historical Society of Pennsylvania, Indian Rights Association, Series 1-C, Letterbook 10, p. 616, Reel 72.

32. Montezuma, remarks recorded in *Proceedings of the Thirteenth Annual Meeting of the Lake Mohonk Conference* (1895), p. 68; Montezuma to Rep. Charles Carter, December 14, 1912, Montezuma Papers, Wisconsin State Historical Society, Box 2.

CHAPTER THREE

1. Carlos Montezuma, testimony in Hearings before the Committee on Expenditures in the Interior Department of the House of Representatives, pp. 360–62 (Washington: Government Printing Office, 1911).

2. Montezuma's addresses are shown in his stationery. He apparently changed his office in the Chicago Loop in 1905.

3. Montezuma, testimony in Hearings before the Committee on Expenditures, 1911, p. 363.

4. Interview with Elsie Elliott Severance, February 26, 1976. Interview conducted by Charles C. Colley, Archivist and Field Collector, Hayden Library, Arizona State University. For Montezuma's financial woes, see his financial records, Carlos Montezuma Papers, Wisconsin State Historical Society, hereafter WSHS.

5. Zitkala-sa, *American Indian Stories*, Publisher's preface, and pp. 36–67.

6. Ibid., Publisher's preface, and pp. 69–81.

7. F. A. Livingston, *The New American* (n.d.); Carlisle records, National Archives.

8. See the letters from Zitkala-sa to Carlos Montezuma, Papers of Carlos Montezuma, WSHS, Box 1.

9. Ibid.

10. Ibid.

11. Ibid.

12. Ibid.; Jessie W. Cook to Carlos Montezuma, June 11, 1903, Papers of Carlos Montezuma, WSHS, Box 1.

13. Zitkala-sa to Montezuma, ibid.

14. Ibid.

15. Carlos Montezuma, "The Indian Problem From An Indian's Standpoint," ibid., Box 5.

16. Ibid.; Carlos Montezuma, "How America Has Betrayed the Indian," Chicago *Tribune*, part 3, editorial section, October 4, 1903.

17. Montezuma, "How America Has Betrayed the Indian."

18. Montezuma, letters to parents of Lillian, n.d., ca. 1904, Papers of Carlos Montezuma, Arizona State University.

19. Montezuma to Richard H. Pratt, October 16, 1899; January 17, 1900; July 1, 1901; September 23, 1901; October 12, 1901; August 2, 1904; all in Richard H. Pratt Papers, Beinecke Library, Yale University.

20. Montezuma to Pratt, November 3, 1904, Carlos Montezuma file, University of Arizona, Box 1, Folder 6.

21. Montezuma to Pratt, January 17, 1900, Pratt Papers.

22. *Arizona Republican* (Phoenix), January 2, 1900.

23. Montezuma to Pratt, October 1, 1901, Pratt Papers.

24. Report from Globe *Silver Belt* in *Arizona Republican*, October 11, 1901; Montezuma to Pratt, October 10, 1901, Pratt Papers.

25. Montezuma to Professor James H. McClintock, June 20, 1906, Papers of Carlos Montezuma, WSHS, unprocessed.

26. Montezuma to Mike Burns, March 28, 1901 and May 2, 1901, ibid., Box 1; Charles Dickens to Montezuma, November 2, 1901, Papers of Carlos Montezuma, Arizona State University, Box 3, Folder 1.

27. *Annual Report of the Department of Interior*, Report of the Commissioner of Indian Affairs, 1905, "Camp McDowell," p. 98.

28. Ibid., p. 98–99.

29. Ibid., p. 100.

30. Ibid., p. 101.

31. Ibid., pp. 101–2.

32. "Purchase of Rights of Settlers on Camp McDowell Reservation, Arizona," U.S. Congress, Senate Committee on Indian Affairs, 58th Congress, 2nd session, Document No. 90, January 15, 1904. See also Record Group 75, Special Series A, Box 10, which deals with settlement claims and issues of fraudulent entry at McDowell.

33. W. H. Gill to Montezuma, October 26, 1903, Papers of Carlos Montezuma, WSHS, Box 1.

34. *Arizona Republican*, July 28, 1903; Gill to Montezuma, October 26, 1903, Papers of Carlos Montezuma, WSHS, Box 1.

CHAPTER FOUR

1. Hazel W. Hertzberg, *The Search for an American Indian Identity: Modern Pan-Indian Movements*, p. 44.

2. Ibid., pp. 38-53.

3. Ibid., p. 32.

4. Donald L. Parman, "Francis Ellington Leupp," in Robert H.

Kvasnicka and Herman J. Viola, eds., *The Commissioners of Indian Affairs, 1824-1977*, pp. 221-24.

5. Carlos Montezuma, A Review of Commissioner Leupp's Interview in the New York *Daily Tribune,* Sunday, April 9, 1905, "On the Future of Our Indians." Papers of Carlos Montezuma, Wisconsin State Historical Society (hereafter WSHS), Box 5.

6. Ibid.

7. Montezuma to Editor of Kansas City *Times,* ca. March 7, 1905 and Montezuma, "The Future of the Indian," Kansas City *Times,* March 7, 1905, p. 12, University of Kansas Library; Montezuma to Editor, Boston *Herald,* February 5, 1907; Montezuma, "Carlisle Indian School Drifting From Its Moorings," Philadelphia *Public Ledger,* July 22, 1907; Montezuma to William Howard Taft, December 24, 1908, Library of Congress, Manuscripts, William Howard Taft Papers, Series 3; Montezuma to Ernest Robetail, May 29, 1909, Papers of Carlos Montezuma, WSHS, Box 2.

8. Pratt to Montezuma, July 8, 1909; Fayette McKenzie to Montezuma, September 2, 1909; McKenzie to Montezuma, September 14, 1909; all in Papers of Carlos Montezuma, WSHS, Box 2; McKenzie to Montezuma, September 20, 1909, Carlos Montezuma file, University of Arizona Library, Box 2, Folder 1.

9. McKenzie to Montezuma, October 11, 1909; McKenzie to Montezuma, November 1, 1909; ibid.

10. McKenzie to Montezuma, November 14, 1909, ibid; McKenzie to Montezuma, November 29, 1909, Carlos Montezuma file, University of Arizona Library, Box 2, Folder 1.

11. McKenzie to Montezuma, May 31, 1910; McKenzie to Montezuma, October 18, 1910; McKenzie to Montezuma, November 16, 1910; all ibid. Copy of McKenzie to Daganett, June 6, 1910, in Papers of Carlos Montezuma, WSHS, Box 2.

12. McKenzie to Montezuma, November 16, 1910; Copy of Daganett to McKenzie, January 9, 1911; both in Carlos Montezuma file, University of Arizona Library, Box 2, Folder 1.

13. McKenzie to Montezuma, January 23, 1911; Daganett to Montezuma, May 17, 1911; both ibid., Box 2, Folders 1-2. See also Hertzberg, *Search for an American Indian Identity,* p. 36.

14. August Breuninger to Montezuma, March 2, 1911, Papers of Carlos Montezuma, WSHS, Box 2.

15. Pratt to Thomas Sloan, Henry Standing Bear, Charles Eastman, Laura Cornelius, Carlos Montezuma, and Charles Daganett, April 13, 1911, Papers of Carlos Montezuma, WSHS, Box 2.

16. Pratt to Montezuma, April 14, 1911, ibid.

17. Daganett to Members of the Temporary Executive Committee, The American Indian Association, April 26, 1911; Pratt to Sloan, April 27, 1911; McKenzie to Montezuma, April 28, 1911; all ibid.

18. McKenzie to Montezuma, May 9, 1911; McKenzie to Montezuma, May 13, 1911, ibid.; Pratt to Montezuma, May 17, 1911, Carlos Montezuma file, University of Arizona Library, Box 1, Folder 1.

19. Daganett to Montezuma, April 26, 1911, Papers of Carlos Montezuma, WSHS, Box 2; Rosa B. LaFlesche to Montezuma, June 29, 1911, Carlos Montezuma file, University of Arizona Library, Box 2, Folder 2.

20. McKenzie to Montezuma, July 11, 1911, ibid., Box 2, Folder 1.

21. Russell White Bear to Montezuma, July 12, 1911; Breuninger to Montezuma, July 21, 1911; Breuninger to Montezuma, July 26, 1911; White Bear to Montezuma, July 28, 1911; Breuninger to Montezuma, August 7, 1911; Papers of Carlos Montezuma, WSHS, Box 2.

22. Pratt to Montezuma, July 4, 1911, ibid.

23. Pratt to Montezuma, August 16, 1911, Carlos Montezuma file, University of Arizona Library, Box 1, Folder 1.

24. LaFlesche to Montezuma, August 12, 1911; Breuninger to Montezuma, September 8, 1911; Daganett to Montezuma, September 13, 1911; Daganett to Montezuma, September 19, 1911; Henry Roe Cloud to Montezuma, October 8, 1911; all in Papers of Carlos Montezuma, WSHS, Box 2; Charles D. Carter to Montezuma, October 2, 1911, Carlos Montezuma file, University of Arizona Library, Box 1, Folder 1; Thomas Sloan, Charles Eastman, Laura Cornelius, Daganett, Henry Standing Bear to Montezuma (telegram), October 11, 1911, Leon Summit collection of Montezuma material, microfilm reel 2.

25. Montezuma to "Dear Sir," September 29, 1911, Papers of Carlos Montezuma, WSHS, Box 2; Montezuma to Daganett, September 25, 1911, Arthur C. Parker Papers, State Museum of New York.

26. Ibid.

27. See Pat Mariella, "Yavapai Farming," in Sigrid Khera, ed., *The Yavapai of Fort McDowell: Outline of Their History and Culture,* pp. 28-31.

28. Ibid.; William R. Coffeen, "The Effects of the Central Arizona Project on the Fort McDowell Indian Community," *Ethnohistory* 19, no. 4 (Fall 1972): 349-51.

29. "Irrigation," in Commissioner of Indian Affairs (Francis Leupp), Annual Report, Annual Report of the Department of the Interior (Washington, D.C., 1906), pp. 82–83.

30. Ibid., p. 83.

31. Ibid.

32. Ibid.

33. Michael Massie, "The Cultural Roots of the Winters Doctrine and Indian Water Rights" (M.A. paper, University of Wyoming, 1980).

34. Ibid.; Norris Hundley, Jr., "The Dark and Bloody Ground of Indian Water Rights: Confusion Elevated to Principle," *Western Historical Quarterly* 9, no. 4 (October 1978): 460–73.

35. Terrence J. Lamb, "Indian-Government Relations on Water Utilization in the Salt and Gila River Valleys of Southern Arizona, 1902–1914," *The Indian Historian* 10, no. 3 (Summer 1977): 39.

36. William H. Code to the secretary of the interior, April 20, 1906. National Archives and Record Services (hereafter NARS), Department of the Interior, Letters Received.

37. Richard Frost, "Fragments of Pueblo History: From BIA Personnel in New Mexico 1890–1930s," paper presented at the annual meeting of the American Society for Ethnohistory, Albuquerque, N.M., October 1976.

38. W. H. Code to secretary of the interior, July 28, 1909; NARS, Record Group (RG) 75, Bureau of Indian Affairs (BIA), Central Classified Files 1907–39, Salt River, 30858-3-10-133. See also Terrence J. Lamb, "Early Twentieth Century Efforts at Economic Development in Nigeria and Arizona" (Ph.D. diss., Temple University, 1978). Some of the same letters to be found in the National Archives, including the above letter by Code, are cited by Lamb in his study. (I thank Terry Lamb for his assistance and encouragement, given at the Organization of American Historians meeting in New York in 1978, when I gave a paper on Montezuma, and in 1980 at the National Archives, when I was completing the research for this book.)

39. See Lamb, "Early Twentieth Century Efforts," pp. 92–175. The preceding three paragraphs are based in part on pp. 122–29.

40. Code to the secretary of the interior, July 28, 1909, NARS, RG 75, BIA, Central Classified Files 1907–39, Salt River, 30858-3-10-133.

41. Ibid.

42. Report of Joe H. Norris, Inspector, Department of the Interior, "General Inspection and Investigation of Conditions at the Camp McDowell Agency and Day School, Arizona, April 9, 1910," NARS, RG 75, BIA, Central Classified Files 1907–39, Salt River, 30858-3-10-133; J. B. Alexander to Commissioner of Indian Affairs, December 9, 1909, ibid.

43. Third Judicial District of the Territory of Arizona, Decision and Decree, *Hurley* v. *Abbott*, Chief Justice Edward Kent, March 1, 1910, p. 19. Copy printed by the Salt River Water Users Association. NARS, Irrigation Service, Arizona Salt River–Verde Correspondence and Reports, 1914–1942.

44. Ibid., pp. 19–20.

45. Norris report, April 9, 1910, NARS, RG 75, BIA, Central Classified Files 1907–39, Salt River, 30858-3-10-133, National Archives.

46. Petition from Fort McDowell Yavapais to Commissioner of Indian Affairs, May 7, 1910, ibid.

47. Charles E. Coe to Commissioner of Indian Affairs, May 7, 1910, ibid.

48. Coe to Commissioner of Indian Affairs, November 22, 1910; Coe to Commissioner of Indian Affairs, December 17, 1910; ibid., 92542-10-313, National Archives.

49. See, for example, Montezuma to Hiram Price, c/o Charles Dickens, July 18, 1910, Carlos Montezuma file, University of Arizona Library, Box 1, Folder 7; Charles Dickens to Montezuma, May 5, 1911, NARS, RG 75, BIA, Central Classified Files, 1907–39, Camp McDowell (Salt River), 30858-3-1910-133.

50. R. G. Valentine to all superintendents and agents, circular no.

497, December 23, 1910; NARS, RG 75, BIA, Central Classified Files 1907–39, Pima, 63455-121174.1.

51. R. A. Ballinger to Montezuma, January 27, 1911; NARS, RG 75, BIA, Central Classified Files 1907–39, Camp McDowell (Salt River), 30858-3-1910-133.

52. Montezuma to Ballinger, January 30, 1911, ibid.

53. Carl Gunderson to Commissioner on Indian Affairs, February 10, 1911; ibid., 92542-10-313.

54. Coe to Commissioner of Indian Affairs, February 16, 1911, ibid.

55. Montezuma to Hon. John Stephens, March 4, 1911, Papers of Carlos Montezuma, Arizona State University, Box 5, Folder 2.

56. R. G. Valentine to Montezuma, March 11, 1911; NARS, RG 75, BIA, Central Classified Files 1907–39, Camp McDowell (Salt River), 30858-3-1910-133.

57. Montezuma to Valentine, March 31, 1911, ibid.

58. Coe to Commissioner of Indian Affairs, May 9, 1911; Assistant Commissioner Hauke to Coe, June 2, 1911, 44049-11-056.

59. See Minutes Committee on Expenditures in the Interior Department, 1st session, National Archives. See also "Hearings Before the Committee on Expenditures in the Interior Department of the House of Representatives on House Resolution No. 103 to Investigate the Expenditures in the Interior Department," Washington: Government Printing Office, 1911. Leupp's interrogation by Latimer took place on June 8, 1911, and may be found on pp. 85–102.

60. See the testimony of Montezuma in the "Hearings," ibid. Montezuma testified on June 16, 1911. For Graham's remarks, see James Graham to Commissioner of Indian Affairs Cato Sells, May 21, 1914, NARS, RG 75, BIA, Central Classified Files 1907–39, Salt River, 1387-11-313. Other material relating to the Yavapai situation at this time may be found in "Memorial and Papers from the Mojave-Apache Indians of McDowell Reservation, Arizona, in Relation to Their Removal from McDowell Reservation to the Salt River Reservation, Arizona," 62nd Congress, 1st Session, House of Representatives, Committee on Indian Affairs, Washington, 1911. The "Memorial" includes some of the correspondence cited in this chapter. A copy of the "Memorial" is in Papers of Carlos Montezuma, Arizona State University Library, Box 12, Folder 1.

CHAPTER FIVE

1. Charles Eastman to Carlos Montezuma, ca. January 27, 1911; Papers of Carlos Montezuma, Wisconsin State Historical Society (hereafter WSHS), Box 2; Eastman, *The Indian To-day: The Past and Future of the First American*, pp. 121-22.

2. Arthur C. Parker to Montezuma, March 4, 1912, Papers of Carlos Montezuma, WSHS, Box 2.

3. Parker to Montezuma, March 28, 1912, ibid.
4. Fayette McKenzie to Montezuma, August 17, 1912; Parker to Montezuma, August 19, 1912; Carlos Montezuma file, University of Arizona Library, Box 2, folder 1; Parker to Montezuma, August 27, 1912; Papers of Carlos Montezuma, WSHS, Box 2.
5. McKenzie to Montezuma, August 30, 1912; Henry Standing Bear to Montezuma, September 4, 1912; Papers of Carlos Montezuma, WSHS, Box 2.
6. For a review of the 1912 conference, see Hazel Hertzberg, *The Search for an American Indian Identity: Modern Pan-Indian Movements*, pp. 84–101. See also Carlos Montezuma, "Light on the Indian Situation" (address to the second conference), *Quarterly Journal of the Society of American Indians* 1, no. 1 (January–April 1913): 50–55. The proceedings of the conference may be found in vol. 1, no. 2 (April–June 1913). Both issues are in the Newberry Library, Chicago, Ill. McKenzie to Montezuma, October 13, 1912, Montezuma file, University of Arizona Library, Box 2, folder 1.
7. August Breuninger to Montezuma, December 17, 1912; Papers of Carlos Montezuma, WSHS, Box 2.
8. Parker to Montezuma, February 19, 1913; ibid.
9. Pratt to Montezuma, March 24, 1913; Sherman Coolidge to Montezuma, April 20, 1913, *The Tomahawk*, April 10, 1913, ibid.
10. Pratt to Montezuma, May 7, 1913; Pratt to Parker, May 7, 1913; Pratt to Parker, April 24, 1913; Arthur C. Parker Papers, State Museum of New York (hereafter SMNY).
11. Pratt to Montezuma, July 17, 1913, Montezuma file, University of Arizona library, Box 1, folder 2; Parker to Pratt, August 13, 1913, Arthur C. Parker Papers, SMNY.
12. Parker to Montezuma, August 14, 1913; Parker Papers, SMNY.
13. Montezuma to Parker, August 19, 1913; Parker Papers, SMNY; Parker to Montezuma, Papers of Carlos Montezuma, WSHS, Box 3.
14. Montezuma to Parker, September 10, 1913; Parker Papers, SMNY.
15. Parker to Montezuma, September 16, 1913; Parker to Pratt, September 24, 1913, ibid.
16. Elsie E. Severance, interview conducted by Charles C. Colley, February 26, 1976, Calexico, California. Text provided by Dr. Colley, archivist and field collector, Hayden Library, Arizona State University.
17. Montezuma to "My own Dutchie," September 22, 1913; Papers of Carlos Montezuma, WSHS, Box 3.
18. McKenzie to Montezuma, October 23, 1913; ibid.; Pratt to Montezuma, November 7, 1913, Montezuma file, University of Arizona Library, Box 1, folder 2.
19. Parker to Montezuma, February 2, 1914; Montezuma, draft of letter in response to Parker, n.d. (1914); Pratt to Montezuma, February 6, 1914, all in Papers of Carlos Montezuma, WSHS, Box 3.
20. Parker to Montezuma, February 17, 1914, ibid.

21. Montezuma, "The Reservation is Fatal to the Development of Good Citizenship," *Quarterly Journal of the Society of American Indians* 2, no. 1 (1914): 69-74, Papers of Carlos Montezuma, Arizona State University Library, Box 9, folder 3.

22. Parker to Members of the Society of American Indians, March 16, 1914; Parker to Montezuma, April 18, 1914; Sherman Coolidge to Montezuma, April 20, 1914; Rosa La Flesche to Montezuma, May 12, 1914; La Flesche to Montezuma, May 26, 1914; all in Papers of Carlos Montezuma, WSHS, Box 3.

23. Montezuma to Mr. and Mrs. Daniel Smiley, October 1, 1914, Quaker Collection, Haverford College; Hertzberg, *Search for an American Indian Identity*, pp. 125–28; Montezuma to Parker, December 7, 1914; Parker Papers, SMNY.

24. Parker to Montezuma, January 22, 1915; Papers of Carlos Montezuma, WSHS, Box 3.

25. Montezuma, "What Indians Must Do," *Quarterly Journal of the Society of American Indians* 2, no. 4 (October–December 1914): 294–99.

26. Sherman Coolidge to Montezuma, April 16, 1915; Montezuma to Coolidge, April 17, 1915; Papers of Carlos Montezuma, WSHS, Box 3.

27. Parker to Montezuma, April 20, 1915; Parker to Montezuma, April 26, 1915; Montezuma to Parker, April 29, 1915; ibid.

28. Parker to Montezuma, June 7, 1915; ibid.

29. Parker to Montezuma, July 10, 1915, July 25, 1915, and August 26, 1915; ibid.

30. Henry Standing Bear to Montezuma, July 26, 1915; Thomas Sloan to Montezuma, August 14, 1915; ibid.

31. Parker to Montezuma, September 10, 1915; ibid.

32. Parker to Montezuma, October 11, 1915; Marie L. B. Baldwin to Montezuma, November 18, 1915; Sloan to Montezuma, December 28, 1915; Sloan to Montezuma, January 8, 1916; ibid.

33. Parker, "Certainly Abolish the Indian Bureau," *Quarterly Journal of the Society of American Indians* 3, no. 4 (October–December 1915), pp. 261–63.

34. Montezuma, "Let My People Go," read before the annual conference of the Society of American Indians at Lawrence, Kansas, September 30, 1915. Privately printed. Copy in Papers of Carlos Montezuma, WSHS, Box 5.

35. Montezuma to L. V. McWhorter, July 13, 1916; L. V. McWhorter Papers, Washington State University Library, Box 13.

36. Elsie E. Severance interview, February 25, 1976, conducted by Charles C. Colley.

37. *Wassaja* 1, no. 1 (April 1916), Papers of Carlos Montezuma, Arizona State University Library.

38. *Wassaja* 1, no. 2 (May 1916), Newberry Library, Chicago.

39. Ibid.

40. *American Indian Magazine* 4, no. 2 (April–June 1916), pp. 170–71, Newberry Library.

41. "Open Debate on the Loyalty of Indian Employees in the Indian Service," *American Indian Magazine* 4, no. 3 (July–September 1916); Hertzberg, *Search for an American Indian Identity*, pp. 148–49.

42. Montezuma, "Address Before the Sixth Conference," *American Indian Magazine* 4, no. 3 (July–September 1916), pp. 260–62.

43. *Wassaja* 1, no. 7 (October 1916), Papers of Carlos Montezuma, WSHS, Box 5.

44. Ibid., no. 10 (January 1917); ibid.

45. Ibid., no. 7 (October 1916); ibid.

46. Ibid., no. 10 (January 1917); ibid.

47. Ibid., no. 4 (July 1916); ibid.

48. Ibid., no. 6 (September 1916); ibid.

49. Ibid., vol. 2, no. 1 (April 1917); ibid.

50. Ibid., vol. 2, no. 3 (June 1917); ibid.

51. Hertzberg, *Search for an American Indian Identity*, p. 172; *Wassaja* 2, no. 7 (October 1917), Papers of Carlos Montezuma, WSHS, Box 5.

52. *Wassaja* 2, no. 1 (April 1917); ibid.

53. Ibid., no. 7 (October 1917); ibid.

54. Ibid., no. 10 (January 1918); no. 11 (February 1918); no. 12 (March 1918), vol. 3, no. 4 (July 1918); ibid.

55. Ibid., vol. 3, no. 1 (April 1918); ibid.

56. Ibid., no. 5 (August 1918); ibid.

57. Ibid., no. 1 (April 1918); ibid.

58. Ibid., vol. 2, no. 10 (January 1918); vol. 3, no. 1 (April 1918); ibid.

59. Ibid., no. 4 (July 1918); ibid.

60. Ibid., no. 5 (August 1918); no. 6 (September 1918); ibid.

61. Gertrude Bonnin to Society of American Indian members, July 25, 1918; Bonnin to Montezuma, August 26, 1918; Bonnin to Montezuma, September 11, 1918; WSHS, Box 3.

62. Program, Seventh Conference, Society of American Indians, Pierre, South Dakota, September 25–28, 1918, ibid.

63. Gertrude Bonnin, "Editorial Comment," and "Indian Society is Welcomed to City," the latter extracted from the Pierre *Daily Capital Journal*, *American Indian Magazine* 6, no. 3 (July–September 1918), pp. 113–14, 117–19, Newberry Library, Chicago.

64. Program, SAI Conference, 1918, and *Wassaja* 3, no. 7 (October 1918), in Papers of Carlos Montezuma, WSHS, Box 3 and Box 5.

65. *Wassaja* 3, no. 7 (October 1918), WSHS, Box 5.

66. Gertrude Bonnin to Philip Gordon, October 14, 1918; Bonnin to Montezuma, October 22, 1918; Bonnin to Montezuma, Novem-

ber 6, 1918; Bonnin to Montezuma, December 6, 1918; WSHS, Box 3. For a different perspective on the conference, critical of the "radicals" and sympathetic to Parker, see Hertzberg, *Search for an American Indian Identity*, pp. 175–78.

67. *Wassaja* 3, no. 7 (October 1918), Papers of Carlos Montezuma, WSHS, Box 5.

CHAPTER SIX

1. George Dickens to Carlos Montezuma, January 18, 1916; Papers of Carlos Montezuma, Arizona State University (hereafter ASU) Library, Box 4.

2. Montezuma to Herbert Marten, March 7, 1912; Montezuma to Frank Andreas, March 11, 1912; Montezuma to Chief Juan Andreas, April 16, 1912; papers of Carlos Montezuma, Wisconsin State Historical Society (hereafter WSHS), Box 2.

3. Montezuma to Marten, March 10, 1912; ibid.

4. Montezuma to Marten, March 7, 1912; ibid.; Joseph W. Latimer R. H. Valentine, June 20, 1912; National Archives and Records Services, Record Group 75, Bureau of Indian Affairs Central Classified Files 1907–39, 63455-1912-174.1, Pima (hereafter NARS, RG 75, BIA, CCF).

5. C. F. Hauke to Latimer, July 2, 1912, ibid.

6. Montezuma to Marten, March 14, 1912; Papers of Carlos Montezuma, WSHS, Box 2.

7. Walter L. Fisher to Latimer, August 6, 1912; NARS, RG 75, BIA, CCF 1907–39, 63455-1912-174.1, Pima.

8. Charles E. Coe to Commissioner of Indian Affairs, June 27, 1912; Calvin Emerson, et al., to Commissioner of Indian Affairs, June 7, 1912; NARS, RG 75, BIA, CCF 1907–39, 63455-1912-174.1, Pima.

9. Charles E. Roblin to Commissioner of Indian Affairs, February 2, 1912; NARS, RG 75, BIA, CCF 1907–39, 8376-11-313, Salt River.

10. See, for example, first assistant secretary to Latimer, August 12, 1912, ibid.

11. Fisher to Latimer, August 10, 1912; ibid.

12. Ibid.; Valentine to Coe, August 21, 1912; Coe to Commissioner of Indian Affairs, October 10, 1912; ibid.

13. Samuel Adams to Commissioner of Indian Affairs, December 4, 1912; ibid.

14. Coe to Commissioner of Indian Affairs, November 6, 1912; ibid.

15. *Arizona Republican*, September 15, 1912; Montezuma to Lancisco Hill, September 4, 1912; Papers of Carlos Montezuma, WSHS, Box 2.

16. Montezuma to William Johnson, Pedro Garcia, and John Allison, January 4, 1913; Papers of Carlos Montezuma, WSHS, Box 2.

17. Montezuma to Joe Ross, January 5, 1913; ibid.

18. Coe to Commissioner of Indian Affairs, July 10, 1912; NARS, RG 75, BIA, CCF 1907–39, 10041-11-063, Salt River.

19. F. H. Abbot to Coe, September 23, 1912; ibid.

20. Coe to Commissioner of Indian Affairs, June 6, 1913; ibid.

21. Montezuma to Cato Sells, September 11, 1913; Sells to Montezuma, September 16, 1913; NARS, RG 75, BIA, CCF 1907–39, 111718-13-063, Salt River.

22. Coe to Commissioner of Indian Affairs, September 24, 1913; George H. Gebby to Sells, October 31, 1913; Sells to Gebby, November 17, 1913; ibid.

23. Jose King, et al. to Montezuma, June 7, 1914; Montezuma to E. B. Meritt, June 7, 1914; Sells to Montezuma, June 20, 1914; ibid.

24. Coe to Commissioner of Indian Affairs, July 8, 1914; Coe to E. B. Linnen, August 24, 1914; Linnen to Sells, September 4, 1914; Coe to Commissioner of Indian Affairs, September 5, 1914; NARS, RG 75, BIA, CCF 1907–39, 111718-13-063, Salt River.

25. Meritt to Jose King, et al., September 16, 1914; Sells to Montezuma, September 22, 1914; Sells to Coe, September 22, 1914; NARS, RG 75, BIA, CCF 1907–39, 111718-13-063, Salt River.

26. Ibid.

27. Frank A. Thackery, telegram to Indian Office, September 28, 1913; Sells to Montezuma, September 29, 1913; NARS, RG 75, BIA, CCF 1907–39, 63455-12-174.1, Pima. Thackery had been in touch with the commissioner's office the month before about representation for the Pimas, suggesting that there was no need for additional help. Thackery to Commissioner of Indian Affairs, August 16, 1913; C. F. Hauke to Thackery, August 28, 1913; ibid., 102637-13-174, Pima.

28. Montezuma to Joe Ross, January 5, 1914. Leon Summit microfilm collection, reel 4.

29. John Baum to Sells, August 26, 1914; NARS, RG 75, BIA, CCF 1907–39, 42803-1914-155, Salt River.

30. Otis B. Goodall to Commissioner of Indian Affairs, June 9, 1914; Shafer to Goodall, July 7, 1914; NARS, RG 75, BIA, CCF 1907–39, 42803-1914-155, Salt River.

31. C. T. Coggeshall to Sells, May 17, 1916; ibid., 63769-16-700.

32. Ibid.; Coggeshall to Commissioner of Indian Affairs, November 24, 1916; ibid., 97255-16-700.

33. Coggeshall to Sells, January 17, 1917; ibid., 10106-17-061.

34. Ibid.

35. Coggeshall to Sells, March 20, 1917; ibid., 28651-17-134.

36. Byron Sharp to Commissioner of Indian Affairs, August 3, 1917; ibid., 77682-1917-155.

37. Richard H. Pratt to Montezuma, January 3, 1914; Carlos Montezuma file, University of Arizona Library, Box 1, folder 3.

38. Pratt to Montezuma, March 13, 1918; ibid., Box 1, folder 4.

39. Pratt to Montezuma, January 15, 1916; ibid., Box 1, folder 3. See also Pratt to Montezuma, February 16, 1915; ibid.: ". . . I do not esteem their landed rights comparable to their rights for the individual ability to become full-fledged American citizens."

40. Pratt to Montezuma, November 2, 1912, July 17, 1913, September 3, 1913, and January 3, 1914; ibid., Box 1, folders 2–3.

41. S. M. Brosius to E. B. Meritt, August 26, 1914; NARS, RG 75, BIA, CCF 1907–39, 42803-1914-155, Salt River.

42. Yuma Frank to Montezuma, February 15, 1913; Papers of Carlos Montezuma, WSHS, Box 2.

43. Ibid.

44. Juan Andreas and Jose Easchief to Montezuma, March 19, 1913; Carlos Montezuma file, University of Arizona, Box 1, folder 10.

45. Montezuma to Sells, May 12, 1914; NARS, RG 75, BIA, CCF 1907–39, 42803-1914-155, Salt River.

46. Ibid.

47. Charles Dickens, et al., to Montezuma, July 10, 1915; see also George Dickens to Montezuma, August 28, 1915; Papers of Carlos Montezuma, Arizona State University (hereafter ASU) Library, Box 4, folder 1.

48. Yuma Frank to Montezuma, November 15, 1914; NARS, RG 75, BIA, CCF 1907–39, 42803-1914-155, Salt River.

49. Montezuma to Chief Yuma Frank, November 21, 1914; Papers of Carlos Montezuma, WSHS, Box 3.

50. Ibid.

51. Meritt, memorandum for Commissioner, September 15, 1914; NARS, RG 75, BIA, CCF 1907–39, 42803-1914-155, Salt River.

52. Ibid.

53. N. W. Irsfeld to C. R. Olberg, January 25, 1915; ibid.

54. W. M. Reed, memorandum for Sells, February 10, 1915; ibid.

55. Fayette McKenzie to Montezuma, April 25, 1915; McKenzie to Montezuma, April 26, 1915; George Dickens to Montezuma, July 10, 1915; Papers of Carlos Montezuma, ASU Library, Box 4, folder 1.

56. Montezuma to Charles Dickens, et al., August 17, 1915; Papers of Carlos Montezuma, WSHS, Box 3.

57. Ibid.

58. Sells to George W. P. Hunt, March 16, 1916; NARS, RG 75, BIA, CCF 1907–39, 24099-16-313, Salt River.

59. George Dickens to Montezuma, March 28, 1916; Papers of Carlos Montezuma, ASU Library, Box 4, folder 2.

60. Charles Dickens to Montezuma, September 9, 1916; Richard Dickens et al., to Montezuma, September 18, 1916; ibid.

61. Montezuma to Meritt, October 9, 1916; Meritt to Montezuma, October 25, 1916; Montezuma to Meritt, November 6, 1916; Meritt to Montezuma, November 17, 1916; Montezuma to Meritt, November 20, 1916; Meritt to Montezuma, November 24, 1916; Montezuma

to Meritt, December 5, 1916; Meritt to Montezuma, December 9, 1916; NARS, RG 75, BIA, CCF 1907–39, 114979-15-424, Salt River.

62. Sells to Coggeshall, February 19, 1917; ibid., 10106-17-061.

63. Sells to Coggeshall, March 19, 1917; ibid., 28651-17-134.

64. See Frederick E. Hoxie, "From Prison to Homeland: The Cheyenne River Reservation Before WWI," *South Dakota History* 10, no. 1 (Winter 1979).

65. *Wassaja* 3, no. 8 (November 1918); Papers of Carlos Montezuma, WSHS, Box 5.

66. Ibid., no. 6 (September 1918); ibid.

CHAPTER SEVEN

1. *Wassaja* 3, no. 10 (January 1919); Papers of Carlos Montezuma, Wisconsin State Historical Society (hereafter WSHS), Box 5.

2. Ibid.

3. Ibid., no. 11 (February 1919); Ibid.

4. Ibid., vol. 4, no. 2 (May 1919); Carlos Montezuma file, Chicago Historical Society.

5. *American Indian Magazine* 7, no. 2 (Summer 1919); Newberry Library.

6. Gertrude Bonnin to Montezuma, June 27, 1919; Papers of Carlos Montezuma, WSHS, Box 4. Other letters from Bonnin to Montezuma were written January 24, 1919; February 8, 1919; February 14, 1919; March 12, 1919; March 28, 1919; April 28, 1919; August 21, 1919; September 8, 1919.

7. For a detailed description of the decline of the Society of American Indians, see Hazel Hertzberg, *The Search for an American Indian Identity: Modern Pan-Indian Movements*, pp. 179–209. This paragraph is based in part on pp. 184–93. See also *Wassaja* 5, no. 4 (July 1920) and no. 8 (November 1920); Papers of Carlos Montezuma, WSHS, Box 5.

8. *Wassaja* 6, no. 4 (July 1921); National Archives and Records Services, Record Group 75, Bureau of Indian Affairs, Central Classified Files, 1907–39 (hereafter NARS, RG 75, BIA, CCF), 67496-1917-341, Salt River II.

9. *Wassaja* 7, no. 11 (November 1921); Susan J. Allen Collection, Panhandle-Plains Historical Museum (hereafter PPHM), Canyon, Texas. Somehow, by this point, the volume and number of *Wassaja* had become incorrect and remained so during the final year of its publication.

10. Ibid.; Montezuma to Richard H. Pratt, November 6, 1921; Richard H. Pratt Papers, Beinecke Library, Yale University.

11. *Wassaja* 7, no. 12 (December 1921); vol. 8, no. 19 (September 1922) and no. 20 (October 1922), Papers of Carlos Montezuma, WSHS,

Box 5. Hertzberg omits consideration of the Kansas City meeting but says the Chicago meeting was scheduled at the invitation of Montezuma. Hertzberg, *Search for An American Indian Identity*, p. 197.

12. *Wassaja*, 3, no. 10 (January 1919).

13. Ibid., no. 12 (March 1919).

14. Ibid., vol. 5, no. 1 (April 1920); Allen Collection, PPHM.

15. Ibid., vol. 6, no. 1 (April 1921); NARS, RG 75, BIA, CCF 1907–39, 67496-1917-341, Salt River II.

16. Montezuma inaugurated this drawing in the January 1921 *Wassaja*, but returned in April 1921, to the old picture of him with other Indians preparing a battering ram to knock down the Indian Office door. He resumed the drawing in August 1921, and continued to employ it until the last issue in November 1922.

17. Montezuma to E. B. Meritt, August 2, 1915; Meritt to Montezuma, August 9, 1915; NARS, RG 75, BIA, CCF 1907–39, 84801-15-052, San Carlos.

18. Montezuma to Meritt, May 24, 1920; ibid., 45642-1920-052, San Carlos.

19. Meritt to Montezuma, June 17, 1920, ibid.

20. Montezuma to Meritt, November 13, 1920; Meritt to Montezuma, November 17, 1920; Montezuma to Meritt, November 24, 1920; Meritt to Montezuma, November 29, 1920; C. F. Hauke to A. H. Symons, January 12, 1921; ibid.

21. Symons to Commissioner of Indian Affairs, January 17, 1921; Meritt to Symons, February 2, 1921; Symons to Commissioner of Indian Affairs, May 14, 1921; ibid.

22. Symons to Commissioner of Indian Affairs; ibid.

23. Hauke to Byron Sharp, June 10, 1921; Yu-co-dep-pah, affidavit, September 9, 1921; ibid. The Bureau had already received affidavits from Montezuma, and from two elderly residents of McDowell, To-mol-giah and Su-ke-yal-vah. To-mol-giah, about ninety years old, said she knew Montezuma's father, Co-lu-ye-vah, well and knew his mother, too; she affirmed that Montezuma was a Pinal Apache, now known as Mohave Apache. Su-ke-yal-vah stated she was an aunt of Montezuma, and had known him as a boy before he was captured and corroborated To-mol-giah's testimony. Montezuma presented autobiographical details, including the fact that Charles Dickens's mother was his aunt, as his mother's sister. He noted that since his relationship had been reestablished at McDowell he made "frequent visits to my people and live with them for such periods I can spare from my professional duties"; ibid.

24. Ernest Stecker to Commissioner of Indian Affairs, December 15, 1921; ibid.

25. Charles Burke to Charles L. Davis, February 23, 1922; ibid.

26. Davis to Burke, March 2, 1922; ibid.

27. "Report of Hearing Held at San Carlos, Arizona, March 7, 1922, by Charles L. Davis, Superintendent, Wherein Certain Witnesses

Were Examined in Connection With the Application of Dr. Carlos Montezuma for Enrollment as an Indian"; ibid.

28. "Report of Hearing Held by Charles L. Davis, Supt., at Fort McDowell, Arizona, March 10, 1922"; ibid.

29. Davis to Commissioner of Indian Affairs, March 20, 1922; ibid.

30. Montezuma to Meritt, March 21, 1922; Burke to Montezuma, March 25, 1922; ibid.

31. Davis to Commissioner of Indian Affairs, April 25, 1922; "Proposed Interrogations for Dr. Montezuma," April 15, 1922; ibid.

32. Davis to Commissioner of Indian Affairs, April 15, 1922; ibid.

33. Ibid.

34. Burke to the Secretary of the Interior, June 12, 1922; ibid.

35. Burke to Montezuma, June 17, 1922; Montezuma to Burke, June 21, 1922; ibid.

36. Montezuma to Latimer, June 22, 1922; Montezuma to Pratt, July 11, 1922; Pratt Papers.

37. Montezuma to Frederick Webb Hodge, July 7, 1922; Smithsonian Institution, National Anthropological Archives, Bureau of American Ethnology, Correspondence, 1909–49.

38. Montezuma to H. W. Dorsey, July 24, 1922; ibid.

39. E. N. Sweet, Jr., "Allotments," Salt River, February 21, 1919; NARS, RG 75, BIA, CCF 1907–39, 20125-19-313, Salt River.

40. Sweet, "Law and Order," Salt River, February 21, 1919; ibid., 20122-19-170, Salt River.

41. Sweet, Report, November 28, 1917; ibid., 113357-17-160, Salt River; Mike Burns to Montezuma, February 1, 1919, April 11, 1919; Papers of Carlos Montezuma, Arizona State University (hereafter ASU), Box 4, folder 5.

42. Charles Dickens to Montezuma, February 23, 1919; Papers of Carlos Montezuma, ASU, Box 4, folder 5.

43. George Dickens to Montezuma, September 8, 1919; NARS, RG 75, BIA, CCF 35263-19-155, Salt River; Meritt to Montezuma, September 23, 1919; Sharp to Commissioner of Indian Affairs, November 5, 1919; Meritt to Montezuma, November 19, 1919; ibid., 79374-19-155, Salt River.

44. Sharp to Commissioner of Indian Affairs, January 16, 1920; ibid., 6186-20-320, Salt River.

45. Samuel Ladlow and Santiago Baptisto to Montezuma, December (n.d.) 1919; Montezuma to Meritt, December 12, 1919; Sharp to Commissioner of Indian Affairs, January 14, 1920; ibid., 106678-19-225, Salt River.

46. *Wassaja* 5, no. 7 (October 1920); Allen Collection, PPHM.

47. *Wassaja* 5, no. 10 (January 1921); University Archives University of Illinois, Record Series 26/4/1; Carlos Montezuma, "Montezuma, Carlos, 1884, Wassaja, Publications."

48. *Wassaja* 5, no. 12 (March 1921); NARS, RG 75, BIA, CCF 1907–39, 67496-17-341, Salt River II.

49. Montezuma to Charles D. Carter, October 28, 1917; Carl Hayden Papers, ASU, Box 623, folder 22.

50. *Wassaja* 6, no. 2 (May 1921), Papers of Carlos Montezuma, WSHS, Box 5; Carl Hayden to Avery Thompson, May 23, 1921; Thompson to Hayden, May 28, 1921; Thompson to Latimer, May 28, 1921; Carl Hayden Papers, ASU, Box 622, folders 16, 25.

51. Burke to Commissioners of City of Phoenix, September 26, 1921; Willis H. Plunkett, Mayor, Phoenix, to Burke, September 28, 1921; Burke to Plunkett, October 12, 1921; Carl Hayden Papers, ASU, Box 622, folder 16.

52. Hayden to John H. Page, November 9, 1921; ibid.

53. Montezuma to Pratt, February 28, 1921; Pratt Papers; Pratt to Montezuma, March 10, 1921; Carlos Montezuma file, University of Arizona Library, Box 1, folder 4.

54. Meritt to John Baum, June 22, 1920; reprinted in *Wassaja* 6, no. 2 (May 1921); Papers of Carlos Montezuma, WSHS, Box 5.

55. Meritt to Montezuma, April 1, 1921; NARS, RG 75, BIA, CCF 1907–39, 67496-17-341, Salt River I; Latimer to Burke, April 12, 1921; reprinted in *Wassaja* 6, no. 2 (May 1921), Papers of Carlos Montezuma, WSHS, Box 5.

56. Albert B. Fall to Montezuma, April 30, 1921; NARS, RG 48, Office of the Secretary of the Interior, Indian Office, Salt River Allotments, January 19, 1916-April 14, 1927.

57. Latimer to Fall, May 12, 1921; NARS, RG 75, BIA, CCF 1907–39, 67496-17-341, Salt River II.

58. Montezuma to Warren G. Harding, May 23, 1921; ibid.

59. Montezuma to Burke, May 24, 1921; Burke to Latimer, June 13, 1921; ibid. Secretary of the Interior to Latimer, June 21, 1921; ibid., 58145-11-313, Salt River. Latimer to Burke, June 22, 1921; ibid., 53376-21-123, Salt River.

60. Montezuma to Marie Montezuma, June 23 and June 24, 1921; Papers of Carlos Montezuma, WSHS, Box 4.

61. Ibid.; Burke to Latimer, June 24, 1921; NARS, RG 75, BIA, CCF 1907–39, 53376-21-123, Salt River.

62. Burke to Latimer, June 24, 1921; ibid.; Latimer to Harding, June 25, 1921; NARS, RG 75, BIA, CCF 1907–39, 67496-17-341, Salt River II.

63. Montezuma to Marie Montezuma, June 27 and 28, 1921; Papers of Carlos Montezuma, WSHS, Box 4. See also his letters of June 26 and June 29.

64. Montezuma to Marie Montezuma, June 28, 1921; ibid.

65. Montezuma to Marie Montezuma, September 3, 1921; ibid.

66. Montezuma to Marie Montezuma, August 19, 1921, and September 3, 1921; Marie Montezuma to Montezuma, September 13, 1921; ibid.

67. Montezuma to Marie Montezuma, September 5, 1921; ibid.

68. Montezuma to Marie Montezuma, September 5, 1921 and August 22, 1921; ibid.

69. Frank A. Virtue to Commissioner of Indian Affairs, April 10, 1922; NARS, RG 75, BIA, CCF 1907–39, 23143-22-155, Salt River.

70. Ibid.

71. Meritt to Charley George, April 29, 1922; ibid.

72. Montezuma to Pratt, May 29, 1922 and June 13, 1922; Pratt Papers.

73. Montezuma to Pratt, October 4, 1922; ibid.

74. *Wassaja* 8, no. 20 (October 1922), Papers of Carlos Montezuma, WSHS, Box 5.

75. Ibid. On November 17, 1922, he wrote to L. V. McWhorter that he had "been ill for several months, slowly stronger." L. V. McWhorter Papers, Washington State University, Box 7, folder 405.

76. *Wassaja* 8, no. 21 (November 1922), Papers of Carlos Montezuma, WSHS, Box 5.

77. Montezuma to Bill Persell, August 13, 1922; ibid., Box 4.

78. Montezuma to Marie Montezuma, n.d.; ibid. Montezuma to Marie Montezuma, January 4, 1923; Leon Summit microfilm collection, reel 3. Marie Montezuma to L. V. McWhorter, ca. February 1923; McWhorter Papers. See also R. J. Stroud, "The 'Last Days' of Carlos Montezuma, M.D.," *Southwestern Medicine,* November 1937. A reprint of this one-page article is in the Arizona Collection, Arizona State University Library. Stroud was the contract physician for McDowell. He says that Montezuma had pulmonary tuberculosis. According to Stroud, Montezuma thought he might have diabetes as well, but the Tempe physician could not confirm this diagnosis. Stroud notes that Montezuma told him he expected to die; otherwise he would have remained in Chicago.

79. *Wassaja* 8, no. 21 (November 1922), Papers of Carlos Montezuma, WSHS, Box 5.

CHAPTER EIGHT

1. *Arizona Republican,* February 2, 1923; Arizona State University Library.

2. *Arizona Republican,* February 5, 1923; Anna Moore Shaw, *A Pima Past,* p. 163.

3. Shaw, *A Pima Past,* pp. 163, 247.

4. *Arizona Republican,* February 5, 1923.

5. "To the Memory of Dr. Carlos Montezuma," Society of American Indians, n.d. Copy in Will C. Barnes Collection, Arizona Collection, Arizona State University Library.

6. "To An Indian Leader (Was-sa-j-a)," The Society of American Indians, February 6, 1923; ibid.

7. Edward H. Spicer, *Cycles of Conquest: The Impact of Spain, Mexico, and the United States on the Indians of the Southwest, 1533–1960,* pp. 530–31.

8. Lawrence M. Hauptman, "Alice Jemison, Seneca Political Activist, 1901–1964," *The Indian Historian* 12, no. 2 (Summer 1979), pp. 18–21; idem., "The American Indian Federation and the American Indian Movement: A Comparative Analysis," paper presented at a meeting of the American Society for Ethnohistory, October 1979, Albany, New York.

9. James E. Murphy and Sharon M. Murphy, *Let My People Know: American Indian Journalism*, pp. 30–85; see also issues of the new *Wassaja*.

10. Sigrid Khera, ed., *The Yavapai of Fort McDowell: Outline of Their History and Culture*, p. 16. See also Sue Abbey Chamberlin, "The Fort McDowell Indian Reservation: Water Rights and Indian Removal, 1910–30," *Journal of the West* 14, no. 4 (October 1975): 27–34, and William R. Coffeen, "The Effects of the Central Arizona Project on the Fort McDowell Indian Community," *Ethnohistory* 19, no. 4 (Fall 1972): 345–77.

11. Interview with John Williams, Fort McDowell, January 5, 1978; interview with John Smith, Fort McDowell, January 7, 1978.

12. Smith interview.

13. See Carolina Butler, "Fort McDowell and Orme Dam," "Speech Given by Tribal Councilman Hiawatha Hood," and "Letters on Orme Dam Written by Fort McDowell Residents," in Khera, *Yavapai of Fort McDowell*, pp. 17–23, 63–70.

14. Williams interview.

15. *Wassaja* 1, no. 3 (June 1916); Papers of Carlos Montezuma, Wisconsin State Historical Society, Box 5.

Bibliography

ARCHIVAL MATERIALS

Arizona State University Library
  Arizona Collection
  Carl Hayden Papers
  Papers of Carlos Montezuma
  Will C. Barnes Collection
Chicago Historical Society
  Carlos Montezuma File
Federal Archives and Records Center, Seattle
  Records of the Bureau of Indian Affairs (Record Group 75)
Haverford College Library
  Quaker Collection
Historical Society of Pennsylvania
  Indian Rights Association Papers (microfilm edition)
Huntington Library
  Horatio Rust Papers
Leon Summit
  Private Microfilm Collection, Carlos Montezuma Papers
Library of Congress
  William Howard Taft Papers
National Archives
  Records of the Bureau of Indian Affairs (Record Group 75)
    Letters Sent, 1870–1908
    Letters Received, 1881–1907

Central Classified Files, 1907–39, Pima
Central Classified Files, 1907–39, Salt River (including Fort Mc-
    Dowell)
Central Classified Files, 1907–39, San Carlos
Special Series A, Box 10
Records of the Department of the Interior (Record Group 48)
    Irrigation Service Reports
    Letters Received
Oklahoma Historical Society
    Indian Archives Division
        Sac and Fox–Shawnee Agency, Miscellaneous Correspondence
Panhandle-Plains Historical Museum
    Susan J. Allen Collection
Smithsonian Institution
    National Anthropological Archives
        Bureau of American Ethnology, Correspondence, 1909–49
State Museum of New York
    Arthur C. Parker Papers
University of Arizona Library
    Carlos Montezuma File
University of Illinois Library
    Carlos Montezuma, Publications
University of Oregon Library
    Ruth Underhill Papers
Washington State University Library
    L. V. McWhorter Papers
Wisconsin State Historical Society
    Papers of Carlos Montezuma
Yale University
    Richard H. Pratt Papers

GOVERNMENT DOCUMENTS

U.S. Congress. House. Committee on Expenditures in the Interior
    Department. "Hearings on House Resolution 103." 62nd Cong.,
    1st sess., 1911.
U.S. Congress. Senate. Committee on Indian Affairs. "Purchase of
    Rights of Settlers on Camp McDowell Reservation, Arizona."
    58th Cong., 2nd sess., 1904.
U.S. Department of the Interior. Annual Reports.

NEWSPAPERS AND CONTEMPORARY JOURNALS

American Indian Magazine
Arizona Republican (Phoenix)
Boston *Herald*

Chicago *Tribune*
Kansas City *Times*
Philadelphia *Public-Ledger*
Pierre Daily *Capital-Journal*
Quarterly Journal of the Society of American Indians
Wassaja

INTERVIEWS

Elsie Elliot Severance, February 26, 1976 (conducted by Charles C. Colley).
John Smith, January 7, 1978.
John and Minnie Williams, January 5, 1978.

DISSERTATIONS

Adams, David Wallace. "The Federal Indian Boarding School: A Study of Environment and Response, 1879–1918." Ed.D., Indiana University, 1975.
Gilcreast, Everett Arthur. "Richard Henry Pratt and American Indian Policy, 1877–1906: A Study of the Assimilation Movement." Ph.D., Yale University, 1967.
Hoxie, Frederick E. "Beyond Savagery: The Campaign to Assimilate the American Indians, 1880–1920." Ph.D., Brandeis University, 1977.
Lamb, Terrence James. "Early Twentieth Century Efforts at Economic Development in Nigeria and Arizona." Ph.D., Temple University, 1978.
Ryan, Carmelita. "Carlisle Indian Industrial School." Ph.D., Georgetown University, 1962.

UNPUBLISHED PAPERS

Frost, Richard. "Fragments of Pueblo History: From BIA Personnel in New Mexico, 1890–1930s." Presented at meeting of the American Society for Ethnohistory, October 1976.
Hauptman, Laurence M. "The American Indian Federation and the American Indian Movement: A Comparative Analysis." Presented at meeting of the American Society for Ethnohistory, October 1979.
Massie, Michael. "The Cultural Roots of the Winters Doctrine and Indian Water Rights," M.A. Paper, University of Wyoming, 1980.

BOOKS AND ARTICLES

Chamberlin, Sue Abbey. "The Fort McDowell Indian Reservation: Water Rights and Indian Removal, 1910–30." *Journal of the West* 14, no. 4 (October 1975): 27–34.

Coffeen, William R. "The Effects of the Central Arizona Project on the Fort McDowell Indian Community." *Ethnohistory* 19, no. 4 (Fall 1972): 345–77.

Eastman, Charles. *The Indian To-Day: The Past and Future of the First American.* Garden City, New York: Doubleday, Page and Co., 1915.

Gifford, E. W. "The Southeastern Yavapai." In A. L. Kroeber, Robert H. Lowie and Ronald L. Olson, editors, University of California Publications in American Archaeology and Ethnology, vol. 29 (1930–32), pp. 177–252.

———. "Northeastern and Western Yavapai." In A. L. Kroeber, Robert H. Lowie, and Ronald L. Olsen, editors, University of California Publications in American Archaeology and Ethnology, vol. 34 (1934–36), pp. 247–354.

Hauptman, Laurence M. "Alice Jemison: Seneca Political Activist, 1901–1964." *Indian Historian* 12, no. 2 (Summer 1979): 15–21, 60–63.

Hertzberg, Hazel W. *The Search for an American Indian Identity: Modern Pan-Indian Movements.* Syracuse, N.Y.: Syracuse University Press, 1971.

———. "Nationality, Anthropology, and Pan-Indianism in the Life of Arthur C. Parker (Seneca)." *Proceedings of the American Philosophical Society* 123, no. 1 (February 20, 1979), pp. 47–72.

Hoxie, Frederick E. "From Prison to Homeland: The Cheyenne River Reservation Before WWI." *South Dakota History* 10, no. 1 (Winter 1979): 1–24.

Khera, Sigrid, editor. *The Yavapai of Fort McDowell: Outline of Their History and Culture.* Fountain Hills, Arizona: Fort McDowell Mohave-Apache Indian Community, 1979.

Kvasnicka, Robert M. and Herman J. Viola, editors. *The Commissioners of Indian Affairs, 1824–1977.* Lincoln: University of Nebraska Press, 1979.

Lamb, Terrence J. "Indian-Government Relations on Water Utilization in the Salt and Gila River Valleys of Southern Arizona, 1902–1914." *The Indian Historian* 10, no. 3 (Summer 1977): 38–45, 61–62.

Murphy, James E. and Sharon M. Murphy. *Let My People Know: American Indian Journalism.* Norman: University of Oklahoma Press, 1981.

Pratt, Richard H. *Battlefield and Classroom.* Edited by Robert H. Utley. New Haven: Yale University Press, 1964.

Proceedings of the Eleventh Annual Meeting of the Lake Mohonk Conference of Friends of the Indian (1893).

Proceedings of the Thirteenth Annual Meeting of the Lake Mohonk Conference of Friends of the Indian (1895).

Prucha, Francis Paul, editor. *Americanizing the American Indian: Writings of "Friends of the Indians," 1880–1900.* Cambridge, Mass.: Harvard University Press, 1973.

————. *The Churches and the Indian Schools, 1888–1912.* Lincoln: University of Nebraska Press, 1979.

Schroeder, Albert H. "A Study of Yavapai History." In David Agee Horr, *Yavapai Indians.* New York and London: Garland, 1974.

Shaw, Anna Moore. *A Pima Past.* Tucson: University of Arizona Press, 1974.

Spicer, Edward H. *Cycles of Conquest: The Impact of Spain, Mexico, and the United States on the Indians of the Southwest, 1533–1960.* Tucson: University of Arizona Press, 1962.

Webb, George. *A Pima Remembers.* Tucson: University of Arizona Press, 1959.

Zitkala-sa (Gertrude Bonnin). *American Indian Stories.* 1921. Glorieta, New Mexico: Rio Grande Press, reprint edition, 1976.

Index

residence near by Yavapais, 42–43;
use of for irrigation, 80; Yavapai
rights to and use of, 83–84, 88, 124,
141, 145, 166–68. *See also* Yavapai
Vest, Pete, 171
Virtue, Frank A., 156, 171

Wabash, Ind., 33
Walapai, 4
Ward, Hiram, 157
Warm Springs, Ore., 23
Washakie, 21
Washington, D.C.: Bonnin's residence
in, 35; site of Bureau of Indian Affairs,
66, 93, 119, 155–56, 176; testimony of
Yavapais in, 89, 139; visit by
Montezuma to, 168–69
Washington, George, 113
Wassaja: Montezuma calls himself, 172;
Montezuma referred to as in tribute,
181; Montezuma signs letters as, 86,
143, 169; Yavapai name of
Montezuma, 3, 5, 176, 185
Wassaja: abolition of Bureau of Indian
Affairs as reason for creation of, 67,
91, 93–94, 106–7; establishment of,
106–7; final issues of, 170, 172–73;
first year of, 108–11; forum for later
views by Montezuma on national
issues, 150–53; forum for views by
Montezuma on Yavapai issues,
145–46, 161, 163–64; inspiration for
contemporary Indian newspaper, 183;
review of role, 178–80; second year
of, 111–13; sent by Coggeshall to
Sells, 133; third year of, 113–15, 117
Water rights. *See* Fort McDowell; Carlos
Montezuma; Salt River
Wavikopaipa, 4
Welsh, Herbert, 28
Western Shoshone Agency, 14–15, 19,
21, 23
Wheelock, Dennison, 27, 69
White Bear, Russell, 72–73
Whiteriver, Ariz., 157
White Rock, Nev., 19
White's Indiana Manual Labor Institute,
33
Williams, John, 183–85
Williams, Minnie, 184
Wilson, Woodrow, 101, 167
Winnebago, 70

Winter, Henry, 78
Winters Doctrine, 82
Winters v. *U.S.*, 78
Wipukyipai, 4
Witter, E. E., 45
Women's National Indian Association, 6
World War I, 112–14, 117, 145
Wounded Knee, S.D., 176
Wright, F. H., 69

Yankton Sioux Agency, 33
Yavapai: mentioned, 7, 29, 74, 91, 93,
102, 107–8, 115, 121, 175; animosity
toward Pima and Maricopa, 4, 83, 121,
143–44; conflict over dances by,
126–29; confusion over Montezuma's
tribal identity as, 153–60; creation of
Fort McDowell reservation for,
43–45; linguistic affiliation of, 4;
Montezuma's final visit to, 173;
Marie Montezuma's visit to, 169–70;
proposed removal of from Fort
McDowell, 81–89, 125, 135–36,
140–46, 161; residence in 1900,
42–43; situation in 1860s, 4–5;
summary of Montezuma's relationship
to, 175, 177, 179–80, 183–84;
testimony in Washington, D.C., by,
89–90; tribe of Montezuma, 3; water
rights issues for, 75–76, 78–85,
87–89, 119, 124–26, 135–36, 139–46,
162–68. *See also* Fort McDowell
reservation; Carlos Montezuma
Yu-co-dep-pah, 155
Yuma, 4
Yuma Dick, 162
Yuma Frank: mentioned, 84; allegiance
of to Montezuma, 139–40, 180;
corresponds with Montezuma, 88,
137–40; criticizes Bureau of Indian
Affairs personnel, 137–38; protests
proposed Yavapai removal, 85,
139–40; role at time of Fort
McDowell's creation, 44; testifies in
Washington, D.C., 89
Yuman, 4, 157
Yumedeppah, 157

Zitkala-sa, 27–28, 33–39, 64. *See also*
Gertrude Bonnin